Venture Capital Redefined

Darek Klonowski

Venture Capital Redefined

The Economic, Political, and Social Impact of COVID on the VC Ecosystem

palgrave
macmillan

Darek Klonowski
Brandon University
Brandon, MB, Canada

ISBN 978-3-030-83386-2 ISBN 978-3-030-83387-9 (eBook)
https://doi.org/10.1007/978-3-030-83387-9

This Palgrave Macmillan imprint is published by the registered company Springer Nature Switzerland AG
The registered company address is: Gewerbestrasse 11, 6330 Cham, Switzerland

Thanks be to God

Preface

Venture capital, which is a global phenomenon that simultaneously maintains a strong local character, is defined as the provision of capital and assistance to private firms by institutional investors. Thus, the industry is influenced by global capital flows, socioeconomic conditions, and the political environment, in addition to local economic growth rates, laws, politics, entrepreneurial dynamics, and institutional infrastructure. Although the venture capital industry was only founded in the late 1960s and early 1970s in the United States (U.S.) and the United Kingdom (U.K.), the total value of private assets under management (AUM) in venture capital is now estimated to equal $3.4 trillion.

On March 11th of 2020, the World Health Organization (WHO) announced to the world the existence of novel coronavirus, which was given the abbreviation "COVID-19." Specialists from Imperial College London released an epidemiological model which estimated that in the absence of strong intervention, the novel virus would result in 7 billion infections and 40 million deaths globally in 2020 alone. As a result, many governments around the globe have engaged in wide-ranging restrictive measures to "flatten the curve"; this practice was initially intended for a period of about two weeks in order to avoid overwhelming the healthcare system, although these restrictions were subsequently extended to remain in place for over a year. As a result, economic activities have been compressed and many industries, sectors, and segments of the economy have been affected worldwide, including the venture capital industry.

Of this book's many objectives, the primary focus has been its use as a tool to understand the severity of the novel coronavirus's impact upon the venture capital industry. Analysis performed for this book project suggests that the industry has undergone profound changes since the early onset of government restrictions designed to halt the spread of COVID-19. A second area of emphasis within this book is an assessment of the potential long-term impact of the economic, political, and social restrictions on the venture capital ecosystem post COVID-response. Thirdly, the perspectives of various stakeholders involved in the venture capital ecosystem, including general partners (GPs), limited partners (LPs), entrepreneurs, and other important stakeholders (including the state) are considered, particularly in the context of the post COVID-response period. Lastly, the ultimate aim of this book is to answer the question of whether current changes to the venture capital industry are likely to renew and promote the industry's overhaul, or simply perpetuate its decline.

The Book's Structure

The book is comprised of four sections and nine chapters. Each section consists of two to four chapters of varying length, with the exception of the last section, as it has only one chapter. There are 25 figures and tables to illustrate and provide further support to key observations.

The introductory section of the book is called "Introduction to Venture Capital and its External Environment in the Age of COVID-response." The first chapter of this section focuses on the definition of venture capital and its characteristics. It provides a brief overview of venture capital and its underlying concepts that serve as a reference point throughout the book; it is important to establish this benchmark because subsequent chapters illustrate changes to the basic concept of venture capitalism in view of COVID-response. Further segments specifically elaborated upon in the chapter include the discussion of venture capital's true contribution to entrepreneurial development, as well as some of the advantages and disadvantages of venture capital as seen from the entrepreneurial perspective. The first chapter will also provide a survey of the historical trends in the global venture capital industry over the last 20 years, with particular attention paid to fundraising and investing activities, including the accumulation of $1.9 trillion in "dry powder." Additionally, the chapter provides a background discussion of venture capital returns in the context of the "promise" made to capital providers (i.e., LPs) by venture capitalists. The chapter ends by providing a summary of venture capital and the significant, fundamental challenges it faced in the pre COVID era, such as its maturation.

The second chapter provides background information on the political reactions and subsequent socioeconomic consequences of COVID-19, as well as a general discussion regarding the implications of government restrictions on venture capital. When the coronavirus initially appeared, the vast majority of political leaders and public officials around the globe moved to implement a range of restrictive public measures, mandates, and orders. Examples of these restrictions include the closure of public spaces (i.e., universities, schools, government offices, courts, etc.), lockdowns, stay-at-home orders, travel restrictions, border closures, forced quarantine, limitations on social interactions, social distancing, mask wearing, and curfews; these reactions are termed "COVID-response" in this book. Although public officials attempted to introduce some measures to counteract the social, economic, and human consequences of the restrictions, the effect of these often strict government mandates was nonetheless devastating. For example, preliminary estimates confirm that in countries belonging to the OECD (Organization for Economic Co-operation and Development), economies shrunk by 4.2%, with Spain and the U.K. experiencing the most significant losses. At the height of the economic crisis, it is estimated that about 500 million people lost their jobs, resulting in a global unemployment rate of 7.2%. However, the small and medium-sized enterprise (SME) sector was one of the hardest hit segments of the economy by far. Furthermore, these restrictions have also negatively impacted mental health and human social behavior. Drawing on this important background analysis, the second chapter begins a discussion of the direct and indirect impact of political, social, and economic changes caused by COVID-response on the venture capital industry, which is continued in more detail in subsequent chapters.

The second section of the book, titled "The Venture Capital Industry Redefined," is comprised of four chapters. The first chapter of this section, or the third chapter of the book, describes the fundamental and inherently complex building blocks of the venture capital ecosystem; it consists of many critical stakeholders, such as GPs, LPs, entrepreneurial firms, banks, consultants, bankers, and governments. In spite of its complexity, the existence of the venture capital ecosystem relies on a delicate balance between LPs' profitability, GPs' returns, and the success of entrepreneurial firms. If this delicate balance is upset, longer term and more profound changes in the industry are likely to emerge, although these trends have beset the industry for some time and were visible prior to COVID-response.

The third chapter also outlines how COVID-response has redefined personal relations in the venture capital ecosystem. Since venture capital is a people-centric business, restrictions have affected virtually every aspect of GPs' interactions with entrepreneurs and LPs, in addition to their in-house operations and relationships with other key stakeholders. Considering recent disturbances to the already precarious venture capital industry, the second part of the chapter extrapolates what the future of venture capital may look like, and describes in detail the stages the industry may evolve through; these include the global consolidation of GP partners (i.e., growing emergence of mega funds), global pooling of LPs (i.e., emergence of global LPs), and the development of more futuristic structures based on the complete digitization of the investment process and the wide-ranging dis-intermediation of GPs.

The fourth chapter broadly discusses the major external undercurrents that have emerged post COVID-response and are likely to impact venture capital in terms of both existing portfolio firms and new investment opportunities. The six major trends detailed include changes to industrial structures, alterations to consumer behavior, mass digitization, the increased role of home as the center of human gravity, public health apprehensions, and the abolition of the middle class in developed countries. Available investment opportunities in specific segments of the economy are also examined as they pertain to each of these key trends. Lastly, the chapter concludes by illuminating the likely sources of venture capital transactions in the COVID era, which may include the privatization of state firms, disposals from major multinationals, and founders.

The venture capital industry has been under pressure post COVID-response, which is a trend that is likely to continue in the future; it is therefore valuable to explore changes to the venture capital investment process, which are analyzed in chapter five. Normal patterns of venture capital's daily operations, deal processing routines, regular habits of communication, and other tacit behaviors that were previously established in the pre-COVID era have been disrupted. Furthermore, state-led COVID restrictions have affected the venture capital community differently from country to country, although the venture capital industry generally went into a retreat-and-hide mode during March and April of 2020. The situation improved in most countries by June, although it was evident by the fall of 2020 that the venture capital community would not be able to engage in its normal processes for the foreseeable future because of the strict COVID-response measures that once again emerged. This chapter discusses the many dislocations to the normal patterns of processing venture capital deals, as well as the challenges experienced within each stage of the investment process (i.e., deal generation, evaluation and screening, financial contracting, monitoring, and exiting). Moreover, the chapter highlights one of the most profoundly affected phases of the investment process, namely due diligence and monitoring, and discusses problems related to portfolio firm underperformance and valuation.

The sixth chapter of this book identifies the future of venture capital performance (i.e., financial returns) by further analyzing the LP-GP relationship. The chapter begins with a discussion of fund formation and the provision of capital by LPs to the venture capital ecosystem. It is stressed that LPs can contribute to the deterioration of financial performance by providing capital to suboptimal GPs, performing poor due diligence on funds, tolerating limited access to information, and so on. The chapter subsequently discusses the cost of "carried interest" and the provision of venture capital services to LPs, which are two of the most expensive components within the LP-GP arrangement. Moreover, the chapter examines value chain analysis, provides another historical look at venture capital performance, assesses the industry's return prospects in the context of a longitudinal study, and outlines the profiles of superior and inferior GPs.

One of the most important components of the venture capital ecosystem is the SME sector, which, as noted above, was one of the hardest hit segments of the economy post COVID-response. Many entrepreneurial firms were left financially devastated because their profits, savings, and "sweat equity" disappeared within a matter of weeks or months following the introduction of restrictive measures mandated by public officials. Thus, the third major section is called "Entrepreneurship Redefined Post COVID-Response" and consists of two chapters that focus on the critical issues impacting the SME sector, including its ability to access entrepreneurial finance.

The first chapter within the third section, or the seventh chapter overall, concentrates on the entrepreneurial crisis created by COVID-response; evidence suggests that up to 80 percent of firms were affected, with about 40 to 50% of firms impacted so severely that they were unsure of business survival. In the U.S., for example, the number of active businesses declined from 15.0 million to 11.7 million, which represents the largest decrease in the number of operating firms in the U.S.' modern economic history. Furthermore, the harm to the SME sector was indirectly related to the firm size (i.e., larger firms were less impacted by COVID-response). Although firms operating within the SME sector are typically flexible and agile in their ability to pivot and generate revenue through different streams, their capacity to respond was thwarted by the speed and strictness of public restrictions. The negative impact of public restrictions has also affected different market segments to varying degrees, as firms operating in retail, hospitality, restaurant and food services, arts and entertainment, transportation, fitness, and leisure sectors have been disproportionately impacted.

The changing landscape for entrepreneurs, particularly in terms of their ability to procure entrepreneurial finance, is discussed in the eighth chapter of this book. Research indicates that access to finance is one of the most critical challenges for entrepreneurial firms, although there are numerous other issues that have acutely impacted areas of the SME sector post COVID-response. Primarily, many firms have faced a severe decline, or a complete loss, of revenue. SME firms have also experienced significant difficulties covering their fixed financial obligations. The combination of revenue decline or loss with high fixed costs of business operations has directly impacted the profitability, cash flow, and liquidity of SMEs. Secondly, challenges to the businesses' financial parameters have negatively influenced the value of entrepreneurial firms. A third issue that has beset entrepreneurial firms post COVID-response has been their ability to maintain personnel; while many firms initially aimed to sustain their employees, they ultimately resorted to temporary or permanent layoffs due to the firms' abysmal financial position. The full impact of these staffing reductions on unemployment will likely be manifested in the next two or three years.

Additionally, it is noted in chapter eight that many firms from the SME sector were forced to close while large "big box" stores remained open, which created an unequal playing field for smaller firms. There is also preliminary evidence to suggest that the SME sector's ability to secure access to entrepreneurial finance is further challenged post COVID-response, as, for example, data from venture capital firms indicates that deal volume is on the decline. Business angels have similarly reduced their financing activities to instead focus on existing investments, while financial institutions are expected to encounter problems with existing loan portfolios and may be reluctant to extend further debt. Although government programs have developed a wide range of options to support struggling firms, such as payroll protection, commercial rent assistance, wage subsidies, tax deferrals, and property tax postponements, these measures are unlikely to adequately supplement the financial needs of SMEs. Furthermore, entrepreneurial firms' abilities to rely on "bootstrapping" strategies may be limited; they will need to develop and test new tactics in this area. On a positive note, the rapid development of fintech has the potential to financially support entrepreneurial ventures on a wider scale in the future.

The final section, and closing chapter, of the book is called "Revival or Descent of Venture Capital in the Age of COVID" and seeks to answer the key question of whether the venture capital industry's current situation will lead to its revival or ultimate decline. The possibility of either scenario (i.e., revival or descent) is discussed in the context of four pillars of analysis, namely the entrepreneurial sector, GP market, LP segment, and the state. These potential futures of the venture capital industry are also compared to the previous evolution of the industry as outlined in chapter three. This concluding chapter ends with an estimation of the key statistics in the industry (i.e., fundraising and investing) over the next 20 years.

The Contribution of This Book

The topic of venture capital and private equity is a popular subject for books, as it has been subject to a plethora of in-depth academic investigations since the industry's inception in the early 1970s. In the last few years alone, there have been more than forty books written about venture capital. And yet, despite the multiplicity of books written in the areas of private equity and venture capital in recent years, there appears to be a steady demand for further publications on these subjects. Furthermore, some of these existing books deal with highly specialized issues in venture capital, such as buyouts, due diligence, financial contracting, or specific geographic markets, while still other books deal with venture capital in a more generalized manner. This project is the first book on venture capital since the onset of COVID-response.

The book provides many advantages to readers, the primary of which is its ability to provide further understanding and context to academics, students, practitioners, and especially entrepreneurs in the area of the venture capital investment model's underlying changes post COVID-response. Additionally, the book aims to outline some of the difficulties the venture capital industry has faced in the past, as well as new challenges that have emerged post COVID-response. This book also draws from multiple sources, including academic studies, industrial assessments, mainstream media, and directly from the venture capital industry. However, by providing a hypothesis regarding what the industry may look like in the future through the extrapolation of long-term tendencies, recent occurrences, and trends that were triggered by COVID-response, this book serves as a valuable tool for academics and entrepreneurs alike as they seek to navigate the future of the venture capital industry.

Despite its advantages, it is important to note that analytical book projects written at a time when new trends and undercurrents are just beginning to impact an industry may have a number of shortcomings; this project is no exception.

Future Research

Venture capital has been a topic of academic inquiry for a long period of time. Debate on this subject has been both useful and productive; it has provided many comprehensive perspectives on various aspects of the venture capital investment process, including screening and evaluation, financial contracting, and investee firm-GP relationships. Furthermore, academic inquiry has not omitted some of the most difficult topics within the industry, such as the divergence of interest between GPs and LPs, declining venture capital performance, and the extent of GPs' effectiveness in their assistance of investee firms. However, due to current changes to the venture capital industry as a result of COVID-response, academic inquiry into venture capitalism is in many ways at a point of partial restart.

There are at least five critical areas of academic investigation that should be considered moving forward, with the first and most important area of research undoubtedly related to the redefinition of the relationship between GPs and investee firms. Venture capital prides itself on the provision of assistance to entrepreneurial firms, in spite of the often imperfect nature of this aid. As outlined in chapters three and five, this critical relationship in the venture capital ecosystem has very evidently been redefined post COVID-response. Thus, the key questions that should now be asked are as follows: How effective are new modes of online interaction between GPs and investee firms? Are GPs capable of providing effective assistance to investee firms post COVID-response, and if so, what are the crucial areas of assistance that investee firms require? Are there new areas of investee firm assistance that have been previously overlooked by GPs?

A second fruitful area of new research should explore the future of venture capital financial performance. In the past, there have been multiple studies that provide a historical perspective on venture capital performance, many of which reach differing conclusions as to whether or not GPs are able to deliver returns in excess of those available in public equities markets. If GPs are unable to generate repeatable returns that exceed returns from public equities markets, the entire venture capital ecosystem would continually be upset and thus subject to LPs satisfying their automatic "bucket filling" allocations in the asset class without much reflection. The vital questions regarding venture capital performance should be as follows: What are the key determinants of returns across various types of private capital investing (i.e., buyouts, expansion capital, seed and early-stage capital, etc.)? In what ways could the venture capital change to generate better and more consistent returns? What are the returns post COVID-response, and how do they differ from those obtained during other economic crises? Has the divergence between top quartile performance and the remaining GPs decreased or widened?

The third facet of study that has arisen post COVID-response specifically relates to the SME sector, which has disproportionately experienced operational challenges, market uncertainties, financial difficulties, and problems with financial management, which, in turn, have elevated the sector's difficulties in accessing finance. Important questions pertaining to entrepreneurial finance could include: What are the key bootstrapping strategies entrepreneurial firms can still rely on, and how has bootstrapping changed for the SME sector? Can fintech fill the intermediate gap by providing finance to entrepreneurial firms? Are there any new forms of entrepreneurial finance that are likely to emerge post COVID-response? What is the new role of the state in assisting the SME sector with regard to the provision of finance? Are government loan guarantee programs sustainable alternatives to bank lending?

A fourth area of possible research relates to actual GP operations. As noted in chapters three and five, in-person interaction has been the bread-and-butter of the venture capital industry; this form of interaction has now been entirely redefined. Significant thought should be given to the effectiveness of GPs' interactions with their portfolio firms, LPs, and other important stakeholders, as well as to the overall value of their role in entrepreneurial finance.

Lastly, since the hypothetical progression of the venture capital industry's evolution has been outlined, the impact of an expected climax in the dis-intermediation of GPs should be considered. Therefore, important questions in this area would be as follows: Is there increasing empirical or circumstantial evidence pointing to further consolidation of the venture capital industry? Can we observe an emergence of a handful of GP leaders in the venture capital industry as has been observed in other segments of the financial services industry? What are the profiles of these market leaders and how unique are their operations? Is there evidence to support the idea that the simplification of the venture capital industry in terms of its structure would be beneficial? Is there tangible proof of GP consolidation and LP pooling? How would the role of the state change if the structure of the venture capital industry were to be re-adjusted?

Acknowledgments

I wrote this book during the period of subsequent COVID-response restrictions (between January and May of 2021), after having read about 70 or so newspaper, magazine, and Internet-based articles on the topic over the Christmas break; this was a useful starting point in my inquiry, as it allowed me to dive further into the study of this new and ever-changing subject. The daily grind of working on this project proved to be interesting, challenging, and thought provoking. The old Benedictine monks' axiom of *ora et labora* has been valuable in keeping this project moving forward.

While preparing the initial manuscript, I benefited from informal (email) discussions with Thomas Meyer (SimCorp) and Mike Casey (Portico). Discussion with Stephen Richmond (Abris Capital), who has provided many favors over the years, has also been extremely beneficial; he has been a go-to person whenever I needed feedback and insight from real practitioners within the venture capital industry. I have relied heavily on my previous research, contemplation, and writing while completing this book, namely *Strategic Entrepreneurial Finance* and *The Venture Capital Deformation*.

I would like to express gratitude to senior administrators at Brandon University, and especially Steve Robinson, who have supported this book project through a research appointment. I would also like to thank

Marissa Stelmack, who has provided careful, detail-oriented, and invaluable editorial assistance; Marissa has made numerous corrections to the manuscript and caught many of my omissions and outright errors. This level of attention to detail may be difficult to find in young people today. Of course, any omissions and shortcomings in this book are solely my own.

I would like to thank Palgrave MacMillan, and particularly Tula Weis, for providing an opportunity to publish yet another book related to entrepreneurial finance. I appreciate a quick turnaround on a book proposal and project approval, as waiting for reviewers' reports is both exciting and nerve-racking. Furthermore, I would like to convey thanks to the anonymous reviewers of the book proposal for their insightful comments and analysis; this was much appreciated. Lastly, I would like to thank those who were involved in the financial copyediting and production of the project, namely Punitha Balasubramaniam, and Karthika Purushothaman. Thanks to you all!

Brandon, Canada
May 2021

Darek Klonowski

Contents

List of Figures

List of Tables

PART I

Introduction: Venture Capital and Its External Environment in the Age of Covid

CHAPTER 1

Venture Capital Prior to the Age of COVID

Venture capital is a global phenomenon, which simultaneously maintains strong local characteristics; it is influenced by global capital flows and trade, socioeconomic conditions, and the political environment, in addition to local economic growth rates, laws, politics, entrepreneurial dynamics, and institutional infrastructure. This introductory chapter will provide a brief overview of venture capital and its underlying concepts that will serve as a benchmark reference point throughout the book. It is important to establish this initial marker because subsequent chapters would illustrate changes to this basic concept in view of COVID-response.

Venture Capital: Definitions, Characteristics, and Publicity

Venture capital can be described as the provision of capital, know-how, and hands-on involvement to entrepreneurial firms by institutional investors. These assets are combined for the purpose of accelerating entrepreneurial development in a pre-planned manner, thereby exploiting opportunities available in the marketplace. Because institutional investors aspire to achieve long-term above-average returns that are in excess of those available in public equities markets, venture capital is thus centered upon risk-equity investing.

D. Klonowski, *Venture Capital Redefined*,
https://doi.org/10.1007/978-3-030-83387-9_1

Similarly, English language dictionaries such as *Collins English Dictionary*, *Cambridge Business English Dictionary*, *Webster's Dictionary*, and the *Dictionary of Business and Management* all describe venture capital as business endeavors involving chance, risk, or even danger; it is defined more specifically as a very risky investment which has the potential to be lost completely. These dictionaries commonly illustrate venture capital as capital invested for an acquisition of shares in speculative entrepreneurial ventures, risky start-ups, and emerging or expanding firms. More simply put, venture capital is capital directed to firms in search of high-return opportunities.

One of the distinguishing features of venture capital is that it can flow into firms at different stages of their development. New venture financing may be offered to young entrepreneurial firms, which is directed to support research and development (R&D), product feasibility studies, or the development of a complete business plan from an initial idea; this type of finance is often referred to as *seed capital*. Early-stage financing, commonly called *start-up financing*, can also be provided to entrepreneurial firms that have a product or service prototype and are ready to test its market potential and understand customer acceptance. *First stage financing* refers to the provision of capital and know-how to firms that have successfully passed the "market test" and are ready to commence large-scale production; this type of financing is often utilized to support the development of a fully functioning business, including production facilities, management, distribution structure, marketing and promotions activities, back office operations, and customer services. *Later stage financing* is directed to entrepreneurial firms that have successfully managed throughout their initial development and "teething problems".

Other forms of venture capital that occur at further stages of a firm's development include *second stage financing*, which is offered to firms that enjoy robust revenue growth and may even be profitable. Here, strong revenue growth necessitates significant investment in working capital, further product or service development, R&D activities, geographic expansion, and improvement to the balance sheet, such as achieving a more manageable debt-to-equity ratio. *Mezzanine financing*, or short-term equity or debt finance provided by institutional investors on a short-notice basis, is a type of aggressively priced financing that may require additional financial arrangements (i.e., interest or coupon payments). *Bridge financing* is directed to entrepreneurial firms aiming to "go public", for the purpose of fulfilling an entrepreneurial firm's finance needs until it receives proceeds from an initial public offering (IPO). On the other hand, *buyout financing* is either provided to management with the goal of acquiring a specific business at which the management works, which is termed *management buyout*, or to allow outsiders (i.e., an independent management team unrelated to the business) to purchase the business, which is termed *management buy-in*. Finally, *leveraged buyouts* are transactions requiring significant amounts of debt, which is used to acquire an entire business or its part.

Furthermore, it is important to make a distinction between various financial terms related to venture capital and private equity, which are commonly used to describe the process of investing institutional capital in firms. In the United States (U.S.), for example, the term "venture capital" is reserved for describing investments in early-stage and expanding entrepreneurial firms while the term "private equity" is used with relation to more sizeable expansion-related transactions, buyout deals, and other types of transactions. The term "private equity" is also used to describe investments related to infrastructure (i.e., roads and highways, hospitals, airports, and seaports, among others), real estate, distressed financial situations (i.e., debt restructuring), specific industrial sectors (such as natural resources, military, energy, or healthcare services), or even state-owned firms. And yet, in contrast to the U.S. and within the European setting, venture capital is defined as capital co-invested alongside the entrepreneur for the purpose of providing capital and know-how to entrepreneurial firms in the early stages of development (i.e., seed, start-up, and first-stage expansion). Invest Europe (IE), formally known as the European Private Equity and Venture Capital Association (EVCA), defines venture capital as a subset of private equity. In this context, private equity is comprised of the following investing behaviors: buyouts, venture capital, growth investment, turnaround financing, private equity secondaries (i.e., LPs sell their stakes in GPs to other LPs), and private equity fund-of-funds. However, to simplify matters for the purposes of this book, the term "venture capital" will be used as the primary description for the act of investing into private firms, whether in their early stages, expansion phases, buyouts or buy-ins, or any other stage of capital provision. This broad-brush definitional treatment of venture capital and private equity reflects the reality that it can be difficult to precisely ascertain where one category of capital investing ends and the next one begins.

Additionally, it is important to consider that venture capital is part of a broader category of so-called closed-end private capital. According to

Prequin, an international firm that provides data, analytical, and information services to GPs and LPs, there are five unique and distinct categories of private capital: private equity (comprised of financing related to buyout, venture capital, growth, turnaround, private equity secondaries, private equity fund-of-funds, and other private equity), private debt (i.e., direct lending, distressed debt, mezzanine, special situations, venture debt, and private debt fund-of-funds), real estate (i.e., private equity real estate, private equity fund-of-funds, and private equity real estate secondaries), infrastructure (i.e., infrastructure, infrastructure fund-of-funds, and infrastructure secondaries), and natural resource (i.e., energy, agricultural and farmland, metals and mining, timberland, water, and natural resource fund-of-funds). This division reflects a more classical definition in the European context. In any case, it is estimated that the total value of private assets under management (AUM) in these distinct categories is equal to about $5.8 trillion.

Finally, it is essential to note that venture capitalists do not manage their own capital. Venture capital firms are commonly structured in the form of limited partnerships, and in such legal structures, there are two classes of partners: general and limited. Limited partners (LPs) normally contribute capital but take no part in the daily operations of the partnership; in other words, they are passive investors. General partners (GPs), on the other hand, are responsible for the day-to-day management of the partnership and are, in comparison, active investors.

Characteristics of Venture Capital

Venture capital can be distinguished from other forms of entrepreneurial finance in numerous ways. For one, as noted above, venture capital is equity oriented and thus aims to provide equity rather than debt. Equity could come in the form of common shares, preferred shares, or convertible preferred shares. Another important characteristic of venture capital is illiquidity. A venture capitalist will stay invested in an entrepreneurial firm for a period of three to five years (or even longer as recent data confirms), which may be further extended if the entrepreneurial firm faces unexpected problems or its operational and financial milestones have not been reached in the desired time period. Commonly, the extended time horizon is dedicated to growing the firm's operations and market penetration, achieving desired levels of profitability and cash flow, and securing a profitable exit. Alternately, investors may prefer to continue their financial involvement beyond their initial period of commitment because of the robust manner in which a firm develops.

Significantly, venture capital is selective in its choice of investee firms; venture capitalists invest in one or two out of every one hundred business plans they review. To filter out the vast majority of potential investment opportunities, venture capitalists use a process known as screening and evaluation to identify any "deal breakers" early in the investment process. These deal breakers can arise either due to the inability of venture capitalists and entrepreneurs to agree to basic deal terms, or due to an entrepreneurial firm's commercial proposition, which may be unattractive.

Implicit in the definition of venture capital is its commitment to contribute more than capital to an entrepreneurial endeavor. In fact, venture capitalists are participants who play active, complex, and multiple roles within the firms they support. They actively participate on the board of directors and may prove to be invaluable "sounding boards" to founders, thereby preventing entrepreneurial firms, especially young ones, from making costly business mistakes. In this case, fledgling entrepreneurs may be forced to more carefully evaluate various potential risks and develop specific plans to avert these risks through their interaction with venture capitalists; of course, more experienced entrepreneurs may do this effectively on their own without the need for external assistance. Because of their board experience, some venture capitalists firmly grasp that intimate, close, and hands-on involvement in entrepreneurial firms may contribute to a firm's improvement in overall operational and financial performance.

In short, venture capital activism may enhance performance and minimize risks if done well. By participating in strategic considerations, revisions to the original business plan, the recruitment of senior management, executing business acquisitions, and raising further external finance (whether through debt or equity), evidence suggests that more reputable and experienced venture capitalists may provide greater improvements to an entrepreneurial firm's efficiency. One common manifestation of venture capital activism is seen in the frequent replacement of existing CEOs (chief executive officer) once a venture capitalist becomes involved. Furthermore, active interaction between venture capitalists and entrepreneurs may lead to the professionalization and corporatization of entrepreneurial firms. This functional interaction may also promote entrepreneurial learning, problem solving, and restrained experimentation on a broader scale within the economy.

Finally, one of the most distinguished characteristics of venture capital is its focus on the disposal of its stake in the firm at the end of the holding period, which is commonly termed as an "exit". Traditionally, venture capitalists pursue two types of preferred exits, which are correlated with the highest valuations of firms and, hence, the maximization of returns. First, venture capitalists may be able to dispose of their shares to a strategic investor, primarily a major international corporation looking to expand its production capabilities, acquire a venture with unique products or services, secure the market share in a desired marketplace, or expand a client base. Venture capitalists may also seek to sell shares to a financial institution, including another venture capital firm, or to the public by offering them on the stock exchange. Other exit options, such as a buyback of the venture capitalist's stake by the founder, share redemption (a purchase of shares by the firm itself), a merger with another business, or a management buyout, are also available, although these exit routes may yield less than desired financial returns. A compromised exit reflects a significant underperformance of the investee firm during the period of a venture capitalist's financial involvement or may occur as a result of a lack of co-operation between existing shareholders or management. However, undesirable exits, which may include liquidation and bankruptcy, are due to the investee firm severely underperforming on all key metrics and result in a struggle for venture capitalists to recover any meaningful part of their original investment.

Venture Capital and Its Contribution to Entrepreneurial Development

Throughout business development and expansion initiatives, entrepreneurs face two major problems: access to finance, which places significant constraints on firms, and access to know-how. Venture capitalists may potentially be able to resolve this dual problem of access to finance and the need for advisory assistance, two problems which are closely related, to become unique providers of capital and knowledge to entrepreneurial firms. Thus, while access to sufficient finance is necessary for the entrepreneurial firm to address operational challenges and effective managerial skill, superior strategic planning and effective execution on the part of the venture capitalist can assure proper utilization of capital.

And yet, in spite of its potential to resolve the duality of problems hindering entrepreneurial development, venture capital has only succeeded in making a small contribution to entrepreneurship. In the U.S., for example, research confirms that only one in 1,541 firms receive venture capital financing; this represents 0.065% of the entrepreneurial firms in the U.S. Thus, 99.93% of U.S. entrepreneurial firms must raise capital from other sources. The impact of venture capital financing upon entrepreneurial firms is seen around the world in similarly underwhelming numbers, with one in 2,379 firms able to secure venture capital in the United Kingdom (U.K.; 0.042% of firms), one in 1,609 in Germany (0.062), one in 2,351 in Holland (0.043%), one in 3,146 in France (0.032%), and one in 4,495 in Canada (0.022%). Other modes of entrepreneurial finance have jointly made a significant impact on business formation and perpetuation far beyond the contribution made by venture capital financing alone. In fact, research confirms that entrepreneurial firms can secure these alternate forms of entrepreneurial finance and successfully grow their ventures without ever accessing venture capital.

It is often argued that venture capital contributes to entrepreneurial and national innovation, and the size of the venture capital industry is furthermore regarded as a reliable barometer of innovation occurring in the economy. Since venture capitalists were early round investors behind a large number of front-page entrepreneurial success stories, such as Google, Groupon, Twitter, Instagram, Zynga, Dell, Intel, and Microsoft, the public are shown a disproportionate contribution of venture capital to the entrepreneurial ecosystem. However, while there is a general perception or association between venture capital and innovation, there is considerable debate whether venture capitalists actually cause innovation in the firms they finance. In fact, evidence suggests that venture capital generally follows innovation, rather than preceding it. After all, the presence of innovation within an entrepreneurial firm is likely to be a key point of attraction for venture capitalists in the first place, so innovation is frequently perfected and converted into products and services long before venture capitalists show up. Therefore, at best, venture capitalists perpetuate and accelerate what has already been discovered, researched, developed, partly (or even fully) commercialized, and paid for. While business perpetuation is an important contribution of venture capital, it is not consistent with claims that venture capital creates or causes innovation in entrepreneurial firms.

There are other reasons why venture capitalists may not be such vigorous contributors to innovation, the first of which is because venture capital's profit maximization, short-term determinism, and exit orientation often result in less investment in long-term R&D, innovation, and commercialization within entrepreneurial firms. In fact, venture capitalists often insist on reducing expenses and capital expenditures associated with innovation in order to maximize profits and cash flow, especially ahead of a desired exit. Secondly, venture capitalists focus on an increasingly narrow range of industries and therefore make a limited impact on the broader economy. Venture capitalists frequently direct their capital toward deals where the innovation cycles (i.e., innovation-to-commercialization) are relatively short; thus, venture capital's desired time frame to exit may simply be too short to develop any long-lasting innovation. Additionally, the cyclical nature of the venture capital industry itself may make any true focus on innovation uneven, unsteady, unstable, and irregular.

Only a limited number of venture capitalists understand that true innovation may come from advances in organizational structures, systems, and approaches rather than technologically driven applications and services. Of course, these organizational innovations cannot be patented and showcased. Instead, "breakthrough" products and services, which venture capitalists often finance, are favored in spite of the fact that they may not grant long-lasting leadership and competitive positions in the marketplace because they can be quickly mimicked by a more efficient service provider or manufacturer. Another claim regularly perpetuated by venture capital is its ability to increase patents in investee firms, which is supposed to be indicative of its contribution to innovation. Of course, the act of encouraging investee firms to register patents for unique products or services that existed prior to venture capital participation should not be confused with the creation of innovation that is frequently allocated to venture capital. An increase in patents following an investment by venture capital may be reflective of the fact that GPs are simply more effective and vigorous in patenting activities. However, patenting may be unnecessary for the majority of firms.

Finally, it is also important to comment on the general contribution of venture capital to the local economy. Despite its frequent claims, venture capital's contribution to employment is questionable, mixed, and controversial. Although venture capital firms frequently report the number of employees employed at their investee firms, in addition to their firm's revenue and profitability, they often fail to disclose the incremental number of employees hired during their tenure. Research suggests that venture capital's contribution to incremental employment growth is not homogenous and depends upon unique circumstances. For example, management buyouts are likely to create jobs while management buy-ins are prone to destroy them. Of course, as stated previously, venture capital seeks to perpetually increase its short-term profits in a rapid manner, and this near-sighted orientation is frequently in conflict with both increasing costs (i.e., hiring more people) and investing in R&D.

Venture Capital in the Mainstream Media

Due to its contemporary proliferation in popular media, it is important to include a brief section about the inclusion of venture capital in popular media and how it is perceived by the general public. Primarily, venture capital and its investments in entrepreneurial firms are mythologized by mainstream media. The popularity of venture capital is frequently showcased to the general public in television programs such as *Shark Tank* and *Dragon's Den*, while venture capitalists like Michael Moritz, John Doerr, Vinod Koshla, Peter Thiel, and many others are often glamorized and maintain "rock star" status in the business community. Furthermore, these individuals are presented as a super-breed class of financial intermediation, artists of deal making, and luminaries of value creation. Of course, the mainstream media promotes venture capital by highlighting only its spectacular successes and megahits, perhaps deceptively implying that these are the standard outcomes of venture capital participation in entrepreneurial ventures; such propaganda is obviously incorrect.

The widespread media promotion of venture capital has also spread the misguided view among entrepreneurs that their expanding business must obtain venture capital in order to become successful. This, in turn, leads many entrepreneurs to internalize the false belief that their ultimate goal is to raise venture capital, further imagining that their firm will just propagate by itself. Therefore, entrepreneurs rarely recognize that their interaction with an average venture capital firm is likely to be a disappointing affair and are not primed to experience such failure because of the skewed perspective perpetuated by mainstream media.

Venture Capital and Entrepreneurial Development: Advantages and Disadvantages

Fundamentally, an entrepreneurial firm will receive capital injection from venture capital in exchange for an equity stake. While entrepreneurial firms at various stages of development may be able to secure other forms of financing, a small number of firms will secure financing from venture capital. It is therefore necessary to explore some of the most important advantages and disadvantages of venture capital financing from an entrepreneur's point of view in the case of the latter, smaller subset of firms.

Venture capital provides a number of critical advantages to founding entrepreneurs and business owners. Primarily, and most importantly, venture capital may be regarded as permanent capital; it does not require repayment, as compared to debt, for example, and there is no expectation of regular interim payments. Venture capitalists also do not require the firm to pay out dividends, nor do they require entrepreneurs to provide any personal guarantees or collateral, which leaves their personal assets intact. Secondly, additional equity capital is likely to increase the firm's creditworthiness by growing its capital base, which is especially important when the firm is seeking to secure bank financing, issue debt, or arrange leasing. In essence, additional equity financing increases leverage potential because higher equity improves the balance sheet of the firm. Financial institutions are especially keen on providing debt to well-capitalized firms, while venture capitalists instinctively understand that firms with a reasonable level of debt financing may be worth more than firms that shy away from debt. However, this form of value creation does not occur automatically, and the firm must first have superior projects to consider and implement. An optimal level of debt in the capital structure, in turn, can further enhance the value of equity.

Equity financing is also likely to improve the firm's credibility with their customers, suppliers, distributors, banks, and other financial institutions. Research has proven that venture capital participation is important during the time of an IPO; venture capital-backed firms normally receive a "certification premium", which is reflected in a higher valuation than would otherwise be achievable. However, recent evidence suggests that this phenomenon may no longer hold true. This credibility certification is based on the general understanding that venture capitalists are highly selective in their investment choices (as noted above) and exhibit a strong preference to invest in firms that have robust growth potential, maintain a strong competitive position (i.e., market share), retain a good management team, and exhibit a proven business model; here, venture capitalists act as "guarantors" and "verifiers" of the quality of the firm. As venture capital record demonstrates, this does not always occur.

Furthermore, due to their hands-on involvement, many venture capitalists can also serve as valuable external consultants to their investee firms. The due diligence process, which requires entrepreneurs to answer multiple questions, rethink expansion plans, and revise financial forecasts, often forces entrepreneurs to evaluate potential business risks more carefully and subsequently develop back-up plans to avert possible hazards in the future. Venture capitalists may be valuable partners, particularly those with strong industry experience, who can contribute to the long-term viability and success of a business. This involvement is likely to not only enhance the operational and financial performance of the entrepreneurial firm, but also to minimize chances of business failure. Venture capitalists likewise aim to develop a solid management team, which is further incentivized by performance-based stock option programs and bonuses. In fact, venture capitalists often insist on establishing a pool of shares (which may be equal to as much as five percent of the firm's equity) dedicated solely to the management team.

However, despite its benefits, venture capital's involvement in the entrepreneurial firm does not come without disadvantages. Firstly, the involvement of venture capitalists in the entrepreneurial venture is dilutive to the founder. Depending on the valuation, venture capitalists are likely to acquire a meaningful minority position in the firm equal to 20 or 30%; of course, there is no dilution of ownership when the firm raises debt. Consequently, due to this dilution, venture capital is often regarded as one of the most expensive forms of entrepreneurial finance. As noted previously, venture capitalists aim to generate above-average returns, which certainly exceed the cost of raising external debt. And yet, the arguments against venture capital's excessive cost may be somewhat exaggerated since venture capital can sometimes be the only form of external financing that a firm is able to secure. Without this capital, the firm may not be able to survive or realize its expansion plans, forcing them to implement a slower development path.

Secondly, the involvement of a venture capitalist means a long-term financial relationship, which will only terminate at exit. While most relationships in the venture capital-backed entrepreneurial firms are effective, nurturing, and cultivating to both sides, difficult operational situations, financial challenges, complex legal arrangements, and various perspectives on strategic planning may strain these relations. Consequently, the behavioral patterns of both parties may become unbearable, intolerable, and destructive. In these difficult circumstances, the founder is not able to simply "fire" his partners or otherwise end the relationship, which can lead to conflicts such as a decision-making gridlock, operational paralysis, and the destruction of entrepreneurial value. These situations are sometimes instigated by the clauses within the legal agreement between venture capitalists and entrepreneurs related to the venture capitalist's ability to approve certain operational, financial, human resource, legal, or contractual decisions. While this is a normal requirement for venture capitalists, it may cause the entrepreneurial firm to become inflexible and slow to respond to customers, changes in the industry, and competitors. In rare situations, venture capitalists' restrictions may even result in founder dismissal, or more simply, firing the founder from the firm they themselves started, as a solution to an intolerable working relationship.

Conflicts Between Venture Capitalists and Entrepreneurs

Conflict in business is common and often unavoidable. It can take the form of obvious verbalized incompatibilities, incongruities, opinions, or simple disagreements and can arise abruptly or unfold slowly over time. There is evidence to suggest that conflict negatively effects business performance, the achievement of financial milestones, and value creation.

The divergence of perspectives between venture capitalists and entrepreneurs can materialize at any point of the venture capital investment process, including, but not limited to, deal closing, operational issues, strategic planning, hiring decisions, and exit considerations. This divergence is often grounded in perceived differences between venture capitalists and entrepreneurs with respect to what is required, necessary, and desired for the firm. For example, conflict can arise due a venture capitalist's insistence on the "professionalization" (or "corporatization") of the entrepreneurial firm. However, operating on the basis of an easy-going internal culture, loosely specified strategies, less established or entrenched management practices, and an informal working atmosphere can be critical to entrepreneurial experimentation and innovation. Thus, a new business construct based on administrative structures and formal procedures, processes, and mechanisms that is frequently insisted upon by venture capitalists may lead to undue bureaucratization, which, in turn, may lead to the destruction of any competitive advantage the firm had previously enjoyed.

Furthermore, while venture capitalists are often skilled in running financial models, structuring transactions, and affecting acquisitions, they typically have relatively "light" operational experience. Entrepreneurs, on the other hand, are generally more knowledgeable than venture capitalists about their specific industry, potential operational issues, and human resource management. Unsurprisingly, the over-analytical handling of entrepreneurial activity by venture capitalists does not pair well with the entrepreneurial process. In fact, an overly analytical approach in which venture capitalists insist on actions that may be suboptimal or even mistaken is directly opposed to the more pragmatic and hands-on entrepreneurial process, and breeds conflict between the two parties. These trends are clearly borne out in numbers, as, for example, evidence suggests that within buyout funds, over 50% of the increase in the value of the firm came from growth in exit multiples and not operational improvements. Other research confirms that more than 75% of buyout-oriented GPs failed to generate operational improvements leading to increased profitability.

Most importantly, as noted earlier, it is the penchant for venture capitalists to dismiss founders. This represents one of the most drastic and forceful manners by which venture capitalists may choose to interact with the founding entrepreneur who initially brought them into the entrepreneurial venture. When justifying such draconian measures, venture capitalists often argue that a new CEO can elevate the firm to new development heights and accelerate the process. However, evidence suggests that such dismissal often coincides with various forms of crisis in the entrepreneurial firm related to compromised financial performance, disrupted operational dynamics, and a poor competitive nature.

Historical Trends in the Venture Capital Industry

The global venture capital industry has grown rapidly in the last fifty years; the industry emerged in the late 1960s and early 1970s in the U.S. and the U.K., accelerated its development in the mid-1980s, and grew exponentially in the 1990s throughout most developed countries. However, the industry entered a period of unprecedented volatility in the early 2000s (see Fig. 1.1(a)). There has also been a robust advent of venture

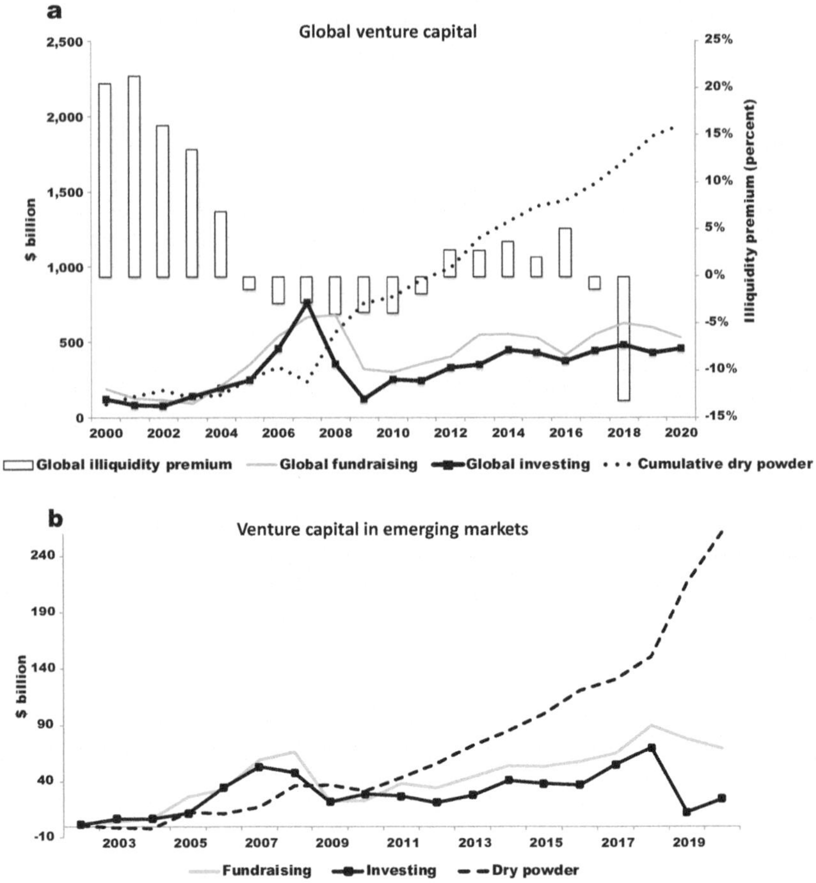

Fig. 1.1 Key statistics in global venture capital (a) Global private equity fundraising, investing, dry powder accumulation, and the illiquidity premium (b) Key data in venture capital in emerging markets (*Source* Various sources, including Prequin, Bain, Cambridge Associates, EMPEA. Updated from Klonowski [2018])

capital in emerging markets throughout this 50-year period, which has grown to account for about 8.7 of global fundraising. Figure 1.1(a) also illustrates the global "illiquidity premium", which is defined as a premium return generated from venture capital returns that is above the returns achieved from public equities markets or alternative asset classes. The U.S. S&P 500 index was selected as the benchmark for approximating these returns from public equities markets.

Figure 1.1(a) illustrates a strong acceleration in global fundraising and investing activities in the middle 2000s, followed by a rapid decline during the 2008 financial crisis. In the last twenty years, between 2000 and 2020, global venture capital firms raised $8,711.0 billion and invested $6,771.1 billion. While the average growth rates in fundraising and investing were equal to 12.9% and 14.9%, respectively, over this twenty-year period, the growth rates in recent years have been irregular, volatile, and inconsistent. For example, between 2000 and 2010, growth rates in fundraising accelerated by 18.0%, while in the following period (2011 to 2020) it was equal to 6.1%, which represents a significant slowdown. The most significant declines in fundraising occurred during and after the "dotcom" crisis, resulting in a 34.5% decline in 2001, and after the 2008 financial crisis, which amounted to a 53.3% decline. Other significant periods of decline in fundraising occurred in 2003 (−19.8%), 2016 (−21.4%), and 2020 (−11.3%).

There have also been periods of rapid increase in fundraising, especially following the dotcom correction (2004–122.6%; 2005–68.6%; 2006–54.2%), as well as in the years after the 2008 financial crisis (2011–17.7%; 2012–15.1%; 2013–35.1%). Meanwhile, the average annual fundraising activities have been equal to $414.8 billion. Investing activities show similar growth and decline patterns, with the most significant decline in investing occurring in 2009 by almost two-thirds from $121.0 billion to $35.0 billion. However, investing activity bounced back to about $254.0 billion the following year in 2010. Additionally, it is important to note that fundraising for younger entrepreneurial firms is one of the fastest growing categories of broadly defined private equity. LPs and GPs generally question whether the industry has reached its peak, and if that is the case, whether this peak is cyclical or more permanent.

Figure 1.1(a) confirms that in the period between the dotcom era and the 2008 financial crisis, average fundraising and investing activities have been well matched. The capital deployment efficiency ratio (CDER), which may be defined as a longitudinal ratio of cumulative investing to fundraising, was equal to 91.5%. The above graph also clearly demonstrates that since the 2008 financial crisis, fundraising has outpaced investing; the CDER ratio post-2008 has been equal to 73.4 (although the CDER ratio over the entire 20-year period has been equal to 77.7%).

This continued divergence between fundraising and investing has led to a substantial accumulation of un-invested capital (i.e., unemployed callable capital or capital committed by GPs that has not yet been called by LPs), commonly known as "dry powder", which is represented by a dotted line in Fig. 1.1(a). So-called dry powder refers to the historic military practice of stockpiling dry gunpowder, which would be ultimately employed for ammunition. In any case, at the end of 2020, dry powder was equal to an estimated $1,939.9 billion, although other estimates suggest that it has already reached $2,500 billion; either way, evidence confirms that dry powder accumulates at the rate of $92.4 billion per annum. The most substantial accumulation of dry powder occurred in 2001, with an increase of 62.1%, but also pre- and post-2008 financial crisis, with a 70.0% increase in 2005 and a 139.3% increase in 2008. Since the average level of investing is equal to $322.4 billion per annum, the cumulative value of dry powder at the end 2020 was equal to 4.2 times the annual value of investments (note that the average value of dry powder to annual investment is equal to 2.6 for the entire time period). In other words, dry powder increased at a rate previously seen over a two-year period of annual investing activity in just 2020 alone or more precisely about 31 months' worth of investment.

The accumulation of dry powder not only occurs on a global scale, but also in emerging markets, because these markets are perceived as one of the most attractive market segments in the global venture capital landscape. The primary attraction of emerging markets reflects the fact that many countries in these markets have been able to achieve strong economic growth due to a dedicated manufacturing and service orientation, a vigorous expansion of the middle class, substantial local investments, extraordinary rural-to-urban migration, a reduced dependence on exports, and responsible public finance. Furthermore, venture capital investors are attracted to the opportunity within emerging markets to employ capital at higher increments within key sectors of the economy (i.e., financial institutions, energy, transportation and distribution, telecommunications, etc.), thus earning returns above those available in developed countries. And yet, despite these potentially attractive characteristics, the flow of venture capital into emerging markets has been slow. For example, the cumulative value of investing was equal to $569.0 billion between 2002 and 2020, which represents only 9.4% of cumulative global investing, while the level of cumulative fundraising over this period was equal to $830.2 billion, accounting for 11.0% of global fundraising. This commitment of venture capital to emerging markets is relatively small given that emerging markets account for about 60% of global GDP (gross domestic product). The difference between the two cumulative fundraising and investing values, which is equal to $261.2 billon, demonstrates the value of dry power accumulation in emerging markets, which, as presented in Fig. 1.1(b), has also been steadily growing since 2005.

There are various conflicting interpretations of the increased presence of dry powder in the industry. Some commentators suggest that an excess value of dry powder in the industry may be interpreted as a useful and handy cash inventory ready for future deployment. Expectedly, venture capital claims that this accumulated capital would be deployed to outstanding deals at acceptable valuations, assuming that venture capital firms can find and secure them, which could ultimately generate superior returns. As careful observers readily note, venture capital firms can easily create an attractive storyline, investment thesis, or compelling investment case when fundraising for a new fund; thus, this "cash overhang" may also be viewed as an example of investors behaving in a responsible, cautious, and prudent manner. By not pursuing investment opportunities at excessively high entry valuations, at the top of the business cycle, or in high competition for deals, a claim can be made that venture capitalists are waiting for valuations to decline to more reasonable levels. Indeed, the EV/EBITDA (i.e., enterprise value to earnings before interest, taxation, depreciation, and amortization) multiples on entry valuations have increased from about 6.4 in 2009 to over 11 times in 2020 (11.4 times in the U.S. and 12.6 times in Europe), with the average over this ten-year period equal to 9.2. While the average EV/EBITDA multiples have been rapidly growing, the percentage of transactions with EV/EBITDA multiples in excess of 11 times exceeded 60% in 2020. Of course, these elevated EV/EBITDA multiples are problematic to venture capitalists seeking to deploy capital into investee firms but benefit those who dispose of investments, although the effect of elevated entry valuations is ultimately destructive to financial returns. Moreover, one could argue that because fundraising historically kept pace with investing, the divergence between the two figures would eventually be self-corrected and normalized (of course, this is not supported by evidence since the 2008 crisis as demonstrated by Fig. 1.1(a)).

Additionally, a further potential benefit of dry powder accumulation is that it can be used for unforeseen circumstances, especially when venture capital funds consider providing further financial assistance to existing investee firms in their portfolio. The accumulation of dry powder may also be explained by the widespread availability of debt at near-zero-interest rates. In other words, GPs are using more debt rather than equity in transactions, which is reflected in a growing number of deals with debt multiples in excess of seven times EBITDA (earnings before interest, taxation, depreciation, and amortization) and a declining number of deals with debt multiples less than six times EBITDA.

Of course, steadily accumulating dry powder has further implications. An obvious conclusion is that dry powder accumulates because investing continues to be disconnected from fundraising activities; this may arise from the fact that GPs are raising excessive funds in relation to the deal opportunities available in the marketplace. In congruence with this initial issue is the fact that GPs may have problems identifying suitable investment opportunities, which can be due to unfavorable economic conditions, poor deal flow, strong competition for high-quality deals, or a problematic exit environment. This could even be a classic case of "too much money chasing too many deals", which is a problem the industry regularly experiences. However, research is clear that overheated entry valuations have one predictable outcome: depressed returns.

Excess fundraising may be indicative of GPs' inherent desire to perpetually raise subsequent funds, which will provide guaranteed fixed fees over a pre-defined period of time. Some observers argue that GPs may be more focused on amplifying their own income rather than maximizing returns for LPs; such behavior may be especially prevalent in GPs with weaker track records of returns. Understandably, these types of situations lead to a distorted LP-GP motivational structure that is filled with agency issues. At the core of such compensation issues is the fact that LPs pay fees on un-invested capital, or as one academic rightly observes, "money for nothing", and there is some evidence in the industry of "zombie" funds, which focus on fee extraction. Additionally, there is the question as to why GPs are actively raising additional incremental capital in the marketplace if they are unable to invest capital already under management. The persistence of dry powder may also alienate LPs, who expect a timely deployment of capital. Lastly, there is a relationship between accumulated dry powder and illiquidity premium as demonstrated in Fig. 1.1(a). This relationship is negative ($\sigma = -0.54$), which signifies that when the value of dry powder increases, the GPs' ability to generate "excess returns" (i.e., illiquidity premium) is compromised.

Venture Capital Returns: A Historical Perspective

Evidence suggests that private equity, like many other industries, is a cyclical business. In this case, the cycle typically begins with a limited number of GPs realizing strong returns after making successful investments and securing suitable exits. At this stage in the industry cycle, deal generation may seem effortless and GPs are able to acquire ownership stakes in investee firms at discounted valuations in what is clearly a capital supplier market. Encouraged by the success of the existing market participants, new venture capital firms enter the market. LPs, who are eager to provide excess capital to the asset class, effectively flood the market with capital and initiate a change in the private equity cycle. Over time, high amounts of capital in the market ultimately create more competition for deals, especially for high-quality investment opportunities; in short, "too many dollars are chasing too few deals". At this point in the cycle, GPs either pursue transactions at excessively high entry valuations or pursue inferior investment opportunities (i.e., "lemons"). Some investments lead to bankruptcies, liquidation, or outright write-offs, which are scenarios likely to generate depressed returns and ultimately discourage LPs from providing more capital to the industry. Poorly performing GPs are thus unable to complete successful fundraising and may close, while others complete capital raising but may not be able to meet fundraising targets. Over time, the quantity of capital available in the marketplace declines and a new cycle begins; it is in this context of the venture capital cycle that financial returns will be discussed.

The most common methods to measure venture capital returns, which can be expressed in gross or net values, include an internal rate of return (IRR), distributions to paid-in capital (DPI), and public market equivalents (PMEs). IRRs are implicit rates of return earned from an investment over a specific period of time. This relative measure used in venture capital is likely to include drawdowns, distributions, fees, other incomes (i.e., dividends), and residuals values in its consideration. DPI is one of the measures used by LPs to illuminate how many times their initial capital has been multiplied. In this specific case, DPI is defined as the ratio of capital distributed to LPs in relation to the amount of capital LPs actually provided to the GP. Similar measures to DPI that are utilized by LPs are cash-on-cash (C-on-C) return, multiple of invested capital (MOIC), or multiple of money (MoM). Lastly, PMEs describe GPs' actual dollar-denominated returns in relation to dollar returns that would have been generated by investing the same value of capital into public equities markets for the same duration of time. This measure effectively represents the opportunity cost of investing into public equities markets vis-à-vis venture capital.

Before reviewing venture capital returns, it is important to preface this discussion with the fact that as a facet of their co-operation, GPs enter into a legal contract with LPs because GPs are predicated to generate above-average (or outsized) returns or "illiquidity premiums" (as defined above). As a part of the legal arrangement, GPs are entitled to fees and carried interest (i.e., GPs receive 20% of the profit generated by the partnership; profits are defined as the difference between the net realized value of the fund and the value of the LPs' initial contribution). The illiquidity premium represents the "venture capital promise" to LPs, who rightly expect that GPs can realize returns exceeding those from public equities markets by three to five percent (i.e., 300 to 500 basis points), although the minimum illiquidity premium expected from venture capital is widely understood to be equal to three percent.

This illiquidity premium reflects at least four distinct risks that LPs carry, which merit higher incremental return expectations from venture capital. The first two risks relate to general illiquidity inherent in the venture capital investment process, and the remaining two relate to operating and financial risks. Firstly, LPs commit capital to GPs for a pre-defined and lengthy period of time, during which LPs have a limited ability to withdraw or access their invested capital. In rare circumstances, LPs may sell their stakes in GPs on a secondary market, although this may subject their stakes to a severe "hair-cut" in valuation. GPs also invest capital into private firms for three to five years, during which period their capital is similarly illiquid, resulting in a compounded illiquidity risk for LPs. Moreover, the investment of a GP into investee firms is also subject to multiple operational risks, including significant chances of underperformance, bankruptcy, or liquidation of the investee firms. Lastly, there are financial risks related to financing an investee firm, which can occur in times of strong financial performance or outright underperformance, as well as burdening them with excessive debt, which is a frequent occurrence in buyout situations.

A review of academic studies on venture capital returns leads to a number of conclusions. In fact, many studies concluded that returns are dependent upon the time horizon when investments were made, exited from, and when the returns were calculated. Some studies, which predominantly focused on investments made in the 1980s and 1990s, illustrate strong above-average returns; the period encompassing the early to mid-1980s appears to be the most profitable era in the development of the venture capital industry in the U.S., the U.K., and other countries.

In any case, it is important to note that the average GP has not been able to generate the excess returns equal to between 30 and 50% that have often been promoted to the public. For example, one study published by the Kauffman Foundation, which provides an analysis of the foundation's investments into its GPs, reports that only about 25% of 100 GPs in the foundation's portfolio have been able to beat the returns from public equities markets by at least three percentage points; nearly 50% of GPs analyzed were not able to provide any returns on invested capital. Thus, it is not surprising that further evidence shows a significant divergence in the return performance between the top quartile and the rest of the GPs. In other words, there is a significant drop-off in performance between the top and remaining quartiles, and there is no doubt that these top performers unduly influence the industry averages. To illustrate this, for example, the top quartile GPs in 2013 in Europe were able to secure net returns equal to 20.3%, while the second quartile GPs were only able to achieve returns of 5.9%; this represents a difference of 14.4% in performance between the first and second quartile performance.

Additional academic studies further dispute venture capital's ability to generate above-average returns. Figure 1.2 demonstrates a comparison of academic studies on venture capital returns in comparison with returns achieved from public equities markets. The studies are presented in the following five columns: venture capital returns worse than public equities markets; equal to public equities markets; better than public equities markets; better than public equities markets by more than three percent; better than public equities markets by five percent. These studies indicate that venture capital funds have not been able to exceed LPs' minimum requirements in any consistent manner. It is also prudent to note that the right-hand side of the figure is quite empty.

Research furthermore confirms a discrepancy between returns generated by LPs and GPs, indicating that GPs may be able to generate positive returns for themselves, but substantially lower returns for LPs. This is inevitably due in part to GPs' excessive fees and carried interest payouts, which cut into LPs' profits or net returns. Additionally, as noted above,

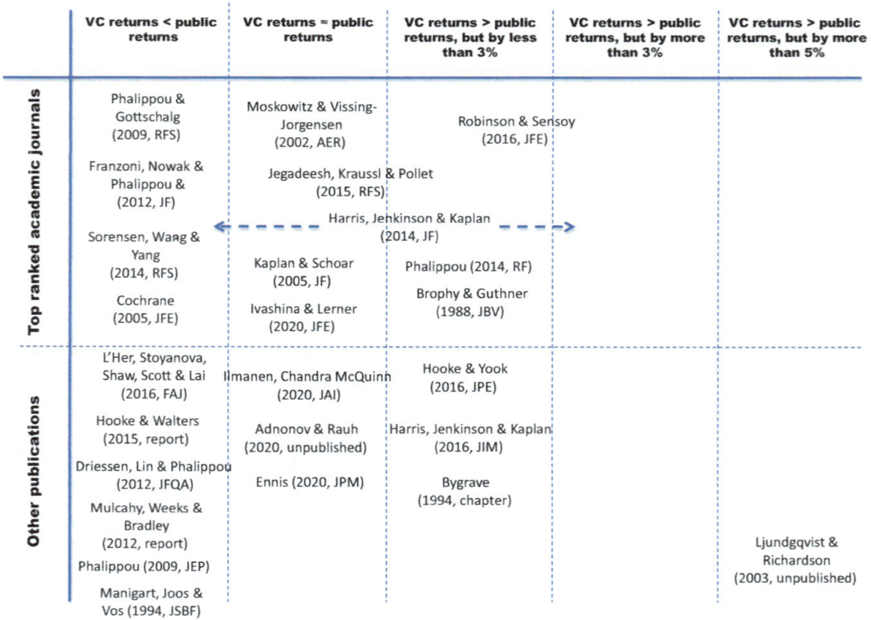

Fig. 1.2 A summary of academic studies on venture capital returns Abbreviations: *AER* American Economic Review, *FAJ* Financial Analyst Journal, *JAI* Journal of Alternative Investments, *JBV* Journal of Business Venturing, *JEP* Journal of Economic Perspectives, *JIM* Journal of Investment Management, *JF* Journal of Finance, *JFE* Journal of Financial Economics, *JFQA* Journal of Finance and Quantitative Analysis, *JPM* Journal of Portfolio Management, *JPE* Journal of Private Equity, *JSBF* Journal of Small Business Finance, *RF* Review of Finance, *RFS* Review of Financial Studies. Updated from Klonowski (2018)

poor GP performance is often associated with strong competition for deals, weaker returns from public equities markets, and larger fund sizes.

A fourth conclusion that can be drawn from studies on venture capital returns is that returns vary from country-to-country and region-to-region. For example, studies confirm that venture capital returns from the U.S. generally exceed those achieved in Europe. There is also a strong potential for emerging market countries to become the next hotbed of above-average GP returns, as, based on 2015 data, ten-year returns were highest in Asia. Finally, however, studies identify that venture capital returns have generally deteriorated over time, which is clearly visible in Figs. 1.3 and 1.4.

In this section, it is important to differentiate between returns from venture capital (i.e., financing younger entrepreneurial firms in the fastest growing sectors of the economy) and private equity (i.e., more substantive expansion transactions with firms at later stages of development). In this context, Fig. 1.3(a) presents a historical perspective on returns from venture capital and private equity in the U.S. between 1986 and 2018, a period of over three decades. Figure 1.3(a) indicates drifts in venture capital returns, particularly when compared to the S&P 500, the most recognized and widely used benchmark index. The graph also illustrates calculations of illiquidity premium, which in this case capture the difference between venture capital returns and returns achieved by investing in the S&P 500 index. Furthermore, Fig. 1.3(a) features a horizontal reference line at the three percent point throughout the entire time horizon to signify the LPs' expectations, although a five-percent reference line would perhaps be more appropriate given the level of risk investing into early-stage entrepreneurial firms.

When analyzing Fig. 1.3(a), it is necessary to mention that the illiquidity premium for venture capital between the period of 1986 and 2018 was equal to 13.0%. However, this average includes the extraordinary excess returns generated in the period between 1995 and 1997. Illiquidity premiums were equal to 69.1% in 1995, 90.6% in 1996, and 87.2% in 1997; such returns and illiquidity premiums have not been achieved since this outlier period. Secondly, venture capital returns have been highly cyclical since 1997, with some visible stability in returns between 2010 and 2017. However, venture capital returns in this period were undoubtedly influenced by a number of outlier returns from novel tech companies. Furthermore, post-1997, there were eight years when

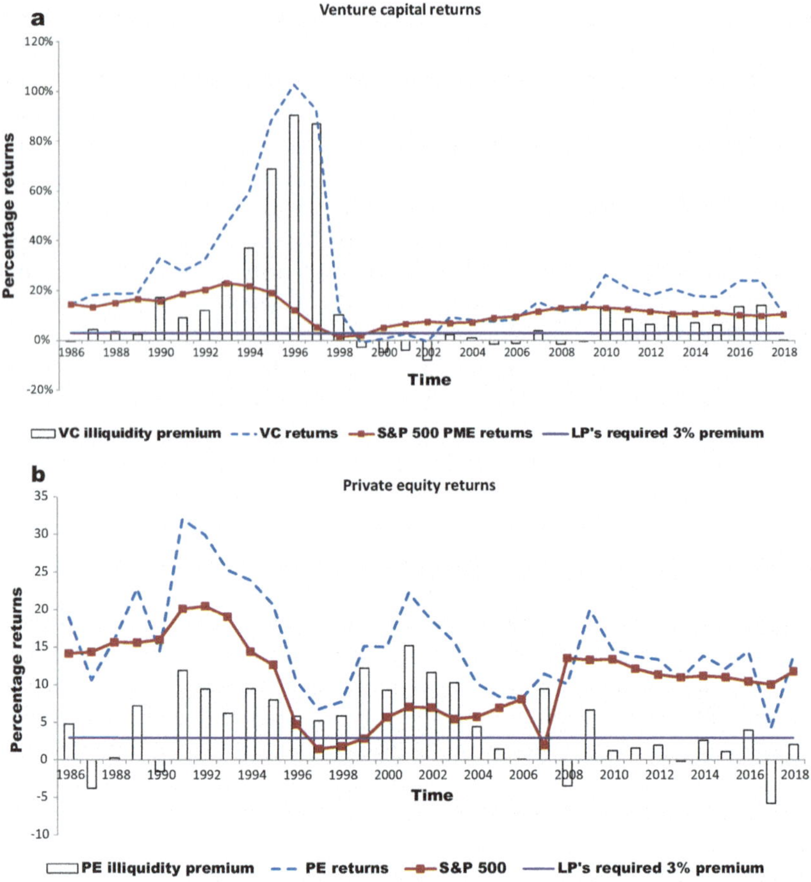

Fig. 1.3 Historical perspective on venture capital and private equity returns in the U.S. (a) Returns from venture capital between 1986 and 2018 in the U.S. (b) Returns from private equity between 1986 and 2018 in the U.S. (*Source* Cambridge Associates. Updated from Klonowski [2018])

the illiquidity premium was outright negative (i.e., 1999–2002, 2005–2006, 2008–2009) and three years when it was below LPs' minimum expected returns (i.e., 2003–2004, 2018). Based on our data, venture capital returns in the U.S. were equal to 3.1% since 1997, which just

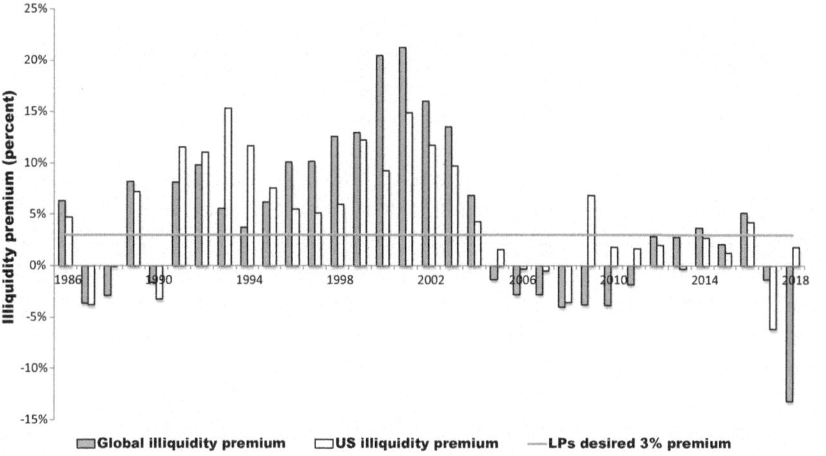

Fig. 1.4 Global perspective on private equity returns in comparison with U.S. returns (*Source* Various sources, including Cambridge Associates, Bain and Company. Updated from Klonowski [2018])

barely meets LPs' minimum return requirement of three percent in the long-term, but is below the reasonable five-percent expectation.

Figure 1.3(b) illustrates returns from private equity investments in the U.S., which is similarly contrasted to the S&P 500 illiquidity premium. In comparison with venture capital, U.S. private equity is also cyclical, choppy, and inconsistent. Although the long-term illiquidity premium between 1986 and 2018 was equal to 4.7%, the ten-year illiquidity premium between 2008 and 2018 declined to a meager 1.1%. Furthermore, the illiquidity premium for this same ten-year period is benchmarked at 2.0 on the S&P 500 index and −0.9% compared to the Nasdaq Composite index, according to the 2020 Cambridge Associates report; this is well below LPs' expectations. Private equity returns also seem less affected than venture capital by the strong volatility of returns as expressed by standard deviation ($\sigma = 5.0$ in private equity; $\sigma = 24.1\%$ in venture capital). Thus, the dispersion of returns from venture capital between different quartiles is much higher than in the case of private equity. For example, the average illiquidity premium in private equity returns was equal to 5.3% between 1986 and 1997, while in the decade between 1998 and 2008 it reached 6.1%. However, the ten-year illiquidity premium between 2009 and 2018 was equal to 1.5%, which is below LPs' required return. There is additional evidence that confirms nearly 70% of IPOs led by GPs underperformed in the market. In these cases, GP certification was ineffectual, while the performance of buyouts overall was even worse.

Lastly, it is also crucial to evaluate the U.S. illiquidity premium in the context of global private equity performance. Figure 1.4 outlines the cyclical nature of both global and U.S. returns, and demonstrates that the returns between the two subsets are highly correlated ($\sigma = 0.73$). The difference between global private equity (excluding the U.S. data) and the U.S.' private equity illiquidity premium is minimal. While U.S. private equity has generated an illiquidity premium equal to 4.7% between 1986 and 2018, the rest of the world produced a similar premium equal to 4.4%. The ten-year illiquidity premium performance for global private equity is equal to −1.1% in the post-2008 financial crisis era (2008–2018).

Maturation of the Venture Capital Industry

The traditional theories of the industry's life cycle suggest that any industry is likely to progress through different stages of development, ending in an eventual decline. This maturation process occurs in distinct phases beginning at the outset of development, during which the industry is often fragmented, and no single firm has a commanding leadership. If the industry grows quickly, its inventors, subsequent entrants, and even late followers may be able to command premium pricing, secure high margins, and generate strong cash flow. Over time, as more competitors enter the market, prices begin to decline and quality may fall; these dynamics are likely to reduce any participant's revenue growth, profit margins, and sustainability of strong cash flow.

As competition increases, market participants aim to differentiate their commercial propositions by re-defining products and services, effecting positive or negative quality adjustments, employing outsourcing tactics, implementing offshoring, revamping the supply chain, or creating new ways to interact with customers; in essence, the entire value chain is overhauled. At the same time as the industry is developing and evolving, buyers become more knowledgeable, demanding, and sophisticated in their purchasing choices. Eventually, industries will mature and become consolidated around a small number of dominant players, while the closure of underperforming firms will initiate industry retrenchment. Of course, this process of maturation is not necessarily unduly negative to the industry, as market participants may choose to retool their operations, rethink their delivery model, or reinvent themselves in other meaningful ways. The impetus for change within the industry may also come from customers who are dissatisfied with the current commercial offers, pricing, quality, and delivery. Thus, while the industry as a collection of firms may resort to basic survival strategies when at the end of its life cycle, it could also lead to the industry's regeneration and revitalization.

There are some parameters that will aid in the evaluation of the venture capital industry's current state. These parameters, which may confirm the industry has already entered its maturity stage, include the size of the industry, diversity, competence, financial performance, and general modifications. In terms of size, although fundraising and investing activities steadily increased until the middle of the 2000s, there is a notable stagnation in both statistics in the last twenty years. This is especially visible in investing statistics, which have been propped up by increased deal sizes in the face of flat or declining deal counts. Deal flow is propelled by public-to-private transactions and venture capital firms recycling investee firms among themselves. Poor deal flow is reflected in the desperation of GPs looking for deals virtually anywhere. For example, with regard to the volume of transactions, the deal count in the buyout space has oscillated around 3,500 in the last decade; thus, a deal flow of high-quality deals is limited compared to the early days of the industry. As noted previously, the net effect of stagnating deal flow is rapidly accumulating dry powder, and this pattern of development is generally indicative of industry maturity.

In relation to the industry's diversity, GPs offer a wide range of services to LPs including participation in early-stage firms (i.e., venture capital), expansion transactions (i.e., private equity), and the outright purchase of firms (i.e., buyouts), in addition to investment opportunities for GPs related to private debt, real estate, natural resources, and infrastructure. There is evidence to suggest that LPs increase their capital allocations to other forms of private capital more readily than to private equity; examples of these disproportionate allocations are found in private debt, natural resource, and infrastructure deals. There is another category of private capital with significant market traction for LPs, namely private debt, which may be particularly attractive to firms in industries such as telecommunications, transportation, and power.

General competence in the industry may be considered as a parameter of the venture capital industry's state with respect to GPs' abilities and skill in managing investee firms and LPs. In terms of capabilities to work with investee firms, only a relatively small group of GPs (about 15%) may truly be able to provide active, realistic, and effective assistance to investee firms; in comparison, other GPs are likely to exhibit significant shortcomings in operational, strategic, and planning assistance. With regard to LP interactions, GPs are assessed on their ability to generate excess returns. While LPs continue to allocate capital toward the sector through "bucket-filling" strategies, there is a significant number of LPs (about 25%) who express dissatisfaction with their returns from the asset class. However, LPs are also disappointed with GP information disclosure, compensation structures, and inherent agency issues, among other problems.

In the matter of financial performance, as noted above, it is evident that GPs struggle to provide strong illiquidity premiums on a consistent and repeatable basis. In fact, research verifies that LPs hardly break even after accounting for fees and carried interest. Evidence also indicates that there is nothing extraordinary about venture capital returns in comparison with public equities markets. In many periods, venture capital returns have been stagnant and declining, which may reflect a general "commoditization" of the industry. Moreover, an increased competition among GPs can similarly lead to declining returns. This, however, does not prevent GPs from generating strong profits for themselves, which raises the question: To what extent is the current business model sustainable in the long-term?

Lastly, regarding the industry's general transition, there are strong undercurrents pointing to slow but consistent consolidation while the industry continues to be fragmented. The most significant of these trends is an increased number of mega-funds equal to between \$5 and \$10 billion in size, which in 2018 accounted for nearly thirty percent of total fundraising; these funds continue to be increasingly appealing to LPs. Moreover, research affirms that the standard GP now manages 4.5 funds on average, in comparison with 3.4 funds ten years ago. In other words, this statistic reinforces the notion that more LP capital flows to fewer GPs. In fact, the top four GPs account for 12.1% of the total assets under management in private equity; this number was equal to 12.4% in 2015. Industry consolidation is also driven by growth in the dispersion of returns between top quartile performance and the rest of the GP pack, which, as noted above, continues to widen in the asset class. Evidence furthermore suggests that LPs increasingly consider top quartile

GPs, but these funds are significantly over-subscribed, so the remaining unsubscribed capital flows to tier two funds (i.e., from the second quartile). The top-performing GPs are rightly able to increase their fund size by about 50% in relation to their predecessor funds.

On the other hand, there are trends, which are contrarian to the consolidation thesis. In the U.S., for example, the number of GPs has doubled in the last ten years or so. The consolidation process is undoubtedly slow due to the longevity of LP-GP partnerships, so although an increase in the number of GPs may be quick, a decline by attrition will be relatively slow. Moreover, while there is some indication that the largest GPs focus on the expansion of human resources, there may be less such indication from smaller GPs. The largest GPs are also implementing some technological changes and digitization improvements, which may lead to increased operating efficiency, improved disclosure to LPs, more timely monitoring of investee firms, stronger analytical capabilities in the investment selection (e.g., in the case of public-to-private transaction space), and more data-driven investment decisions; smaller GPs are simply not able to afford these improvements.

Even though there may not be unequivocal and unmistakable signs of maturity in the venture capital industry, there are distinctive indicators, which point to its movement in this direction. In general terms, the transition to maturity is confirmed by a broad-based slowdown of fundraising and investing, more intense competition for deals, inconsistent and declining returns, an increased number of failed GP fundraisings, and a larger number of mega-funds, among other indications. There are also some signs that venture capital has suffered from a reputation crisis in the eyes of entrepreneurs and LPs.

Summary of Venture Capital in a Pre-COVID Era

Venture capital was struggling prior to the end of 2019, which is reflected by a number of factors. Primarily, despite the generally positive publicity and euphoria it creates, venture capital only makes a very small contribution to the entrepreneurial ecosystem. For example, and as observed previously, venture capitalists finance less than one percent of all entrepreneurial firms in the U.S.; these statistics are even worse in other countries. Moreover, venture capitalists are less true today than in the past to their early-day maxim of being "value creators" and "builders of businesses". Since venture capital often exhibits a "batting average" and "spray-and-pray" mentality toward its portfolio of entrepreneurial firms, it often loses interest in the underperforming investee firms it finances. Thus, venture capital increasingly resembles a roulette-like search for megahits in which underperformers or "casualties" matter less. If the entire asset class behaves in a similar manner, venture capitalists may actually contribute to a general impairment of the entrepreneurial ecosystem. However, due to its limited exposure to entrepreneurial firms, any potential impairment may be limited.

Secondly, there is a significant debate about whether venture capitalists are truly skilled at consistently picking winners. Evidence indicates that venture capitalists may achieve a track record of about two-six-two on their portfolio of investee firms; in other words, venture capital achieves two or even one robust investment, six investments that grossly underachieve, and two or more total write-offs. Therefore, "expert" investors are getting it right approximately one or two times out of ten bets, which is astonishing given that the industry claims to spend significant time and resources on due diligence, making significant value-added contributions to investee firm operations, and planning their exit exceptionally well. It is no surprise that LPs are increasingly questioning the validity and efficacy of the venture capital business model given these lackluster statistics.

Thirdly, venture capital has accumulated significant amounts of dry powder in the last three decades. The estimates of uncalled capital range between $2.0 and $2.5 trillion, which is a historically unprecedented amount in the venture capital industry. This is especially concerning to LPs, who pay approximately $25 billion in fees to GPs on this unemployed capital. Although there may be various explanations for this cash overhang, it is important to question whether GPs may be unduly attracted to the management fees they accumulate. It is also intriguing why GPs are raising more funds if they are unable to spend cash already on hand. Moreover, beyond the fees accrued on their un-invested capital, VC firms are breaking one of their most fundamental promises relating to returns for LPs, who expect to generate returns at least three percent higher than returns from public equities markets to compensate for the additional risk and long periods of illiquidity. While, for example, the long-term illiquidity from private equity in the U.S. is equal to 4.7% in our dataset, the ten-year average (2008–2018) is equal to a meager 1.1%; this underperformance is also borne out in data from other sources.

Fourthly, it is valuable to mention that the venture capital industry has not experienced any significant disruptions to its business model. Changes in the industry have been slow and the business model has remained consistent over time.

Finally, this section concludes with an analysis to underline the excessive size of the global venture capital industry, which is based on an analysis performed by Portico Advisers and its managing director Mike Casey. Let's use the logic applied by Portico here. If it is assumed that global venture capital raises $404.5 billion from LPs on average, and there is an expectation to generate three times cash-on-cash returns for LPs, venture capital firms are effectively required to convert $404.5 billion into $1,213.5 billion of exit value on an annual basis (subject to management fees and other costs chargeable to the fund). In other words, over one trillion dollars of exit value should be realized annually. And yet, evidence suggests that the average value of exits between 2005 and 2019 was equal to $312.6 billion (based on buyouts), which exceeds the exit value that could be reasonably expected by a factor of 3.9 times. In other words, given that the global venture capital industry can generate exit values in excess of $300 billion per annum, the amount of global venture capital fundraising that the industry can absorb should be equal to roughly round up to one hundred billion dollars. Therefore, the annual fundraising value should not be $404.5 billion, meaning that the industry is currently four times too large. Even if it is assumed that LPs can reasonably expect cash-on-cash returns of two times, a recalculation would suggest that the industry is still excessively big by a factor of nearly 2.5 times. Of course, GPs are unconcerned by an over-allocation of capital to the industry; they are content to take the money, which freely arrives to them in the form of management fees and potentially lucrative payments from carried interest. GPs are in fact addicted to these guaranteed cash flows, which may represent as much as two-thirds of GPs' total compensation.

Bibliography

Arundale, Keith and Colin Mason. 2020. Private equity & venture capital: Riding the COVID-19 crisis. In *Innovation in Business, Economics & Finance 1*, eds. Monica Billio and Simone Varotto, 193–220. Ca' Foscari University Press: Venice.

Bain & Company. 2020. Global Private Equity Report. www.bain.com.

Braun, Reiner and Ingo Stoff. 2016. The cost of private equity investing and the impact of dry powder. *Journal of Private Equity*, Spring, 22–33.

Brown, Gregory W., Oleg R. Gredil, and Steven N. Kaplan. Do private equity funds manipulate reported returns? *Journal of Financial Economics*, 132: 267–297.

Cambridge Associates. 2020a. U.S. private equity index and selected benchmark statistics. June 3.

Cambridge Associates. 2020b. U.S. venture index and selected benchmark statistics. June 30.

Cambridge Associates. 2020c. Private equity: Index and selected benchmark statistics. 2020. June 30.

Cambridge Associates. 2014a. U.S. private equity index and selected benchmark statistics. March 31.

Cambridge Associates. 2014b. U.S. venture index and selected benchmark statistics. March 31.

Casey, Michael. 2017. Portico perspective: Does the emerging markets private equity asset class scale up? December 2017. www.porticoadvisers.com.

Klonowski, Darek. 2018. *The Venture Capital Deformation: Value Destruction throughout the Investment Process*. New York: Palgrave MacMillan.

Klonowski, Darek. 2013. *The Venture Capital Investment Process: Principles and Practice*. New York: Palgrave MacMillan.

Korteweg, Arthur and Morten Sorensen. 2017. Skill and luck in private equity performance. *Journal of Financial Economics*, 124: 535–562.

Lamber, Marie. 2020. Agency costs of dry powder in private equity funds. September 21. University of Liege. Working paper.

M.C.K. Private equity: The propaganda versus the facts. 2017. *The Economist*. September 21, 2016.

Mulcahy, Diane, Bill Weeks, and Harold S. Bradley. 2012. We have met the enemy…and it is us: Lessons from twenty years of the Kauffman Foundation's investments in venture capital funds and the triumph of hope over experience. Washington: Ewing Marion Kauffman Foundation. May.

McKinsey & Company. 2019. Private markets come of age. McKinsey Global Private Equity Markets Review. 2019.

Prequin. 2019. 2019 Private equity & venture capital fundraising & deal update. www.prequin.com.

Prequin. 2018. 2018 Fundraising update. www.prequin.com.

Prequin. 2018. 2018 Prequin alternative assets performance monitor. www.prequin.com.

Riback, Chris. 2018. What will private equity do with 'dry powder'? November 28. www.workingcapitalreview.com.

Sraders, Anne. 2020. Private equity firms are sitting on $1.5 trillion in unspent cash, and looking to raise more. January 25. www.fortune.com.

Van Hoegarden, Georges. 2012. The big venture capital mistake. www.venturecompany.com.

Wright, Mike, Sarika Pruthi, Kevin Ames, and Yan Alperovych. 2019. Private equity: Where we have been and the road ahead. *Venture Capital: An International Journal of Entrepreneurial Finance*, 21: 51–64.

CHAPTER 2

Political Reactions and SocioEconomic Consequences of COVID: Implications for Venture Capital

On March 11 of 2020, the World Health Organization (WHO) announced to the world the existence of novel virus, which was given the abbreviation COVID-19. The initial predictions regarding its impact on humanity were grave. Just 15 days later on March 26, Neil Ferguson, together with his colleagues from Imperial College London, released an epidemiological model with a chilling estimate: "in the absence of interventions, COVID-19 would have resulted in 7.0 billion infections and 40 million deaths globally this year" (Imperial College COVID-19 Response Team, 2020, p. 1). It is worthwhile to reiterate that these severe estimates were for 2020 alone. In their report, Ferguson and his team also compared the potential impact of this novel coronavirus to the devastation caused by the H1N1 influenza, or Spanish flu, of 1918. However, it is important to clarify that the report, its claims, and its modeling codes were not independently verified, peer reviewed, or otherwise academically challenged.

The cornerstone of the suppression strategy recommended by Ferguson and his colleagues included protection for the elderly, the institution of wide-scale social distancing measures, isolation of the sick, household quarantine, and the closure of schools. These measures were intended to be implemented swiftly and for a period of at least 18 months, the probable length of time required to develop a vaccine.

D. Klonowski, *Venture Capital Redefined*,
https://doi.org/10.1007/978-3-030-83387-9_2

However, Ferguson and his team did not recommend complete lockdowns, stay-at-home restrictions, or work-from-home measures; rather, public authorities in specific countries have implemented these restrictive measures and developed significant add-ons to Ferguson's initial model. The recommendation from Imperial College was to slow down the spread of COVID-19, but not to suppress it entirely (as currently insisted upon by many public health officials and political leaders) in order to avoid overwhelming the healthcare system during the initial stages of viral spread. This suppression strategy was based on the initial evidence from China that 80% of coronavirus transmissions occurred within a household setting. Ferguson and his colleagues clearly stated that the recommended strategy did not estimate "wider social and economic costs of suppressions", or in other words, the strategy that at its core recommended the disruption of millions of lives had no related background analysis of socioeconomic consequences (Imperial College COVID-19 Response Team, 2020, p. 2). It is unclear whether public authorities around the world have ever conducted such analysis on their own.

Political Reactions: The COVID-Response

It is necessary to primarily distinguish that the cause of the socioeconomic afflictions experienced by the population and the economy is a direct or indirect response of public policy. In other words, what individuals and economies experienced is directly connected to political decisions. Viruses have been a regular part of human existence, and these viruses, including the current coronavirus, have been doing what viruses normally do; they cause sickness, mutate to survive and expand, and, unfortunately, result in human deaths despite high rates of vaccination.

What is atypical in the case of novel coronavirus is the response of public authorities in many countries to what is perceived as a health crisis; this is what will be termed as "COVID-response". Public authorities had numerous policy alternatives to choose from, with countries such as Sweden, Norway, and Japan, for example, taking different stances and policy approaches toward the coronavirus that were grounded in allowing businesses to operate, keeping schools and universities open, avoiding other personal restrictions; in other words, there were no lockdowns. The public authorities in such countries recommended basic hygiene measures, individual precautions, and requested that their citizens behave in a responsible manner.

Lockdowns, Social-Distancing, and Masks

When the coronavirus initially appeared, the vast majority of political leaders and public officials around the globe moved to implement a range of restrictive public measures, mandates, and orders. Examples of such restrictions included the closure of public places (i.e., universities, schools, government offices, courts, etc.), stay-at-home orders, travel restrictions (both domestic and international), border closures, and the forced home quarantine of healthy people. Other preventive actions included restrictions on social interactions and gatherings (including visitations of family members and friends), the implementation of curfews, and the enactment of social distancing measures. Most businesses were not allowed to operate or were forced to operate on a restrictive basis. Moreover, the decision of public officials to restrict business operations was made on the basis of somewhat artificial conceptions of what may be essential or non-essential services; non-essential services were mandated to shut down. For example, liquor and cannabis stores were determined to be essential services and were allowed to remain open, while "optional" medical procedures or appointments, including surgeries or physiotherapy, were disallowed.

Of course, the demarcation between essential and non-essential businesses may be flawed because the various fragments of the economy are inter-connected. In other words, it is unlikely that public authorities understood that restrictions on different parts of the economy have spillover effects, such as a healthcare professional needing their car fixed, kitchen appliance repaired, or children to be supervised. Consequently, due to their demarcation of essential and non-essential services, public authorities closed recreational facilities, retail outlets, and religious places, while cultural, music, sport, and educational events were cancelled. Some businesses were allowed to operate on a curb-side pickup basis, while others, due to the in-person nature of their services, had no such luck.

To counteract the effects of their own restrictive measures, public officials focused on assistance in a number of areas. For individuals, public authorities provided social security payments, extended and increased unemployment compensation, offered direct payments, instituted eviction bans, postponed student loan payments, and extended food assistance programs. Tax payment deferrals, grants, loans and loan guarantee programs, eviction prohibitions, foreclosure bans, and interest payment deferrals were offered to businesses.

Social and Human Implications of Restrictions

Fear is one of the most human consequential outcomes of COVID and the COVID-response. Throughout 2020, fear of disease appeared to be more pronounced than the disease itself. However, this fear was not static; it evolved in accordance with the political restrictions and social atmosphere. Like frequently changing blood pressure in the human body, oscillating levels of fear can also have grave physical and mental effects on human health. There are many manifestations of such changing levels of fear, including the fear of contagion, emergence of new strains of the coronavirus, its general advancement in the community, and general uncertainty about life going forward, especially with respect to health, economic wellbeing, employment, and the ability to pay off one's mortgage; the fear often perpetuated in mainstream media has also resulted in protracted levels of chronic stress. Secondly, there has been fear surrounding the possibility of one's own death, or the death of their loved ones. Elevated levels of fear, in turn, led to a sense of helplessness, a loss of person freedom, a loss of control, and outright anger. Fear has also redefined human relations, which may create difficulty when individuals attempt to return to normal patterns of human interaction. This experience may lead to decreased empathy for one another, which, in turn, may translate into a permanent state of social disengagement, lack of public gatherings, and self-isolation. Because fear has created disruptions in family life, the educational system, criminal justice (i.e., suspended jury trials), and the legal and court system, it is unclear how societal and social structures may be redefined in the future.

The net effect of these fears is not difficult to predict, with research confirming that the consequences of continued chronic stress, social isolation, separation from loved ones (especially children from elderly parents or grandparents, and other family members from each other), social distancing, and financial uncertainty include the deterioration of physical health, increased chances of substance abuse, and an amplified probability of domestic violence and aggression (i.e., physical and emotional abuse). Specifically, COVID-response has resulted in declining wellbeing and mental health, elevated levels of loneliness, poor community relations, family separations, and increased mental illness and emotional stress, such as anxiety, depressive behavior, and post-traumatic stress disorder. Practice-based evidence confirms relapses into addictions, depression, and mental illness.

Research has further verified that individuals are at a higher risk for suicide; undue stress will likely result in 50,000 excess suicides, which could affect young people more drastically. For example, a study by the Centre for Disease Control and Prevention (CDC) conducted in June 2020 indicated that 24.1% of young people between 18 and 24 years old had suicidal thoughts, while only about 11% of older adults reported similar feelings. Evidence from Europe has similarly confirmed that children and young adults are especially vulnerable to developing long-lasting psychological symptoms post-COVID, with children suffering from difficulties in concentration, general irritability, anxiety, constant worries, nervousness, and restlessness. These studies have also found that parents had significant concerns about their children's mental health, general well-being, and emotional stability due to an onset of rapid changes, social isolation and dislocation, and a lack of access to normal social structures. These consequences occurred in spite of widespread access to the Internet, social media, and Internet-based activities; these modes of interaction are clearly ineffectual and do not provide the social interaction required for children and young adults. Furthermore, research has found that young adults were likely to consume more alcohol and be less physically active due to their isolation and will struggle to secure permanent employment.

There have also been predictions that COVID-response will result in increased cases of post-traumatic stress disorder (PTSD), mental burnout, emotional exhaustion, relational disassociation, and human separation. Research confirmed that the coronavirus has affected the psychological wellbeing of the vast majority of the population, which is reflected in increased levels of medical consultations related to stress, calls to mental health helplines, and psychological counseling. As an example, visits to mental health professionals in Canada are expected to double from baseline averages of 4.0 million visits per annum, and there is also evidence to support the increased use of anti-depressants. However, the full impact of chronic stress on the mental and physical health of individuals because of the coronavirus is likely to be fully manifested in the near future.

COVID-response has created significant disruptions in access to healthcare, with many elective surgeries and medical appointments simply cancelled, and individuals with non-COVID illnesses experiencing appointment delays or cancellations. A significant portion of healthcare providers also moved to telemedicine, where they provided services and offered medical advice via telephone, teleconferencing (i.e.,

Zoom), or other means without seeing the patient or conducting physical examinations. The widespread public fear also meant that a significant part of the population, which reached 50% in some instances, avoided accessing health services entirely. Some sub-segments of the healthcare system, including dentists, optometrists, chiropractors, or physiotherapists, continued to deliver services on an emergency or as-needed basis, and their facilities were open with some restrictions.

Education was another area of human life affected due to the widespread closures of schools and universities. It was estimated that some 1.5 billion students worldwide, or about 90% of the student population, were impacted. There are significant concerns about educational outcomes as a direct result of the restrictions, which have also affected the quantity and quality of academic research.

Lastly, in the case of individuals who commonly rely on routine religious engagement, COVID-response led to social and human dislocation. Churches, synagogues, mosques, and temples were all required to close. Although some religious leaders offered opportunities for online worship instead of regular in-person congregation, public restrictions also meant the elimination of religious pilgrimages, festivals, and other spiritual activities.

Economic Consequences of Political COVID-Response

COVID-response by public officials came at a time when national economies had not yet fully recovered from the 2008 financial crisis. At the onset of the current version of the coronavirus, most economies were vulnerable and effectively unable to defend themselves in any meaningful manner; in other words, the timing was imperfect. Preliminary estimates confirm that member economies belonging to OECD (Organization for Economic Co-operation and Development) shrunk by 4.2% on average in 2020. Countries with the highest declines in gross domestic product (GDP) were Spain (–11.6%), the United Kingdom (–11.2%), Greece (–10.2%, which was the years ninth recession in the last 13), and Mexico (–9.2%). The least affected countries were Korea (–1.1%), Norway (–1.2%), Turkey (–1.3%), Sweden (–3.2%), and Ireland (–3.2%). The clear victor is China, which grew its economy by 1.8% and is the only country with positive economic growth among OECD countries, although this is much below its ten-year average of 6.8%. While the major

OECD economies were far removed from their normal economic growth patterns, China returned to its normal economic trajectory by the end of 2020.

The net effect of a global economic slowdown was a decreased demand for raw materials, weakened consumer spending, reduced investments, and lowered cross-border trade (i.e., both import and export activities). There has also been an unprecedented disruption to local, national, and global supply chain structures. While some economists are optimistic about the potential for a quick economic rebound, others see a risk of sustained or even permanent damage to the global economy. Furthermore, COVID-response has impacted all components of the GDP, with the exception of government spending.

There are a variety of options public authorities may resort to post COVID-response, although the focus will likely be on monetary and fiscal policies. In terms of the monetary policy, even with interest rates near zero, states could print more money, although the predictable consequence of this policy is sustained inflation in the long term. The fiscal policy may result in massive state spending on social support, unemployment protection, infrastructure, and so on. Of course, elevated public spending would lead to increased budget deficits, more debt (and increased debt-to-GDP ratios), and higher taxes. Therefore, no matter what public policies are implemented, they may not be sufficient to offset declines in the business sector.

The most visible impact of COVID-response was unemployment on a massive scale; at its height, there was a stunning estimate that 500 million people lost their jobs, with only about half regaining their employment back over time. Job losses materialized quickly and reached levels not seen in decades. In some nations, like the United States (U.S.), job loss also coincided with the loss of healthcare protection. The global unemployment rate in OECD countries increased from 5.2% in December 2019 to 7.1% in November 2020. In comparison, unemployment in OECD nations after the 2008 crisis was equal to 8.5% (2010) and 10.2% in the European Union (2010). However, the 2008 financial crisis most heavily impacted the Baltic nations (i.e., Lithuania, Latvia, and Estonia), which experienced unemployment rates exceeding 15%.

Currently, many countries have experienced high incremental increases in unemployment, such as Columbia, which increased by 5.2%, Lithuania (by 4.8%), the U.S. (by 3.1%), and Spain (by 2.7%), although these figures do not account for people on unpaid leaves of absence. In the U.S., for example, it was estimated that 24 million jobs were lost in a few months, with the unemployment rate reaching 14.8% by April; this is about ten percentage points higher than in the previous year. The most disproportionately affected were young adults, who experienced visible displacement in the labor market. Globally, it is estimated that about 260 million young people were unemployed and were not attending any post-secondary training in 2019; the current COVID-response has only further aggravated this situation. In any case, it is presently unclear whether these job losses are permanent or transient. However, it is important to note that sustained levels of unemployment, falling wages, loss of healthcare, and declining standards of living can lead to social unrest.

High rates of unemployment further perpetuate the mental health problems already exacerbated by chronic stress from public restrictions. Persistent unemployment is a major source of distress, which has been well documented in economics. The vast majority of job losses occurred in the service sector, of which retail and wholesale trade are the most significant components; this is consistent with previous recessions, as, for example, over 90% of job losses in Canada due to the 2008 financial crisis occurred in the service sector. High unemployment rates have also led to a significant decline in individual and family incomes. Evidence from the U.S., for example, suggests that nearly twenty percent of families were not able to meet their basic needs, including housing, food, and utilities, which constitutes an extra financial burden in addition to the high levels of debt that families already carry. Of course, the actual impact on developing countries has been much more severe than what has been seen in developed countries.

Small Business in Crisis

The economic impact of COVID-response is visible everywhere, with public restrictions having affected individuals, families, communities, businesses, and societies alike. The small and medium-sized enterprise (SME) sector was one of the hardest hit segments of the economy, which has only increased the high unemployment rate because the SME sector normally generates over 95% of private sector employment. For example, small businesses (1–99 employees) account for 97.9% of employment in Canada, while medium firms account for an additional 1.9%. In the U.S., the SME sector creates 99.7% of jobs, of which small firms account for 98.2% and firms with fewer than 20 employees generate 89.0%.

The SME sector is responsible for about two thirds of newly created jobs and generate between 40 and 50% of the national GDP in most nations. Furthermore, the SME sector contributes significantly to innovation, research and development, invention, and new product development. Most importantly, however, the SME sector provides employment opportunities in many underserved communities.

The SME sector has been affected by political COVID-response in multiple ways, most significantly through enormous dislocations between SME firms. In many cases, the profits, savings, and "sweat equity" disappeared within a matter of weeks after the introduction of restrictive measures mandated by public officials, leaving firms financially devastated. Evidence suggests that up to 80% of SME firms were affected, with about 40 and 50% of firms impacted in a severe manner; one study conducted by Goldman Sachs confirmed that three quarters of SME firms were unsure of their business's survival. Furthermore, COVID-response redefined or even destroyed existing business models, business economics, and survival statistics, which may still be difficult to precisely quantify. The question of business survival is critical to SME firms because they have limited financial protections to withstand external shocks. For example, evidence from the U.S. indicates that the number of active businesses declined from 15.0 million to 11.7 million, which represents the largest decrease in the number of operating firms in the United States' modern economic history (the majority of these firms were unincorporated).

Of course, any external, financial, or operational turbulence can disproportionately affect business survival for smaller firms. More sizeable firms are normally endowed with more cash on hand and short-term assets, both of which can be liquidated, and they may have more options to borrow. These assertions have been borne out in research, which reveals that the level of harm to the SME sector is indirectly related to the firm size; in other words, larger firms are less impacted by COVID-response. Evidence also corroborates the idea that many of these struggling firms are likely to exhaust cash in a few months, which would eliminate their chances of survival before economic recovery arrives. Thus, the impact on the SME sector was disproportionate since private firms did not have time to strategize, plan, prepare, or develop any back-up alternatives in view of quickly mandated public restrictions. While small firms are typically effective at being flexible and agile, their capacity to respond in this case was thwarted by the speed and strictness of public restrictions. Many business owners were subsequently forced to pour their entire life savings into the business in order to keep it afloat, the psychological impact of which has yet to be determined.

The negative impact of public restrictions has also affected different market segments to varying degrees. For example, firms operating in retail, hospitality and accommodations, food services, arts and entertainment, casinos and gaming, transportation (i.e., taxis, airlines, public transit), automotive, oil and gas, repair and maintenance, leisure and recreational facilities, and various forms of manufacturing, have been disproportionately impacted. On the other hand, firms that focus on the provision of professional services, financial services (i.e., insurance), government services, and construction were among the least affected segments. Revenue growth was also recorded in the agriculture, mining, and utilities industries. With regard to corporate business, the clear beneficiaries from the COVID-response were major retail outlets, social media firms, and online shopping operators.

There are at least five main areas within the SME sector that were affected by COVID-response, the first of which was the severe decline or even complete loss of revenue many firms experienced. Evidence suggests that revenue losses are inversely related to the size of the business, which is defined by the number of employees; thus, revenue declined by more than 50% for smaller firms, while it declined by only 30% for larger firms. Smaller firms simply did not have sufficient financial resources to offer their products online in comparison to larger firms. On a positive note, evidence indicates that some firms have been able to identify innovative ways to generate new revenue streams by pivoting into alternate business segments. It is unclear, however, whether these new revenue streams are sustainable in the future.

Secondly, there are a significant number of fixed financial obligations that the business must cover on a monthly basis, including rent and interest payments on loans. While some protection was offered by public officials to businesses for these payments, assistance is unlikely to be sustained over the period of time necessary for these firms to survive. Additionally, revenue loss combined with high fixed costs has a direct impact on profitability and cash flow. A reduction of cash flow and profit subsequently led to a loss of value and reduction of business valuations. Although business owners generally aimed to maintain staff, evidence suggests that between 30 and 40% of firms eventually resorted to layoffs and cutting wages in order to minimize cash burn. Many firms implemented strategies of selling inventory at reduced prices, taking advantages of federal programs, deferring tax payments, and raising external debt to remain open. As stated previously, the full impact of these employment reductions in the SME sector has yet to be determined, although economic evidence has indicated that the worst impact on employment will be manifested in the next two or three years. A final issue is related to the major retail chains, which were allowed to operate without many restrictions while the SME sector struggled during the onset of the coronavirus; there is evidence confirming that mega-corporations took business away from the SME sector.

Public authorities have attempted to resolve some of the challenges facing the SME sector, although it is worthwhile to re-iterate that this was a problem of their own making because it was these same officials who implemented the strict government restrictions. Many countries resorted to unprecedented stimulus packages directed towards businesses that maintain interest rates at near-zero levels. The core measures of these assistance packages included payroll protection, commercial rent assistance, wage subsidy, tax deferral, and property tax rebate postponement. Additionally, some states established SME relief funds, but there is concern whether these arrangements will provide the necessary assistance in time. Officials also instituted bans on commercial evictions while some financial institutions offered temporary moratoriums on loan repayments. Unfortunately, access to these public programs was predicated on meeting pre-defined criteria and requirements, which excluded many firms in the SME sector from benefiting from the programs.

Socioeconomic Drifts Post COVID-Response: Implications for Venture Capital

This chapter aims to provide background information about the coronavirus, but more importantly, about its major impact on virtually every aspect of human life, including business. In this part of the chapter, the impact of political, social, and economic changes on the venture capital industry will be considered. The influence of political and socioeconomic changes on the broader entrepreneurial ecosystem will also be discussed, which is an integral part of the venture capital industry. Table 2.1 presents a brief analysis of the potential impact of these changes on venture capital.

Table 2.1 Political, social, and economic impact of COVID-response to entrepreneurs and venture capitalists

Area	*Key developments*	*Practical consequences*	*Impact on venture capital*
Political	• Public officials mandate lockdowns, masks, curfews, limits on travel, and other restrictions • Closure of schools and universities • Transitioning government offices, judicial system, and social support to online delivery models; this likely to be less citizen friendly • Increased infringement on basic human rights and freedoms	• More centralization of political power (i.e., central planning) • More forceful insistence by the state on certain desired policies and ESG protocols (i.e., environmental, social, and governance) • More reliance on fiscal policies • Possible tax increases • More control, restrictions, and regulations in various aspects of human life • Potential for increased personal invigilation through contact tracing and information censorship • Likely more reliance on public–private partnerships • Amplified influence of mega-corporations on public authorities	• Likely more restriction on and scrutiny of the venture capital industry • More requirements to implement ESG protocols and other state policies; these requirements are likely to increase cost of doing business • Additional politically driven reporting requirements • Opportunities to participate in privatization of state-owned assets and natural resources • Venture capitalists likely to experience problems with existing portfolio firms, which may struggle to redefine themselves post COVID-response

Area	*Key developments*	*Practical consequences*	*Impact on venture capital*
			• Newly established market segments may present attractive investment opportunities, but profitability may be uncertain
Social	• Social distancing, stay-at-home, and work-from-home restrictions • Fear of socialization due to contagion • Limits to in-person human interactions • Disruptions of normal patterns of life • Interference to familial interactions • Increased teleconferencing in key aspects of human life (i.e., healthcare, education, state services, counseling, etc.)	• More real desire for in-person human interactions, but less such desire due to fear of contagion • Less in-person shopping and more online consumption • Human isolation • Risk of chronic mental health issues, including suicide • Risk of domestic violence, which may lead to family separation and break-ups • Potential for substance abuse • Likely compromised educational outcomes • Likely increased crime and incarceration rates • Increased poverty rates globally	• Impact on various phases of the venture capital investment process, especially those that require significant in-person contact • Deal generation and monitoring are most affected stages of the investment process due to highly interactive component • More reliance on online interaction may lead to compromised investment decisions • Limited in-person interaction may negatively influence access to finance for entrepreneurs; this may also impact venture capitalists when additional fundraising is required

(continued)

Table 2.1 (continued)

Area	*Key developments*	*Practical consequences*	*Impact on venture capital*
Economic	• Changes to economics of many sectors and industries; some industries are likely to struggle for long periods of time while others may be small-sized • Increases in unemployment • Reduction of income for families • High cost of emergency borrowing for families • Downward pressure on wages • High business failure in specific sectors • Lower economic productivity (i.e., employee anxiety and stress) • Increased personal debt • Increased public debt	• Sustained economic under-performance (i.e., reduced consumption and investments are unlikely to be offset by increased state spending) • Likely continued high unemployment, low wages, and declining family income • Unemployed individuals may seek other sources of income • Possible introduction of guaranteed "basic income" • High failure rates in new venture formation • Entrepreneurial resistance to new venture formation • Age of mega-corporations (i.e., increased profits and valuations, more bargaining power, and social influence) • Significant negative impact on the middle class	• Problems with business formation and lower survival rates may contribute to weak deal flow • Poor small business economics may prevent venture migration (i.e., from small to medium to large firms); less high quality deal flow for venture capital • Some sectors of the economy are unlikely to be investable • Entire sectors of the economy may lose appeal to venture capitalists while other sectors may increase in prominence • Sustained problem may encourage entrepreneurs to sell their ventures at lower valuations • Likely low exit valuations, but also low entry valuations; this may favor venture capital funds seeking investment opportunities

The Impact of Political, Social, and Economic Changes on the Venture Capital Industry

As observed earlier in this chapter, political reaction (or over-reaction) has a plethora of direct consequences on normal patterns of life; these political measures included lockdowns, social distancing, mask wearing, stay-at-home mandates, and curfews, just to mention a few. These measures undoubtedly led to the centralization of political power, the introduction of state controls, and the institution of new regulations and bylaws. Some public officials have also experimented with increased personal invigilation (i.e., contact tracing), restricted access to information, and even censorship (i.e., silencing opposing viewpoints). These measures represent an infringement on basic human freedoms and rights, and if the progression of these public measures were to persist, it could represent a more pronounced shift to the left of the political spectrum, where the state plays a more intrusive role in the society and the economy. Moreover, public officials have yet to address slow economic growth, persistent unemployment, decreased wages, and low family income; these realities may lead to the introduction of a guaranteed basic income, which is a concept that has been contemplated on the left side of the political spectrum for decades. If this political shift toward the left continues, there could also be the introduction of higher taxes, more business over-regulation and control, and other policies. In practical terms, public policy may devolve into private–public partnerships while the role of mega-corporations is increased to more strongly influence government policy and political processes. Lastly, it is important to note that regardless, the public policy course would eventually need to be reversed toward debt reduction, austerity, and privatization.

The SME sector typically does not operate well in an over-regulated, restrictive, and unstable environment where political decisions can make or break firms. Therefore, added restrictions, regulations, and requirements are likely to negatively influence new business formation and discourage existing business owners from expansion. Business owners may be particularly discouraged if political decisions are perceived to unduly promote mega-corporations, as it has occurred in 2020. Moreover, political mandates and restrictions not only impact individual firms, but they also shift, transform, and redefine the economic wellbeing of entire industries. As noted previously in this chapter, COVID-response disproportionately impacted some industries, industrial sub-segments, and market niches; for example, lockdowns, stay-home restrictions, and remote-work requirements led to a rapid increase and demand for Internet services.

The redefined business realities occurring within the broader entrepreneurial ecosystem have both positive and negative implications for venture capital. In terms of pessimistic implications, if the political shift to the left continues to progress, the venture capital industry is likely to face more extensive regulatory and legal oversight from the state; this has already significantly increased since the 2008 financial crisis. These regulations, reporting necessities, and other requirements (including these related to environmental, social, and governance [ESG] protocols) are costly and onerous for the venture capital industry. Moreover, venture capitalists must deal with significant strategic, operational, and financial challenges related to existing portfolio firms. In contrast, there are some positive opportunities for the industry should the political shift persist. For example, pressure to reduce public expenditure may lead to the privatization of various state assets such as crown corporations, natural resources, or even entire sectors of the economy (i.e., healthcare, education, social assistance, public infrastructure, or parks and recreation). Of course, many of these state-oriented opportunities would be available to well-connected firms, which are often mega-funds that employ former politicians on their boards of directors. Privatization can also create investment opportunities in newly emerging market segments.

COVID-response and its social impact, which has been discussed previously, have a multidimensional effect upon entrepreneurship. Primarily, firms that rely on significant in-person interactions with their clients are disadvantaged, due to the fear of contagion, social distancing, stay-at-home measures, and other restrictions detailed earlier. These public mandates to limit direct human contact negatively impact operations in specific sectors of the economy such as retail trade, restaurants and bars, recreational and sports facilities, and so on. Other industries that involve various forms of consultancy, such as healthcare professionals (i.e., dentists, chiropractors, optometrists, therapists, naturopath doctors, and traditional medical doctors), lawyers, accountants, or financial advisors, have been forced to conduct online interactions, which can only fulfill a limited function or purpose. In short, the operations of many industries are likely to be negatively impacted by mandated restrictions.

By limiting in-person human interactions, disrupting normal patterns of life, interfering in familiar interactions, and creating human isolation, it is all but guaranteed that there will be a negative impact on in-person business interactions as well. This could manifest in the form of decreased productivity, less innovation, and a discouragement of close co-operation. Team development, cohesion, and unity will similarly be adversely impacted, while a fear of contagion is likely to create distrust among individuals. A lack of in-person interaction may also hinder an entrepreneur's access to finance because social interaction is such a critical part of venture analysis and assessment.

In-person interactions at each step of the venture capital process are integral, which is why limits and restrictions are detrimental on a fundamental level. Strong interpersonal relations are critical in the primary stages of venture capital networking, deal generation, and screening; they are also essential during the monitoring stage when unanticipated problems need to be resolved. Social collaboration is similarly important during fundraising because venture capitalists present to and need to form positive relationships with, new investors (i.e., limited partners). The development of new relationships, especially for those venture capital firms, which were unable to show top-quartile performance, may be challenging in the most opportune circumstances, and are therefore undoubtedly hindered by interpersonal restrictions.

Despite these challenges, the venture capital industry must quickly analyze, re-think, and re-imagine which sectors of the economy are likely to be performing well and on a consistent basis not only during the time of COVID-response, but also in the long-term. Entire sectors of the economy may lose their appeal while other may gain in prominence over time. Venture capital firms will also need to discover or re-imagine new ways of working inside of their own firm to correspond with their unique strengths, capabilities, and competencies. Restrictions upon in-person interactions will similarly force venture capitalists to rapidly develop new and effective methods of communicating with their investee firms and capital providers.

COVID-response and associated restrictions have tangible financial implications for the entire economy, while public policy decisions have led to economic slowdowns, rising unemployment, widespread small business closures, and public debt growth. However, it is worth reiterating that some economists predicted an economic slowdown was likely to occur even in the absence of the coronavirus; of course, COVID-response accelerated and intensified this slowdown. Economic slowdown and rising unemployment are likely to create a downward pressure on wages and family incomes, leading some unemployed individuals to seek alternative sources of income in entrepreneurial ventures, while others will gravitate toward social assistance. Sustained high levels of unemployment could lead to the introduction of guaranteed basic incomes to a disproportionately large part of the society; states with significant socialistic orientations have already freely promoted this model. Significantly, it is the middle class that has been devastatingly impacted by the COVID-response thus far.

In terms of the impact on entrepreneurship, public officials have effectively pre-determined which sectors of the economy are likely to do well and which are destined to struggle with revenue generation, profit generation, and value creation. Therefore, it is difficult to predict the faith of the SME sector, but in the most general terms, there may be poor business survival and a reduction in new business formation. The firms, which survived the initial shock brought about by political COVID-response, and endured through their financial struggles, may have less appetite to grow and expand their ventures; the current crisis is likely to leave minor scars or deep wounds on the entrepreneurial psyche. Many of these entrepreneurs had to struggle with the most basic unit economics, rightsizing their operations to market demand, and fundamental business uncertainties. Those who contemplate a new venture creation may be dissuaded by the additional risks of operating a small business even if they lose their current employment and are desperate to find new revenue streams. Individuals who are unable to find employment may be similarly deterred from entrepreneurship by a guaranteed basic income. These dynamics are likely to have an injurious and long-term impact on the entire entrepreneurial ecosystem. While new opportunities may, of course, emerge, the general propensity for entrepreneurship will be limited for a foreseeable period. There is also a problem related to the drifting patterns of small firms as, in the past, there has been a persistent migration of small business into medium-sized firms, while those that exhibit a propensity to become large ones do so in due course; this entire entrepreneurial migration may be frustrated and even suppressed under the current restrictions and challenges to entrepreneurship.

Persistent economic slowdown creates significant problems for venture capitalists, whose operations are sensitive to changes in the economic framework. An initial negative impact a poor economic situation can have on the venture capital industry is a reduction of venture capital financing toward the entrepreneurial ecosystem, in spite of record levels of dry powder accumulation in the industry (as noted in Chapter one).

Secondly, reduced economic growth may adversely affect stock markets and valuations of public firms. Declines in stock market capitalization may also negatively impact limited partners' commitments of capital allocation to the venture capital industry. In other words, when stock markets decline, it results in an immediate and automatic over-allocation of limited partners' funds in venture capital, which, in turn, can cause difficulties in venture capital fundraising. Additionally, in an attempt to reduce perceived risks, venture capitalists may shift their focus to financing later stage firms rather than early-stage firms; this would also adversely affect entrepreneurs.

Most importantly, weak economic growth is often correlated with weak consumption, which arises from suppressed wages and family incomes. Weak spending power can similarly result from personal debt payments taking an increasing part of the family income, thereby leaving less income for other discretionary spending, or because of high unemployment rates and poor job prospects. Moreover, as noted above, the number of high quality and investable entrepreneurial firms may decline, which will impact venture capital deal flow and increase competition for available deals; this, in turn, may have an adverse impact on returns. Lastly, however, the venture capital industry has been occasionally subject to intense scrutiny and investigation by public officials. The industry has also witnessed some political backlash due to its limited transparency, unethical behavior, and illegal conduct, which has resulted in the introduction of additional regulations, reporting requests, and other requirements. There is the potential for similar tensions to re-emerge in the current environment.

On a more positive note, venture capitalists may encounter more willing sellers, whether these are founders who, in the normal course of business development, would likely look for a generational transition but are now incentivized to act due to frustrations with business post COVID-response, but owners may also wait for more suitable timing of disposal. There may also be large multinational corporations which are in the process of re-shuffling their own divisions and re-designing new product and service offers. Venture capitalists may be able to acquire these firms at low valuations. Of course, lower valuations may be problematic for these venture capital firms, which are currently ready to monetize portfolio firms.

Bibliography

Alexander, Craig. 2020. Economic impact of the coronavirus outbreak. February 27. www.deloitte.com.

Bartik, Alexander W., Marianne Bertrand, Zoe Cullen, Edward L. Gleaser, Michael Luca, and Christopher Straton. 2020. The impact of COVID-19 on small business outcomes and expectations. *Proceedings of the National Academy of Science,* 117: 17656–17666.

Braun, Reiner and Ingo Stoff. 2016. The cost of private equity investing and the impact of dry powder. *Journal of Private Equity*, Spring: 22–33.

CBIZ. 2020. Small businesses feel biggest impact of coronavirus pandemic. October 8. www.cbiz.com.

Centre for Disease Control and Prevention. 2020. Mental health, substance abuse, and suicidal ideation during the COVID-19 pandemic—United States, June 24–30. *Morbidity and Mortality Weekly Report*, 69, www.cdc.gov.

Centre on Budget and Policy Priorities. 2020. Tracking the COVID-19 recession's effects on food, housing, and employment hardships. January 28. www.cbpp.org.

Deloitte. 2020a. *The social impacts of COVID-19. Reset not restart: Taking advantage of a crisis for social change*. August. www.deloitte.com.

Deloitte. 2020b. *Uncovering the hidden iceberg. Why human impact of COVID-19 could be a third crisis*. August.

Imperial College COVID-19 Response Team. 2020. Report 12: Impact of non-pharmaceutical interventions (NPIs) to reduce COVID-19 mortality and healthcare demand. March 26. Imperial College London.

Martin, Amory, Maryia Markhivda, Stephane Hallegatte, and Brian Walsh. 2020. Socio-economic impacts of COVID-19 on household consumption and poverty. *Economics of Disaster and Climate Change*, 4: 453–479.

Meckbach, Greg. 2020. Intact warns of indirect economic impact from COVID. September 29. www.canadianunderwriter.ca.

Otar, Chad. 2020. The impact of the coronavirus on small business. May 29. www.forbes.com.

Patterson, Andrew J., Shaan Raithatha, Adam Schickling, Maximilian Wieland, and Beatrice Yeo. 2020. Estimating the economic impact of the COVID-19 shock. June. Vanguard research.

Polyakova, Maria, Geoffrey Kocks, Victoria Udalova, and Amy Finkelstein. 2020. Initial economic damage from the COVID-19 pandemic in the United States is more widespread across ages and geographic than initial mortality impacts. *Proceedings of the National Academy of Science (PNAS)*, 117: 27934–27939.

Radicioni, Brianna. 2020. New research: The real impact of COVID-19 on small business. September 29. www.entrepreneurship.babson.edu.

Statistics Canada. 2020. Impact of COVID-19 on small business in Canada. May 11. www.statcan.gc.ca.

Wang, Jilian, Jeyul Yang, Benjamin Iverson, and Raymond Kluender. 2020. Bankruptcy and the COVID-19 crisis. Harvard University. Working paper 21–041.

Yeuh, Linda. 2020. Looking ahead to 2021 and the economic impact of Covid-19. December 15. www.forbes.com.

PART II

The Venture Capital Industry Redefined

CHAPTER 3

Transformations in the Venture Capital Ecosystem Post COVID-Response

The General Structure of the Venture Capital Industry

The venture capital ecosystem and the affiliations among its different participants create a symbiotic architecture that is inherently complex, which is demonstrated in Fig. 3.1. The main stakeholders in the venture capital ecosystem include limited partners (LPs), general partners (GPs, i.e., fund managers), and entrepreneurial firms (i.e., investee firms). The system also includes other providers of finance such as banks and financial institutions, business angels, public equities markets, corporate partners, and crowdfunding platforms. Additionally, each of the three major stakeholders (i.e., LPs, GPs, and entrepreneurial firms) may rely on their own unique set of external stakeholders who could be invited to participate in individual projects or be involved on a perpetual basis. As an example, in order to develop a high caliber deal flow, GPs may rely on a wide network of external contacts or stakeholders, including portfolio firms, investment bankers, deal brokers, commercial bankers, lawyers, accountants, recruitment specialists, or consultants, among others. To perform their due diligence, GPs may invite various technical experts, environmental specialists, lawyers, or accountants to be stakeholders, while during the exit phase, underwriters, investment bankers, or other specialists could be included. Similarly, an entrepreneurial firm may invite expert advice from tax professionals, financial specialists, investment bankers,

D. Klonowski, *Venture Capital Redefined*,
https://doi.org/10.1007/978-3-030-83387-9_3

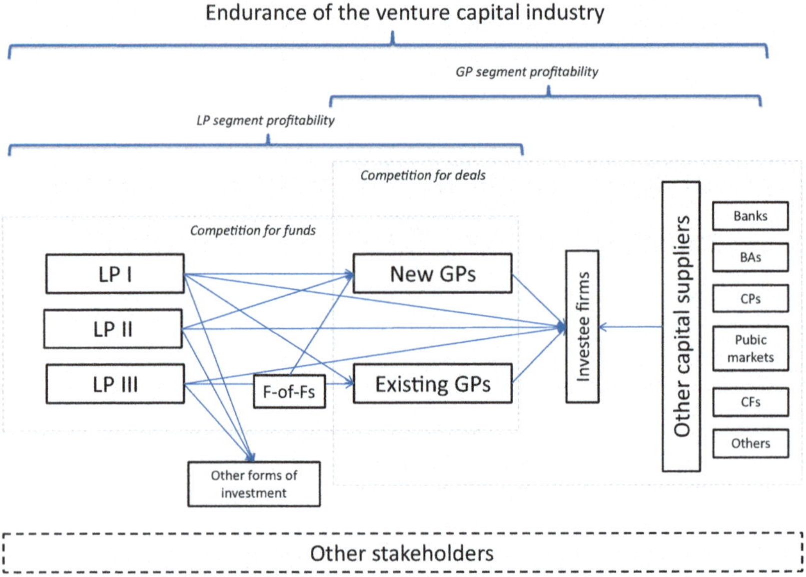

Fig. 3.1 The major stakeholders in the venture capital ecosystem (Abbreviations: *BAs* business angels, *CPs* corporate partners, *CFs* crowdfunders, *F-of-Fs* fund-of-funds, *GPs* general partners, *LP* limited partner)

lawyers, accountants, or consultants. LPs, on the other hand, may rely on their own distinctive advisors, including lawyers, accountants, and various consultants. LPs also depend upon "gatekeepers", who act as intermediary consultants between LPs and GPs, to screen potential GPs and make partnership recommendations to LPs.

LPs, which may take the form of endowments, pensions funds, insurance companies, wealthy individuals, corporations, financial institutions, or banks, direct capital to either newly formed or existing GPs. The decision to spread capital among various GPs serves to diversify LPs' exposure to various funds, which may have a unique investment thesis, market approach, or investment strategy. This broad-based exposure to various GPs should, at least theoretically, improve LPs' returns from the asset class. However, LPs may be unable to obtain exposure to all GPs as the most successful are often oversubscribed. Other investment opportunities LPs may consider pursuing include public equities markets, different segments of private capital markets (i.e., private debt, real estate, infrastructure, and natural resources), and other investment opportunities (i.e., hedge funds). Regardless, LPs often rely on co-investment agreements with GPs to direct additional capital to investment opportunities for the purpose of extending their exposure to a specific firm, market segment, or industry. LPs may also dedicate capital to GPs indirectly, which often occurs through fund-of-funds.

One of the most influential stakeholders in the venture capital ecosystem is the state (i.e., government), whose impact may be either direct or indirect. For example, the state can influence an industry by implementing additional regulations, requirements, and oversights. While the venture capital industry has been historically self-regulatory, GPs in many jurisdictions are increasingly obligated to register with securities regulators and government agencies. Similarly, governments around the world have been re-evaluating their approach to the tax treatment of capital gains from the venture capital industry, information disclosure requirements, and compensation structures, since the 2008 financial crisis. In relation to information disclosure, for example, regulators have discovered serious transgressions occurring in the venture capital industry related to failing to disclose relevant information, reporting false returns, violating portfolio valuation principles and guidelines, engaging directly or indirectly in acts of corruption (especially in relation with foreign officials), misallocating fees, and failing to disclose conflicts of interest. Moreover, some LPs (like CalPERS) needed to resort to freedom-of-information legislation to gain access to relevant information about fund operations.

The result of such poor access to information is that LPs are not able to conduct oversights of GPs' activities or perform their own fiduciary responsibilities; a lack of forthcoming disclosure and transparency in venture capital aids to hide venture capital's underperformance. The problem of information disclosure has led to lawsuits against GPs, which relate to fraudulent disclosure to LPs, withholding important information, manipulating financial statements, distorting information about portfolio firms, and providing materially false and misleading information. Beyond the issues with information access, academics have also documented further negative behavioral patterns of GPs, which include illegitimate transfers of intellectual property between investee firms; investing capital into firms where clear conflicts of interest exist; excessively terminating employees; disposing company assets to pay off debt;

underfunding or even plundering employee pensions; redirecting investment opportunities away from one fund and toward another; using capital from one fund to bail out investee firms of another fund; investing into competitors, including trying to merge their investee firms with competition; and eliminating minority shareholders through dubious means. Academics confirm that some of the largest venture capital firms are at the center of these misbehaviors.

A negative assessment of the venture capital industry has also been fueled by a growing body of academic evidence challenging the actual contributions of venture capital toward economic growth, job creation, and innovation. Because governments increasingly recognize that greater operational freedoms and flexibility, privileged taxation of capital gains, and limited information disclosure granted to the venture capital industry have not translated into the promised above-average returns, their scrutiny of venture capital is likely to increase in the near future. This privileged treatment of venture capital has resulted in multiple abuses of the venture capital ecosystem by GPs, especially in relation to entrepreneurial firms. Examples of these GP misbehaviors include allegations of draining off wealth from founders, unjustified ownership dilution, unfair founder dismissal, expropriations of investee firms' assets, and forced mergers. Such exploitative acts increasingly pressure GPs to employ compliance officers, investor and public relations specialists, and ESG (i.e., environmental, social, governance) specialists.

As Fig. 3.1 further outlines, the venture capital ecosystem is comprised of two interwoven, but distinctly separate, market sub-segments in which GPs compete. In the first case, GPs compete to secure an opportunity to invest in firms. GPs will vie for access to the most appealing, attractive, and profitable investment prospects; this dynamic is captured on the right-hand side of the graph. Competition for deals is fierce, and there is evidence that competition has intensified even further post COVID-response because GPs appear to focus on a limited set of investment opportunities. GPs aiming to increase their catchment areas may also create competition by encroaching on other local regions in which they would not normally be active. Beyond these incumbent players, GPs also must contend with new entrants into the marketplace. The motivation behind these newly established GPs is often financial in nature, related to the possibility of generating strong excess returns, more favorable allocation of carried interest, and higher bonuses. Other non-financial motivators may include operational independence, higher prestige, new opportunities, and personal fulfillment. Additionally, competition may derive from participants who could have worked on the periphery of the venture capital ecosystem such as LPs, consulting firms, data gatherers, business angels, large corporations, or financial institutions, who, incentivized by the potential for high returns and fees, may establish their own in-house operations focusing on venture capital.

GPs can also compete in other aspects of the venture capital investment process, such as the friendliness of various terms and provisions, business valuation, timing of transaction closure, and level of hands-on assistance, to name a few examples. Less competitive GPs may distort the market by undercutting other participants, offering unreasonable, loose terms, and promoting abnormally high valuations; they may also pursue less commercially attractive investment opportunities. Moreover, GPs not only compete with each other, but they also compete with other suppliers of finance. For example, entrepreneurial firms can resort to bootstrapping, which is a process of acquiring, allocating, and coordinating resources within a firm in a way that does not require any external capital. An entrepreneurial firm's aptitude to secure another form of finance depends on its level of development, profitability and cash flow, the industry, the investment program, the firm's preference for working with new partners, and the risk tolerance level of capital suppliers. While many of these financial suppliers manage to work within the venture capital ecosystem in a manner which is complementary to venture capital, there are instances where entrepreneurs actively consider other viable options, resulting in GPs' losing deals to other financiers. However, the position of venture vis-à-vis these capital providers is relatively strong due to the widely held public perception that the mere presence of "smart money" guarantees success. Similarly, venture capitalists often have relatively strong negotiating positions, in comparison with the average entrepreneurial firm, which may have general problems with access to finance and must resort to more creative financing options.

A further facet of the competition GPs encounter when attempting to secure an investment opportunity is poor deal flow. Due to a proliferation of higher quality later stage deals (i.e., flight-to-quality, with quality equating stability), entry valuations continue to rise to new heights, which could, in turn, fuel more mismatch between seller and buyer expectations; hence, fewer deals. It is conceivable that under these conditions, venture capital firms would continue to recycle the same deals between themselves, while other deals would be postponed or cancelled. Although

GPs often wish to develop a proprietary deal flow in attractive market segments, this is difficult to achieve in practice. GPs, who are most effective in deal generation, devote significant resources to this function and are capable of drawing from a wide network of contacts, relationships, and influences (including political connections). Unique deal flow often arises from long-term relationships GPs have with strategic partners and government institutions (i.e., research institutes, agencies, and universities). The best examples of such relationships are Advent International, the Blackstone Group, and the Carlyle Group; these GP-corporate partners often work on an exclusive basis. Some GPs are also able to rely on unique reputations in the marketplace. In comparison with an average GP, who is only able to provide a fairly "commoditized" service to entrepreneurial firms, only the best GPs are able to provide significant hands-on value-enhancing assistance. Given evidence from previous recessions, higher levels of competition and effective narrowing of the deal flow may last for a number of years post COVID-response.

The second market sub-segment in which GPs compete is the flow of capital, which is a fundamental feature of the venture capital ecosystem. In spite of LPs being critical suppliers of capital to the system, LPs have historically held relatively limited bargaining power vis-à-vis GPs because they often have few alternatives for obtaining exposure to the private sector. Thus, while LPs may learn how to become proficient in processing deals relatively quickly, they may have a problem replicating GPs' ability to access attractive firms. Another bargaining weakness of LPs is related to their pre-programmed allocation of funds to venture capital, which occurs on the basis of a percentage of total capital under management; LPs effectively force themselves not to ignore the asset class and instead seek exposure to it. A problem subsequently arises if LPs are not able to place capital in the top quartile performers. In such a case, LPs may alternately pursue second quartile or lower performers, which often proves counterproductive and unprofitable to LPs due to a significant drop in performance between the top quartile and the remainder of GPs. This misallocation of capital to suboptimal GPs is unlikely to change unless LPs actively shift their pre-programmed capital allocation mentality, of which there is increasing evidence; for example, some LPs ignore this asset class entirely. Evidence suggests that this trend may be more pronounced in the future.

In spite of the excess capital available from LPs, there are moments when GPs encounter strong competition in fundraising. This tendency occurs during economic downturns, or when LPs hoard capital, seek exposure to liquid assets, pursue more protected assets (i.e., debt), exhibit a tendency for flight-to-quality and flight-to-safety, or limit their number of partnerships with GPs. Under these circumstances, and in order to achieve successful fundraising, GPs aim to differentiate their commercial propositions through their approach to the type of entrepreneurial firms they pursue (i.e., early stage, later stage), the type of deals they seek (i.e., traditional, buyout, expansion, buy-ins, restructuring, turnaround), the types of industries they are interested in, and the amount of capital per deal. Of course, the real differentiator among GPs is their historical track record of performance, which is the only tangible and verifiable measure of GPs' skill in generating strong deal flow, abilities to effectively work with the investee firm, and talents in grooming the firms for a well-timed exit. And yet, LPs' weak bargaining power is likely to change in the future, which will be discussed shortly, due to GPs' declining returns, excessive fees, amounts of dry powder, information disclosure problems, and other challenges in the LP-GP relationship. However, it goes without saying that GPs often display a natural talent for developing and pitching a persuasive storyline, interesting narrative, and credible description. Guaranteed fees for substantial time periods combined with strong upside potential and relatively minimal downside risk jointly act as further strong motivators for GPs.

Figure 3.1 also illustrates two segments of unique profitability structure in the venture capital ecosystem, namely that profits can accrue to LPs and GPs. While this demarcation may be counterintuitive, it is important to highlight that the goals of LP and GPs, while having many areas of convergence, diverge in terms of financial and non-financial objectives. The LP-GP arrangements rely on a balance in which distinct goals are harmonized, and if this delicate balance is upset or lopsided, the intricate architecture begins to malfunction. Furthermore, this symbiotic balance of incentives, structures, and motivations ultimately determines the long-term survival, endurance, and profitability of the entire industry.

The historical record confirms that the most vocal and public reactions occurred when LPs realized that they had been taken advantage of by GPs. This occurs when GPs produce high compensation while LPs generate weak returns that are uncompetitive with those available in other segments of private capital and public equities markets. In other words, this profitability imbalance in the ecosystem occurs when a financial windfall for GPs does not translate into positive outcomes for LPs as well. This commonly arises during the time when GPs operate follow-on funds, as it is under these circumstances that significant agency issues (i.e., GPs have many conflicts by operating multiple funds at the same time) and moral hazard considerations (i.e., where GPs' effort may be observable but is not verifiable) become apparent. In the case of moral hazard, GPs may actively discriminate where and how much effort they wish to exert in different situations. For example, GPs may commit less effort and resources to previous funds if newly formed funds offer better return opportunities. However, as observed in a general framework for industry analysis, the venture capital industry presents one of the worst-case scenarios for generating sustained profitability: entry barriers are low or moderately low (i.e., it is relatively easy and inexpensive to become a fund manager) and exit barriers are high (i.e., LPs and GPs enter into a long-term relationship). The industry has witnessed this prediction in the last few decades in the form of declining, sporadic, and volatile returns.

GPs persistently struggle to provide superior and optimal services to LPs, and although some LPs continue to positively appraise the asset class, many express dissatisfaction with their returns. LPs are also disappointed and discouraged by GPs' information disclosure, including sensitive questions related to fees charged to investee firms, complex legal structures, distribution of carried interest, allocation of bonuses, and executive succession. Furthermore, GPs choose not to invest in appropriate technological infrastructure to handle complex LP information requests.

However, LPs are also subject to numerous behavioral distortions which have a negative impact on the entire venture capital ecosystem. Firstly, as noted previously, LPs supply capital to underperforming GPs, and given the divergence of performance between top quartile and other GPs, the misallocation may be equal to as much as 50%. In other words, given that LPs normally commit $404.5 billion to GPs globally (on average in the last 20 years), this misallocation may be equal to approximately $200 billion annually. And yet, LPs often fail to perform adequate due diligence on GPs due to a lack of sufficient expertise, know-how, and analytical skills to properly assess GPs' experience, skills, and track record. Finally, LPs do not negotiate sufficient rights in their partnership agreements to properly oversee GPs' actions.

Re-Characterization of Venture Capital Relationships

As outlined in Chapter 2, it is evident that COVID-response has redefined personal relations within society. Thus, the venture capital business was also critically affected by state lockdowns, limitations, restrictions, and other measures because it is a people-centered business; it relies heavily on strong interpersonal relations, close working interactions, and good rapport. Many challenging situations in the venture capital setting are resolved in unstructured, informal, and relaxed meetings conducted over a drink, dinner, a sports event, and other casual settings. Candid, in-depth, and frequent discussions are the cornerstone of the venture capital connection at all stages of the process. During fundraising, for example, venture capitalists commonly deliver in-person presentations about some of the unique features of their next fund. These presentations critically rely upon strong social interactions, so are likely to be less effective in an online setting. The screening and evaluation stages also require venture capitalists to scrutinize entrepreneurs' responses and reactions to questions, small interpersonal cues, and body language. It is during these pre-deal stages that venture capitalists and entrepreneurs effectively test their ability to interact constructively in the future; during such communications, they begin to develop interpersonal "chemistry". The robustness of this relationship determines whether serious conflicts would arise and how they would be resolved. As noted in Chapter 1, these conflicts have serious repercussion on value creation, since unresolved and simmering conflicts can lead to value destruction.

While a lack of in-person interaction in traditional venture capital transactions has a major impact, which will be discussed in further detail below, the negative impact of limited interactions is lessened in buyout situations. In these types of transactions, the interactions of venture capitalists with sellers may be brief and less consequential for future success; a seller's loyalty is often vested with the highest bidder. During buyout situations, venture capitalists buy to sell by relying on paths for rapid improvement to operational and financial performance, in addition to the forceful usage of external debt. Of course, GPs need to interact with their portfolio firms in buyout deals, but they predominantly count on highly motivated and financially incentivized incumbent or new management teams. In the last twenty years, the venture capitalists' hunting ground for buyout deals included public firms, noncore divisions of large corporations, and unwanted assets of multinational corporations. Less in-person interaction may also be acceptable in other segments of private capital in which frequent interactions are not critical to investment success.

There are numerous consequences of suppressed and infrequent in-person interactions between various stakeholders in the venture capital ecosystem. The first and most apparent consequence of limited in-person interaction is the forced digitization of these relationships. Digital forms of communication and remote working translate into the near complete elimination of traditional non-verbal forms of communication, including body language, eye contact, facial expressions, emotional manifestations, gestures, posture, tone, touch, and other non-verbal cues. According to research, these non-verbal expressions account for over 90% of effective human communication. In-person interactions normally relate to the development and enhancement of trust, a demonstration of importance, the enhancement of credibility, and personal validation. In comparison, online interactions lead to an overall decrease in motivation, while interactional digitization has a de-humanizing impact on individuals. It is likely to take time and require a significant adjustment to normal modes of operation, as evidence suggests that investment professionals are currently finding it difficult to engage through virtual channels of communication.

The natural consequence of digital communication is the de-personalization of finance in the entrepreneurial environment. Human interactions, which previously resulted in interpersonal and long-term commercial relationships developed on the basis of catering to unique entrepreneurial needs, are now reduced to singular transactions. Thus, continuity, loyalty, and commitment are slowly becoming less important and unnecessary. De-personalization of finance also implies that transactions in the venture capital ecosystem are likely to be incidental, singular, disloyal, and opportunity-based. Furthermore, other stakeholders operating in the ecosystem are more likely to be invited to investment projects on an as-needed basis to provide assistance in specific areas, such as transaction execution, assistance to entrepreneurial firms, or the provision of expert advice. It is important to note that such profound changes in commercial relations due to the de-personalization of commerce were also initiated in the seventeenth and eighteenth centuries. This style of business has penetrated the field of finance, and changes are likely to continue into the future.

An important component of any business relationship is trust, which, as evidence suggests, is normally based on many interconnected building blocks, including clarity, integrity, character, ethical behavior, compassion, transparency, commitment, interpersonal chemistry, connection, contribution, recognition, validation, and expertise. However, this laundry list of characteristics can be reduced to three simple ideals: stability and consistency, readiness to address complex problems, and, most importantly, clear communication. The last component (i.e., communication) is especially critical since people in every setting are heavily impacted by conflicting messages and interpretations. Therefore, while trust is the cornerstone of long-term, successful, and nurturing relationships, it is evident that the de-personalization of finance and the digitization of relationships in venture capital negatively impact entrepreneur-venture capitalist communications and, consequently, adversely influence trust dynamics. High levels of trust are normally built over time, not only through seemingly tiny and inconsequential actions, small words and gestures, and intentions grounded in consistent behavior, but also when reaching major decisions.

However, trust is based on multiple interactions and it can be ruined quickly; once broken, it is difficult to repair. A lack of trust in a business context translates into uncertainty, the divergence of goals, disengagement, low morale, a "silo" or self-focused mentality, an inability to resolve disputes, and higher turnover. In addition to damaging loyalty and commitment, a lack of trust is also connected with poor business efficiency and financial performance. The absence of trust in a venture capital ecosystem can similarly discourage innovation, prevent measured risk taking, and inhibit sound decision-making. There are also psychological implications of distrust, including high anxiety, stress, worry, and even burnout, which, in turn, reduce the desire for communication and interaction, further perpetuating mistrust. This cycle, which evolves around issues such as doubt, suspicion, anxiety, fear, and self-protection, can continue indefinitely and will eventually lead to relational dissolution. Furthermore, problems with trust amplify agency issues, subsequently leading to increasing monitoring costs, in which an individual's energies, time, and efforts are directed to suspicious scrutinizing rather than more value-creating functions. Unclear communication, invisible compassion, uncertain moral standards, vague commitment, and weak contributions to common tasks are all evident in a reduced in-person interface, which impact the venture capital industry at the time when there have already been alarming levels of mistrust in business relations.

With limited in-person interactions and heightened de-personalization, it is increasingly difficult to build and nurture new relationships in the venture capital ecosystem. As noted previously, new relationships are nurtured and developed over time, through a process based on the continuous exchange of ideas, verbal and non-verbal expressions, and emotion-based interactions. These conditions will most profoundly affect GPs' abilities to establish human connections and develop new relationships with LPs and entrepreneurial firms.

Venture Capitalists and Limited Partners

Interaction with limited partners is become increasingly complex, which, as stated previously, reflects LPs' increased dissatisfaction with the asset class. This discontentment is grounded in declining and non-persistent returns, in addition to worsening economics for LPs in comparison with other segments of private capital and public equities markets. LPs have historically treated GPs with friendliness, flexibility, admiration, and contractual leniency, but this trend is expected to change due to unsatisfactory returns. LPs are less likely to give GPs the benefit of doubt, especially post COVID-response when many LPs have adopted a wait-and-see approach; they also adopt more risk-averse behavior. In fact, many LPs have already become more selective and less loyal to the GPs with whom they worked in the past. For example, LPs are increasingly choosing not to participate in follow-on funds. This has also been exemplified by the actions of CalPERS and CalSTRS, which have either skipped the new fundraising efforts of their loyal GP partners or invested in new partnerships despite refusing previous funding offers. Moreover, LPs may be even less concerned with their ability to secure appropriate capital allocations in the top quartile GPs.

Currently, new entrants into the industry have a relatively easy time in setting up new venture capital operations. The cost of starting a new fund is not difficult to overcome, as the cost of entry into the industry is more or less equal to the cost of conducting fundraising efforts and is typically less than one million dollars. However, this cost could be substantially less if LPs are receptive to new entrants or more desperate to secure their allocations in venture capital. Furthermore, entry expenses can be charged back to the fund after a successful fundraising. Any individual with a few years of professional experience in the industry, good industry contacts, and a previously established network of entrepreneurial firms (which can be converted into a deal flow) can set up independent fund operations; on average, it takes between nine to eighteen months to raise a fund, and intermittent efforts must be sustained. However, these low barriers to entry into the venture capital industry may change. New entrants (i.e., GPs) into the industry are likely to have difficulty establishing new LP relationships post COVID-response due to LPs' discontentment with the contemporary trend of lower-than-expected returns.

Limited in-person interaction negatively affects the propensity of GPs to raise new funds, and, as observed above, this task will be especially difficult for new entrants. An additional obstacle is the need for LPs to re-calibrate their market approach, reassess allocations to venture capital, re-adjust perceptions of geopolitical risks in view of COVID-response, and understand their own liquidity situations. Evidence suggests that LPs are very slow to commit capital to GPs and there may be some re-thinking of previously employed "bucket-filling" allocations. The fact that many GPs will not raise their successor funds is also borne out by research, while others will not reach their fundraising targets. Further research suggests that there may be a wave of adjustments to LP-GP partnership agreements post COVID-response, with the main modifications potentially including extensions of commitment periods and lifespan of funds, requests to recycle realization proceeds, and revisions on the restrictions of debt use. A final key function that is likely to be affected by suppressed in-person interaction relates to the regular quarterly meetings of a fund's board of directors once the newly created fund becomes fully operational. There may also be fewer meetings of supervisory boards, advisory boards, or investment committees, all of which LPs may be involved in.

Venture Capitalists and Entrepreneurs

The relationship between entrepreneurs and venture capitalists is often complicated, in part because it can evolve over time and change abruptly. However, intense interactions between entrepreneurs and venture capitalists occur in four distinct phases of the venture capital investment process. The interactions within these phases have of course been altered post COVID-response, as early evidence suggests that various parts of the investment process completely froze or locked up for a significant number of GPs. In spite of lofty promises and outright propaganda by the venture capital industry regarding their readiness to initiate deals, GPs, similar to LPs, have gone into hibernation mode on new deals.

At the moment, GPs' attention is predominantly dedicated to existing portfolio firms, with their basic objectives here being "damage control" and defense of performance; they intuitively understand that their hope of future fundraisings and survival is currently at stake. On the other hand, newly formed GPs also aim to avoid showing losses early in a fund's life by offering help to firms that should not receive such financial support. Unfreezing their efforts on the new deal front will only occur once GPs reform their approach to the distinct phases of the venture capital process in the wake of COVID-response; these phases will need to be re-conceptualized and re-imagined through bottom-up strategizing, reassessing market opportunities, and devising new sector capital allocations.

The first phase of interaction between entrepreneurs and venture capitalists is the initial relational courtship, which normally occurs at the deal generation phase. Here, each side wishes to present itself through the most positive lens. In this romanticized stage of the venture capital transactional courtship, venture capitalists promote themselves as active, hands-on, and value-added financial backers; their verbal promotional offers often include assurances of frequent attention, assistance to address any anticipated challenges in business development, and operational support. However, as academic research and practice often confirm, venture capitalists may "oversell and under-deliver", resulting in suboptimal value-added contributions due to a lack of operating experience. Moreover, venture capitalists are under pressure not only to participate on the board of directors of their existing portfolio firms, but they are also expected to be actively involved in new deal identification, due diligence, and the negotiation of new transactions. Entrepreneurs, on the other hand, wish to showcase strategic commercial, operational, and financial successes and business savvy during their initial interactions with venture capitalists by, for example, touring newly built plants, promoting recently acquired accounts, or demonstrating new software upgrades. By desiring to obtain authentication and certification of their success by external validators, who are perceived as sophisticated investors, superior builders of entrepreneurial value, outstanding strategizers, and able to bring professionalism into firms, entrepreneurs seek the approval of "smart money". Thus, while venture capitalists often arouse the approbation and even envy of the public, entrepreneurs are similarly in awe of, and desire to please, venture capitalists.

This initial stage of interaction has been substantially redefined post COVID-response because deal-generation interactions traditionally occur in informal settings, casual meetings, networking occurrences, sport events, and other easy-going venues. Due to lockdowns, meeting restrictions, and the fear of contagion, these interactions now either do not occur at all, or take place on a significantly limited scale. Thus, the impact of limited interactions on an industry known for informal networking and schmoozing has been detrimental. Primarily, the negative consequences of limited interaction for venture capitalists are reduced access to deals, less successful conversions of initial contacts into actual deals, fewer chances to showcase their own successes, prolongation of deal completion, and concentration on entrepreneurs and firms where proven relationships exist (while perhaps omitting the development of new relationships). Poor initial interactions also compromise opportunities to establish an initial business magnetism, mutual respect, and a strong relationship. While the value of this initial in-person interface may have been undervalued by venture capitalists, difficulty in subsequent interactions may quickly prove how valuable these interactions once were.

If the initial business courtship is fruitful, both sides proceed to the next phase of the venture capital investment process, namely screening and evaluation. At this stage, venture capitalists aim to investigate and confirm the underlying strengths of the firm through analysis of the venture's commercial areas (i.e., management, market, products and services, competition, finance, and so on). After the initial screening and evaluation, a deeper analysis focusing on a detailed investigation of the firm's financial forecasts and its valuation is performed. The objective of venture capitalists' interactions with the founder at this stage is to understand commercial realities in the context of the financial projections. Intricate deliberations on the achievability of the financial projections will lead to discussions on business valuation, which is often a sensitive and contentious area for the two sides. However, this exercise represents a significant investment of time for both parties; this, in turn, builds commitment, reinforces respect, and constructs loyalty between the entrepreneur and the venture capitalist.

The most significant consequences of limited and poor interaction during the screening and evaluation stage are the misappraisal of the underlying venture's commercial and financial strengths, the misassessment of management, and the establishment of an excessive entry valuation. While data analysis regarding the size of the market, market share, and the financial performance of the firm may be easy through distance interaction and virtual data rooms, ascertaining the skills and capabilities of the entire management team, the dedication of the founder to the venture, and the meaning the founder attaches to their venture may be significantly more difficult. It will also prove challenging to understand the personality, motivations, and ambitions of founders and members of their management team, as such appraisal can only be done effectively in-person.

The impact of suboptimal interactions during the screening and evaluation stage is truly concerning, as in venture capital, ascertaining people is just as important as evaluating data and facts. Research evidence suggests that GPs already struggle to appraise new investment opportunities. Although GPs attempt to compensate for the absence of in-person meetings with increased zoom meetings, reference checks, and background investigations, it is doubtful that the quality of these activities is the same when compared to real face-to-face interactions. For example, GPs would not be able to recognize more nuanced messages, explanations, or details from entrepreneurs. In terms of financial decision-making, compromised interactions during the due diligence phase may lead to suboptimal investment decisions, including inferior investment prospects or passing on superior firms, because misappraisal is probable in an online setting. The chance of these errors is likely to be inversely related to the level and intensity of in-person interactions. This, of course, has negative implications for returns, as screening and evaluation would take more time, effort, and financial resources.

Having established strong rapport, mutual respect for each other's talents and accomplishments, and interpersonal sympathy, both venture capitalists and entrepreneurs naturally proceed to one of the most difficult stages of interaction: negotiating the foundational terms of the transaction. Significantly, deal negotiations can occur at various points of the relationship. The early interactions focus on the most general role the venture capitalist will play in the venture. During these discussions, venture capitalists attempt to identify any deals breakers (i.e., any contractual terms which are unlikely to be accepted by founders). While there are many areas of potential disagreement and dispute, both sides are normally able to resolve these challenges through formal interactions and informal meetings. These early negotiations serve to test-drive the interpersonal chemistry, ability to resolve conflict, and aptitude for both parties to work together under pressure. Arising difficulties force the two sides to demonstrate flexibility, creativity, and compromise, which are tested and re-tested by continued value exchange. Problems can be resolved rather quickly due to face-to-face collaborations, although intense interactions at this stage in the process normally culminate in the signing of sizeable legal documentation. The initial agreement includes complicated terms, conditions, rights, provisions, and obligations, which guide the relationship between entrepreneur and venture capitalist from the preliminary deal signing to the complete monetization of the venture capitalist's stake in the venture.

Frequent interactions at this third stage of the venture capital investment process are likely to moderate any disputes, confrontations, and disagreements during the finalization of financial contracts. This stage particularly relies on venture capitalists' abilities to interpret the feelings, thoughts, gestures, situations, and behaviors of entrepreneurs; entrepreneurs are similarly charged with the reciprocal task. Therefore, infrequent in-person interaction during the negotiation stage can lead to the inability of venture capitalists to address sensitive issues related to some of the more intrusive terms enshrined in legal documentation (i.e., change of control provisions, drag along rights, veto rights, etc.) and resolve any disputes or conflicts. This is likely to affect the speed at which venture capitalists are able to complete deals. Evidence suggests that venture capitalists have toughened their approach to deal negotiations post COVID-response, whose offers now include more veto and approval rights, anti-dilution safeguards, and liquidation preferences.

The most protracted stage of the venture capital process relates to monitoring, which represents a period where entrepreneurs and venture capitalists focus on specific operational milestones as outlined in the term sheet. The key area of concern is whether the investee firm is performing in accordance with the initial investment premise. Regardless of whether the venture capital-backed firm underperforms or over-performs, the venture must look for additional capital not anticipated prior to deal completion. This stage also forces the venture to amend their strategy, hire additional senior members, and address operational issues. However, a significant percentage of venture capitalists (perhaps in spite of their best efforts, intentions, and initiatives) are unable to provide significant contribution to entrepreneurial ventures. We estimate that only about fifteen percent of venture capitalists, most of whom possess relevant knowledge of the industry, real-life operating experience at senior posts, and a track record of value-generating projects, are able to make meaningful, long-lasting, and value-generative contributions to entrepreneurial firms. Thus, the most disappointing moments in the entrepreneurs' relationship to venture capitalists are when venture capitalists openly exhibit their mentality to search for "home runs", abandon underperforming ventures, and promote excessive risks.

The most obvious consequence of limited interaction between these two sides is the destruction of business value. The monitoring phase of the investment process relies on heated and intense exchanges between entrepreneurs and venture capitalists. Disputes and conflicts often emerge over issues related to strategic development, additional rounds of financing (which can be dilutive to entrepreneurs, who do not participate in a capital increase), and management decisions. These disputes can easily lead to distrust, which, if left unresolved by a lack of in-person interaction, can certainly perpetuate conflicts. Despite these challenges, evidence suggests that GPs have barely increased their allocation of time to portfolio firms post COVID-response; this is surprising given that a majority of portfolio firms indicate they have been affected by COVID-response, the full impact of which has not yet materialized.

Venture Capitalists' In-House Operations Post COVID-Response

One of the most important components of successful business operation is the team involved, who, in the venture capital setting, consist of founding partners, managing directors, senior and junior partners, associates, principals, and back-office operations (i.e., finance, administration, legal counsel, and human resources). GPs also increasingly employ ESG specialists and investor relations professionals, although it is questionable whether these individuals actually add any value to the venture capital investment process. Because the entire team contributes to finding, processing, and exiting from deals, the composition of the team and its effective communication is critical to the overall performance of the fund.

Therefore, when face-to-face communication within a venture capital team is infrequent, fund operations are disrupted in numerous ways. Firstly, while there may be different compositions of the team (i.e., fewer or increased numbers of junior and senior staff members), many GPs rely on an organizational construct where two or three founding partners establish their own venture capital firm and subsequently employ a wide spectrum of individuals. Although these team members may have lofty job titles, such as directors, partners, or principals, they effectively constitute an organizational "engine room" responsible for the daily grind of processing deals; this can be termed the associate-based organizational model. Another common approach for organizing the venture fund may be the partners' model, in which senior partners are responsible for all functions of the investment process and there is a limited reliance on junior staff. In practice, many GPs oscillate between these two models over time. The main advantages of the associate-based model are lower costs, more operational flexibility (staff can be hired or let go), less potential for conflict between senior partners, and increased availability of numerous personnel for various functions. However, these individuals normally operate at lower levels of expertise and experience. The main disadvantage is that two or three individuals, who enjoy a disproportionate allocation of salaries, bonuses, and carried interest, monopolize the firm. Lastly, it should be clear that substituting kitchen tables for office desks does not carry the same level of productivity.

While the associate-based organizational structure can work, its effectiveness is predicated on the efficient supervision and training of junior staff. Of course, the system may also be successful on the basis of an effective and systematic downward transfer of tacit knowledge through on-the-job training, mentoring, coaching, counseling, and directing, in addition to apprenticeship opportunities at increasingly higher level of responsibility. The scheme can similarly be supplemented with external training and development. However, the associate-based structure requires a continuous effort for junior partners to become effective deal processors. Under the current circumstances of COVID-response, the process of on-the-job training is likely to be disrupted and dislocated, therefore reducing the scheme's overall success because it is inherently predicated on frequent communication, senior partners engaging with junior partners in high-quality interactions, and in-person attention. The re-adjustment and re-alignment of these interactions could prove to be difficult, and simply put, the vast majority of GPs are not prepared to put in the significant time required for an effective transition to remote work.

There is another key function in the venture capital firm that is critical to its successful operations, and if utilized correctly, can result in strong financial performance. This key function of GP operations is the investment committee, which may be defined as a formal collection of individuals in the venture capital firm. These individuals have the power to legally bind the fund toward an investment, so the general purpose of the committee is to evaluate and consider all new investment opportunities brought to the venture capital fund, and to oversee the firm's existing portfolios. At every phase of the investment process, professionals in the venture capital firm interact with its investment committee by presenting appropriate documents (i.e., preliminary, investment, restructuring and recapitalization, and exit memorandum) for internal approval. The most important parts of the interactions between investment professionals and the investment committee relate to information sharing, during which deal leaders are encouraged to communicate freely, to limit active selling, and to restrict any personal biases toward a deal. These interactions are often informal and can greatly contribute to identifying key deal issues, understanding the potential investee firm's commercial realities, contemplating the value creation process, analyzing potential "growth disruptors", and ultimately making the right investment decision. Less in-person interaction can negatively impact information discovery and cross-sharing processes, which are the foundation of good decision-making, and can result in important information being over-looked or downplayed.

Venture Capital and Its Relations with Other Stakeholders

Another key component of the venture capital ecosystem which requires effective communication is interaction with external stakeholders who participate in the investment process. As noted above, venture capitalists interact with multiple external stakeholders in distinct stages from deal flow generation to exit. Developing a high-quality proprietary deal flow is rooted in networking, informal meetings, and information exchange. During term sheet development, lawyers, accountants, environmental specialists, consultants, and other advisors are employed in the screening and evaluation stage. However, entrepreneurial firms may require expert external assistance during deal monitoring, especially when the firm is away from its anticipated developmental, operational, and financial targets. Exit represents another phase where these external advisors are forcefully involved.

The Venture Capital Industry Re-Imagined

Given the topic under consideration, the goal is to hypothesize what the venture capital industry may look like in the future, and how these changes may be accelerated by COVID-response. While this exercise is grounded in some assumptions, it also reflects more nuanced and stealth-mode undercurrents already occurring in the venture capital industry; these small and more distinct tides have become increasingly visible since the 2008 financial crisis.

As noted in Chapter 1, there are multiple signs of the venture capital industry's maturation, such as a slowdown of fundraising and investing, more intense competition for deals, inconsistent and declining returns, failed GP fundraisings, and a growing number of mega-funds. There are also indicators that the venture capital industry has suffered from a crisis of reputation in the eyes of entrepreneurs, LPs, and other stakeholders (i.e., the state). Therefore, the industry is desperately trying to reinvent itself since there have not been any substantial changes to its basic operations, business model, mode of finance provision, or know-how in recent history. There has been a similar lack of any major innovation, improvement, or modernization in the industry, short of any such actions undertaken by individual funds. For example, the vast majority of GPs have not made any significant commitments to digitization, artificial intelligence, or science-based decision-making; we conjecture that many of these ambitious undertakings will accelerate in the near future.

Figure 3.1, which was included at the beginning of this chapter, is a pictorial representation of the venture capital industry's basic structural blocks in the last five decades and confirms minimal changes have been made within the industry. Numerous observations can be made about the historical architecture of the industry, the most significant of which is the structure's complexity. There are multiple connections between stakeholders in the venture capital ecosystem whose relations need to be constantly adjusted, negotiated, and harmonized; this requires financial resources, time, and effort. More specifically, the financial success of the structure relies heavily on a delicate balance between two segments, LPs and GPs, which have convergent, but also divergent, objectives. The misalignment of these objectives gives rise to multiple agency issues that are inherently difficult to navigate, moderate, and resolve.

Additionally, the web-like design of the venture capital industry is inherently inefficient, primarily because the structure multiplies costs and depresses profits. Its inefficiency is reflected in the frequent, intense discussions between LPs and GPs regarding compensation; in short, many LPs realize that GPs are pricing themselves out of the market. For example, if it is assumed that GPs receive annual fees equal to about 1.5% (this percentage may be reduced over time), the total amount of compensation paid by LPs to GPs would be equal to about $51.2 billion on the total assets under management (AUM), which in turn is equal to about $3.4 trillion (without accounting for carried interest). Similarly, fees on $2.0 trillion of dry powder (i.e., un-invested capital) are equal to $31.4 billion. If we consider that the industry has had about $1.5 trillion of AUM, the total fees paid to GPs in the last 20 years were equal to about $450 billion. This figure is stunning when compared to the financial performance of GPs during this period, some of whom are still in denial regarding their returns.

Of course, when hypothesizing any changes to the current architecture of the venture capital industry, a number of fundamental assumptions must be made. One of the central expectations relates to the role of LPs in the ecosystem, who must have sufficient resolve to address the most serious problems, including compensation and performance. Furthermore, these compensation issues are expected toprod LPs to continually bypass GPs, a trend that has already been visible in the marketplace. For example, in their desperate attempt to disintermediate GPs, LPs have made significant efforts either to establish their own in-house operations or increasingly rely on direct co-investment rights because they intuitively recognize that these efforts are more profitable. LPs' continuous efforts to evade GPs confirm that they have diminished confidence and increased reluctance to support the current venture capital business model; although the current structure has served GPs well, it has been less valuable to LPs. Moreover, we conjecture that LPs' pressure on fees will contribute to market consolidation on the GP side and, ultimately, on the LP side.

However, we anticipate that industry transition is likely to take place in three distinct phases of evolution that will initiate the long-awaited disruption of the current venture capital business model presented in Fig. 3.1. The first two phases are expected to center on consolidations, primarily related to GPs and then, in due course, to LPs. The third, most progressive, and final stage of this transformation would focus on the mass digitization and redefinition of all stakeholder relationships in the entire ecosystem. The contributions of these key stakeholders are often underappreciated and minimized, and although well compensated, they have been perceived as "best supporting actors" in the venture capital ecosystem while the true limelight is accrued to venture capitalists. However, in the final stage of industry progression, this diminished role of stakeholder will be reevaluated. The method in which these stages may be unveiled, and the characteristics of the resulting structures, will be discussed further below.

Global Consolidation of General Partners

In the past, the venture capital industry has continued to operate in a fragmented manner, wherein no GP or group of GPs has been successful in driving the consolidation process. For example, the total market share of the five largest venture capital funds (Carlyle, Apollo, KKR, Blackstone, and Bain), was equal to 15.5% in 2015, while in 2020 it was equal to 14.3%; the industry grew from $2.4 trillion to $3.4 trillion over the same period. However, the most dynamically developing GPs (i.e., Apollo and KKR) have grown significantly. For instance, Apollo increased its AUM in private equity by 2.0 times while KKR increased its AUM by 1.8 times in the last five years. While it is difficult to predict whether this growth trajectory for Apollo and KKR is likely to continue, this trend may represent a slow emergence of market leaders and industry consolidators. Similarly, Carlyle also increased its AUM by 1.2 times, which represents a meaningful increase over others such as Blackstone and Bain, which stayed flat in their respective amounts of AUM.

In the era of post COVID-response, it appears that industry consolidation on the GP side has more chances to succeed because the process is likely to be driven by three interrelated components: return performance, GPs' actual assistance capabilities, and innovation. In the first case, academic and practice-based evidence clearly demonstrates an increasing disparity between top quartile performers and the remaining GPs, which was discussed in detail in Chapter 1. One reason for such poor return performance could be due to the increased competition venture capital is facing from other segments of private capital and private equities markets, which have strong advantages over venture capital.

With regard to GPs' ability to aid entrepreneurial firms, however, only a small fraction of venture capital firms are able to provide value-added services and advice. Unfortunately, as practice demonstrates, many GPs exhibit significant shortcomings in their know-how and assistance efforts to entrepreneurial firms, which reflect a lack of practical experience, poor decision-making capabilities, and suboptimal business judgment. This lack of hands-on competence among GPs is especially evident during periods of rapid change, economic downturns, and severe external shocks; thus, there is no better time than the current period of post COVID-response to test GPs' true skills and capabilities. Unskillful GPs will experience significant problems with their portfolio firms and express paralysis in their actions due to the extent of these challenges.

Thirdly, the increased reliance and testing of remote digital technologies post COVID-response are likely to initiate further progression in this area. While there are clear benefits to in-person human interactions, and there are proven harms arising from online interactions, the venture capital industry is unlikely to resist the temptation to further digitize relationships and the entire venture capital investment process; this probability is in line with the old maxim of "never waste a good crisis". We anticipate that increased digitization will go hand-in-hand with market consolidation on the GP side, ultimately resulting in the emergence of GP mega-funds. In other words, only major GPs with a substantial cash flow would be able to make financial commitments to digitize interactions with stakeholders (including entrepreneurial firms and LPs), screening and evaluation processes, decision-making, and value enhancement during monitoring. The natural consequence of digitization will be a slow but steady disintermediation of many GPs from the ecosystem. This transient industry consolidation structure is presented in Fig. 3.2.

There are some distinctive characteristics of the venture capital industry's projected architecture, such as the expected emergence of mega-fund GPs. These GPs are predicted to maintain strong partnerships with governments, corporate partners, and financial institutions, and are expected to dedicate a full array of financial services and financing choices (i.e., debt, equity, and other forms of entrepreneurial finance) to investment opportunities from a single investment hub (i.e., a mega-fund GP). The process of financial disintermediation in the venture capital ecosystem would affect financial institutions since mega-fund GPs could offer access to other forms of financing, which would similarly entice corporate partners.

Mega-fund GPs are also projected to increasingly rely on technological solutions, such as artificial intelligence, statistical analysis, and science-driven tools in their daily operations, and are likely to digitize the entire

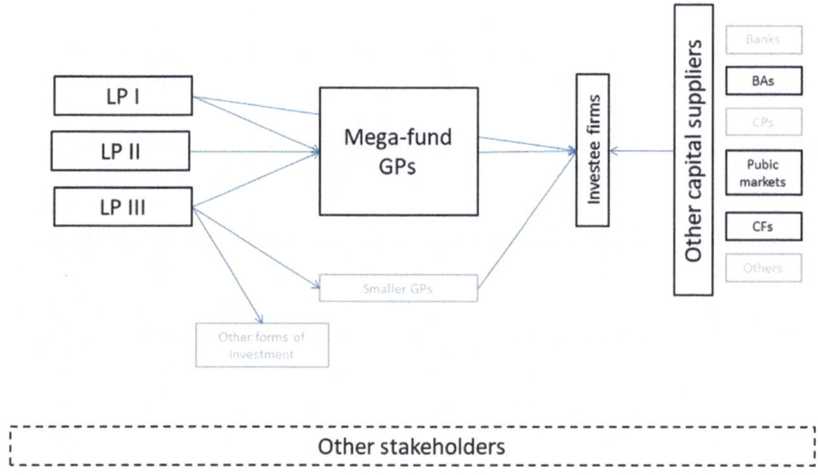

Fig. 3.2 The GP consolidation stage of the venture capital industry (Abbreviations: *BAs* business angels, *CPs* corporate partners, *CFs* crowdfunders, *F-of-Fs* fund-of-funds, *GPs* general partners, *LP* limited partner)

investment process. Newly implemented technological solutions would be used to identify buyout opportunities in the private sector, public equities markets, and search for other types of deals in the business universe. It is estimated that a mere dozen global mega-funds GPs will account for about 60 or 70% of total AUM in global private equity. A small number of regional, independent, and smaller GPs would simultaneously continue to serve unique market niches or market segments omitted by mega-fund GPs.

The transient mega-fund consolidation structure could yield numerous benefits to LPs, although not all current concerns would be resolved; this is in part why further changes to the industry architecture are envisaged. Increased digitization is projected to reduce GP cost related to travel, the number of employees, and fixed structures. Market consolidation would also limit competition and increase monopolization, which would lead to a stabilization of declining returns. LPs would also benefit from no longer having to commit significant human resources, time, and capital to the GP evaluation, selection, and monitoring processes.

The effect of such a transient consolidation structure would be moderate. Although mega-fund GPs could execute buyout transactions well (which currently account for the majority of transactions), they may experience challenges with other types of deals, such as expansion and growth opportunities that may require additional assistance. Within investment opportunities that are characterized by a requirement for hands-on support and active participation, mega-fund GPs could rely on a network of established relationships with consultants, specialists, and advisors. The funds could also draw resources from major accounting and advisory firms such as Accenture, Boston Consulting, McKinsey, Deloitte, KPMG, Ernst & Young, and so on. Firms like these often have significant industry experience and a strong local presence; they already benefit from a relationship with the industry to the tune of between $8.3 and $15.4 billion per annum. Thus, their direct involvement through hands-on assistance, for example, could ultimately prove valuable to entrepreneurial firms.

Lastly, we assume here that fund-of-funds, which are the least efficient and value-added investment vehicles in the venture capital ecosystem, would likely be eliminated altogether.

Global Pooling of Limited Partners

It is anticipated that the second stage of industry consolidation would take place on the supply-of-capital side of the ecosystem. Mega-structures on the LP side are expected to arise as a result of various LPs (i.e., pension funds, endowments, insurance firms, wealthy individuals, corporations, financial intuitions, and others) pooling capital under new financial and management structures. The pooling of capital by LPs is likely to be driven by a number of trends, the first of which is as a response to the growing negotiating power of GPs. There is evidence that the best GP performers have not only been able to maintain their compensation packages, but actually improve them through GP consolidation. Secondly, consolidation on the GP side and the subsequent emergence of mega-fund GPs may not fully resolve LPs' concerns related to performance, as evidence from research suggests that fund size is negatively related to returns. In other words, while market consolidation on the GP side would yield clear benefits to GPs (i.e., higher dollar value of dollar compensation, the ability to reduce operating cost, and so on), it would be initially unclear whether these GP benefits would be shared with LPs. Finally, pooling financial resources would allow an evident reduction of cost for LPs.

Consolidation on the LP side would be a distinct possibility since such structures already exist in other segments of financial markets. An analysis of fund management within the U.S. confirms that three fund managers (i.e., Black Rock, Vanguard, and State Street) effectively directly or indirectly control over 90% of corporations comprising the S&P 500 index, nearly 90% of corporations within Dow Jones 30, and about 80% of NASDAQ 100 firms; these fund managers also control FTSE 100 firms. We conjecture that a similar consolidation and control process is also possible on the LP side of the venture capital industry. Furthermore, one benefit of an LP consolidation is that it would allow LPs to exercise more negotiating power vis-à-vis the consolidated and integrated GP side. An increased reliance on external advisors and lower percentage compensation of GPs will also reduce costs of the venture capital business model and generate more profits for LPs.

The adjusted architecture of the venture capital industry regarding LP-side consolidation is illustrated in Fig. 3.3. The structure is primarily comprised of mega-fund GPs and a declining number of smaller, independent GPs. Figure 3.3 also illustrates a more prominent role of other stakeholders in the ecosystem; here, consultants, advisors, and specialists effectively become an "operating" arm of mega-fund GPs. Therefore,

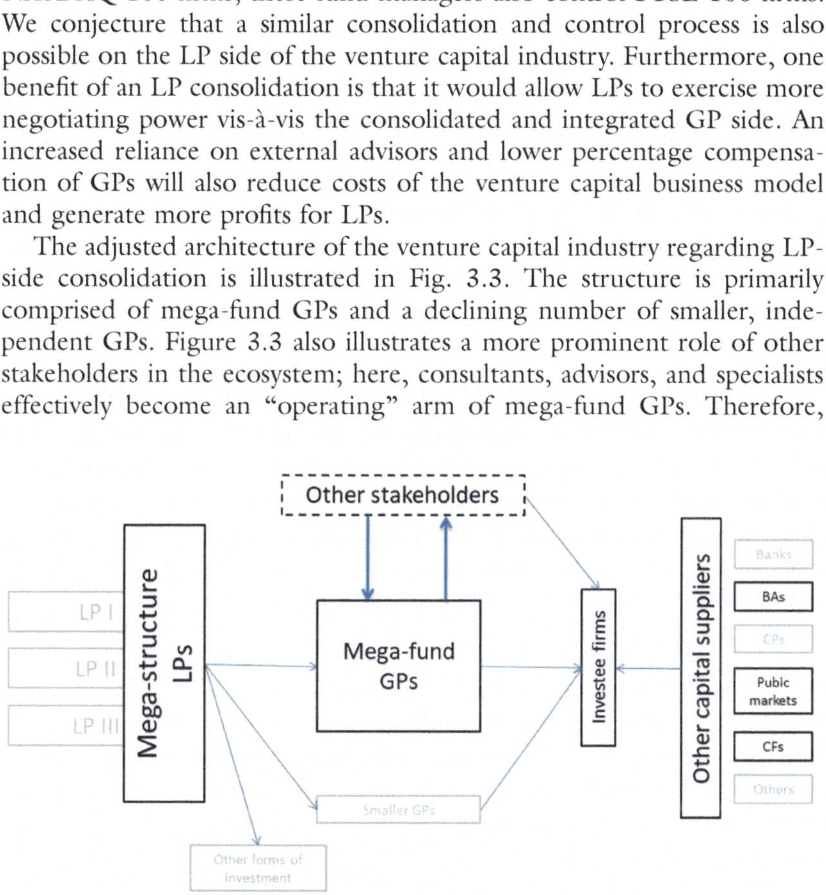

Fig. 3.3 The LP pooling stage of the venture capital industry (Abbreviations: *BAs* business angels, *CPs* corporate partners, *CFs* crowdfunders, *F-of-Fs* fund-of-funds, *GPs* general partners, *LP* limited partner)

mega-fund GPs would continue to offer various financial services to entrepreneurial firms and the advisors would work on a project-by-project basis. In other words, LPs themselves would make decisions about the right composition of debt and equity in a deal without the need to involve external financial institutions, and GPs could generate financial returns on the provision of equity and debt.

As stated previously, external experts (i.e., accountants, lawyers, independent consultants, advisors, and so on) would be more directly involved in the venture capital ecosystem, increasingly substituting the hands-on role of GPs, and could even be responsible for deal sourcing. It is interesting to observe that in buyout transactions, external advisors are already responsible for initiating the purchase transaction, advising the firm when operational and financial issues emerge, and executing the final sale. LPs effectively pay extra for these services as these expenses do not reduce GP compensation, and are instead charged back to the fund or covered by the firm; in these circumstances, it is not entirely apparent what role GPs actually serve.

The Futuristic Architecture of the Venture Capital Industry

We conjecture that the final transformation of the ecosystem would result in complete disintermediation of mega-fund GPs. Such a conclusion would occasion major savings and grant full control of the ecosystem to mega-sized financial managers like Black Rock, Vanguard, State Street, and Fidelity. We anticipate that GPs would either be bought out by these mega financiers, join them, be invited to cooperate under special arrangements, or disappear completely. In the U.S., for example, there were precedents for these types of mega consolidations in the industry and the financial system beginning in the early 1900s.

Figure 3.4 illustrates the adjusted architecture of the venture capital industry in the future. The central component of this futuristic architecture is the complete digitization of the investment process, which would operate on the basis of artificial intelligence systems. A new "smart platform" would be responsible for identifying suitable investments, performing screening and evaluation, offering standardized deal terms, finalizing transactions, monitoring key vital statistics, and exiting, as illustrated in Fig. 3.4. This type of platform is already being used on a smaller scale through crowdfunding, and it fundamentally minimizes human interaction. Only in rare circumstances and when absolutely required

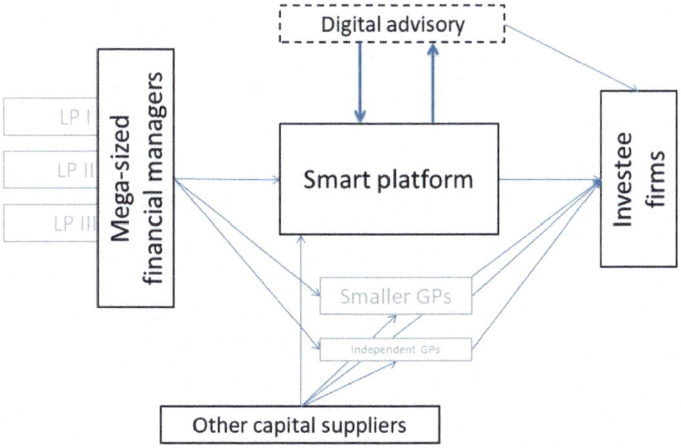

Fig. 3.4 The futuristic architecture of the venture capital industry (Abbreviations: *BAs* business angels, *CPs* corporate partners, *CFs* crowdfunders, *F-of-Fs* fund-of-funds, *GPs* general partners, *LP* limited partner)

would external stakeholders be invited to assist on a project-by-project basis. The platform would connect capital suppliers and demanders (i.e., entrepreneurial firms) without the need for intermediaries (i.e., GPs). As noted throughout this book, GPs are neither true suppliers nor demanders of capital; thus, the venture capital ecosystem can operate efficiently without GPs. Lastly, it is important to note that using sophisticated artificial intelligence to navigate the investment process is not new to global financial management, and the best example of such a system is Aladdin, which was developed by Black Rock.

Another unique feature of the projected futuristic system is that other suppliers of capital, including financial institutions, business angels, and corporate partners, would become an integral part of the smart platform. Although the smart platform, rapid digitization, and the depersonalization of relationships would disintermediate many GPs, we also anticipate the existence of a limited number of smaller GPs. However, stakeholders would further contribute to the disintermediation of GPs by assuming their hands-on roles. If the venture capital ecosystem was reduced in complexity through the complete exclusion of GPs, there would be savings of about $25 billion per annum, short of any cost related to running the smart platform and compensation paid to other stakeholders. In this instance, LPs would assume full control of the venture capital ecosystem.

The Evolution of the Venture Capital Industry and Entrepreneurs

While we discuss the actual impact of future changes in the venture capital industry on entrepreneurs in more detail later in the book, this chapter would not be complete without at least some mention of how these transformations could affect the entrepreneurial environment. For example, an increasing de-personalization of relationships, digitalization of the investment process, and challenges with trust would have a negative impact on entrepreneurial firms. The many benefits of in-person interactions and harms due to a lack of such interface have already been discussed at length in this chapter. While the system of de-personalization and digitalization would be expected to impact many entrepreneurial firms, young entrepreneurial firms would be especially vulnerable to these changes. It is imaginable that the flow of venture capital to the startup ecosystem will also freeze for some time in spite of huge amounts of dry powder on hand. Young firms especially rely on frequent communications, regular contacts and connections, valuable hands-on assistance, and, of course, capital.

Broader changes to the architecture of the venture capital industry are also expected to result in further negative consequences to entrepreneurial firms. Firstly, mega-fund GPswould likely direct their interest toward selected types of opportunities such as buyouts (note that buyout deals already account for the vast majority of transactions), which require relatively limited human interaction, can be sustained without the development of effective long-term relationships, and rely on the extensive use of external advisors. The industry as a whole may become less interested in expansion and growth opportunities or firms in the early stages of development, instead favoring buyouts of later stage firms. Additionally, mega-fund GPs could monopolize access to other forms of entrepreneurial finance, while a smart platform could similarly limit access to alternative financing sources.

However, there may be some advantages of the venture capital industry's architectural transformations. As noted throughout this book, venture capital is responsible for a very small portion of the overall financing needs pursued by entrepreneurial firms. Therefore, diminished chances of obtaining venture capital would not affect over 98% of entrepreneurial firms. Those firms which are impacted could become more prolific managers of internal finance and master bootstrapping techniques. Other viable options could be the increasing reliance on alternate forms of financing such as the already sizeable market of family-and-friends, or the continued usage of crowdfunding. Evidence suggests that business angels have become less active post COVID-response. Despite these options, an important advantage for those entrepreneurial firms that actually obtain venture capital financing is that mega-fund GPs would likely increase their reliance on external advisors, consultants, experts, and specialists, thus providing higher quality and hands-on industry experience compared to the vast majority of professionals employed in venture capital.

Bibliography

Bain & Company. 2020. The impact of Covid-19 on private equity. Brief. www.bain.com.

Barber, Felix and Michael Goold. 2007. The strategic secret of private equity. September. www.hbr.org.

Białek, Józef. 2019. *Czas Niewolników: Jak Świat Stał Się Własnością Kilku Korporacji*. Kobierzyce: WydawnictwoWektory.

Canderle, Sebastian. 2020. Myths of private equity performance: part II. November 25. www.cfainstitute.org.

Fittchner, Jan and Eelke M. Heemskerk. 2018. The NEW Permanent Universal Owners: Index Funds, (im)patient Capital, and the Claim of Long-termism. www.researchgate.net.

Galford, Robert M. and Anne Sibold Drapeau. 2003. The enemies of trust. *Harvard Business Review*. February. www.hbr.org.

Gompers, Paul, Will Gornall, Steven Kaplan, and Ilya A. Strebulaev. 2020. Venture capitalists and COVID-19. October. Working paper. Boston.

Grossman, David. 2019. Face-to-face communication: 6 reasons to lead in person. April 15. www.yourthoughtpartner.com.

Klonowski, Darek. 2013. *The venture capital investment process: Principles and practice*. New York: Palgrave MacMillan.

Klonowski, Darek. 2014. *Strategic entrepreneurial finance: From value creation to realization*. London: Routledge.

Klonowski, Darek. 2018. *The venture capital deformation: Value destruction throughout the investment process*. New York: Palgrave MacMillan.

Michels, David. 2019. The trust crisis in business. June 26. www.bain.com.

Smith, Dustin. 2019. The importance of face-to-face communication in the modern workforce. October 29. www.lifesize.com.
Surpure, Shantanu and Christopher Rasmussen. 2020. How the coronavirus pandemic will affect venture capital dealmaking. March 23. www.vccircle.com.
Vereckey, Betsy. 2020. 5 trends in venture capital (beyond the pandemic). April 22. www.mit.edu.
Woodford, Isabel. 2020. Covid has put VCs under the spotlight, and exposed their vulnerabilities. November 6. www.sifted.eu.

CHAPTER 4

Venture Capital Post COVID-Response: External Environmental Scanning and Investment Opportunities

The objective of this chapter is to discern how key social, economic, and political trends can create opportunities for the venture capital industry. There are many alternative methods to understand the competitive, structural, and economic dynamics in any industry, including Michael Porter's six forces model, SWOT analysis (strengths, weaknesses, opportunities, and threats), STEEP analysis (sociocultural, technological, economic, ecological, and political), and PESTEL analysis (political, economic, sociocultural, technological, ecological, and legal). However, the most traditional analysis of the industry occurs in the context of external environmental scanning. This form of analysis includes the process of detailed examination, assessment, evaluation, and appraisal of key factors, elements, and features occurring, and directly affecting the firm operating, within a task environment. Such analysis detects and illuminates key factors that impact the long-term profitability of the industry and its stakeholders. Significantly, external environmental scanning relates to the following categories: economic (i.e., economic growth, unemployment rate, wages, disposable income, competition, and business environment), technological (i.e., new products and services, research and development, Internet usage and reliance, digitization, and new technological developments), political (i.e., stability of state, political orientation, business regulations, individual rights and freedoms, and constitutional protections), legal (i.e., laws and regulations related to business, tax, immigration,

D. Klonowski, *Venture Capital Redefined*,
https://doi.org/10.1007/978-3-030-83387-9_4

foreign ownership, and trade; judicial and court system), and sociocultural (i.e., lifestyle changes, pace of life, family and its composition, life expectancy, age distribution, healthcare, and education).

Undercurrents in the Peripheral Ecosystem

Chapter 2 highlighted key developments in the external political, social, and economic environments which became most prevalent post COVID-response. On the political front, public mandate lockdowns, mask-wearing requirements, quarantine compulsions, limits on travel, curfews, and numerous other restrictions have led to a massive centralization of political power in 2020. States around the globe have capriciously instituted, suspended, and re-instituted these restrictive measures with limited scientific justification for their decisions. The execution of these arbitrary restrictions represents a visible migration of the political apparatus to the left of the political spectrum because, as stated earlier in this book, these measure not only constitute a significant infringement on basic human rights and freedoms, but also transgress on one's liberties to operate a small business, attend school, or maintain religious services. Therefore, these global political actions represent an infringement of the statutory rights that most constitutions, charters, and declarations aim to protect.

In terms of social transformations, COVID-response resulted in an elevated fear of contagion, which, in turn, led to social distancing, isolation, a lack of socialization, and disruptions to the normal patterns of human life. There is evidence that these reactions initiated an acceleration of mental health issues, as well as increases in substance abuse, domestic violence, and excess deaths (i.e., the number of deaths, which could be expected to be above normal annual averages). COVID-response has impacted human sociocultural behavior by redefining certain values, norms, traditions, and customs; these value changes are likely to prove detrimental for individuals, families, communities, and societies.

With respect to the economy, state-led COVID-response converted into a severe slowdown of economic growth, enormous job losses, and business closures on a massive scale. The economic impact of COVID-response is both broad because it penetrates many industries in fundamental ways, and deep due to it affecting the critical components of industrial value chains. Thus, the economic slowdown is likely to persist for longer periods of time since these structural dislocations post COVID-response are extensive. If these economic realities were to continue in the foreseeable future, there is a likelihood of global, political, and economic polarization and tension, social unrest, mass protests, civil disobedience, and violence.

In this chapter, we continue our discussion regarding the impact of this complex external environment on venture capital. As noted initially, there are many factors that can impact the venture capital industry. However, in reality, it is not practical to monitor all aspects of the external environment with the same level of intensity and depth. Instead, it is important to determine which of these factors have a high probability of occurring, and of these, which are likely to have either a significant positive or negative impact on the industry. For example, scanning the most critical factors in the external environment allows for the evaluation of opportunities that perhaps were not anticipated in the original business plan, which may include new product and service development, acquisition opportunities, new strategic partnerships and alliances, and geographic expansions. Consequently, monitoring these factors should become the center of analysis. This chapter also expands the discussion of key external environmental factors to include other critical undercurrents which naturally flow from the political, social, and economic drifts stated above. The six factors discussed here in detail consist of changes to industrial structures, alteration to consumer behavior, digitization of the human universe, home as the center of human gravity, the deterioration of public health (especially mental health), and the abolition of the family; these factors are presented in Fig. 4.1.

Figure 4.1 is the priority milieu of the venture capital industry post COVID-response. At the top left corner are factors in the venture capital ecosystem which are judged to have a medium-to-high chance of occurring with a similarly medium-to-high impact on venture capital. The matrix confirms that the key economic indicators (i.e., unemployment, wages, and incomes) are likely to have a broad-based impact on the economy, and hence on the venture capital industry. Uncertainties in these areas are anticipated to lead to a postponement of consumption and major expenditures, reshaping family budgets, re-prioritization of spending, and adjustments to savings. Governments have been similarly impacted and, as a result, have encumbered their budgets with significant debt. However, with an increased centralization of decision-making, governments are expected to play a critical role in the external environment; their impact may only be truly assessed when more normal patterns of life re-emerge, and current restrictions are lifted.

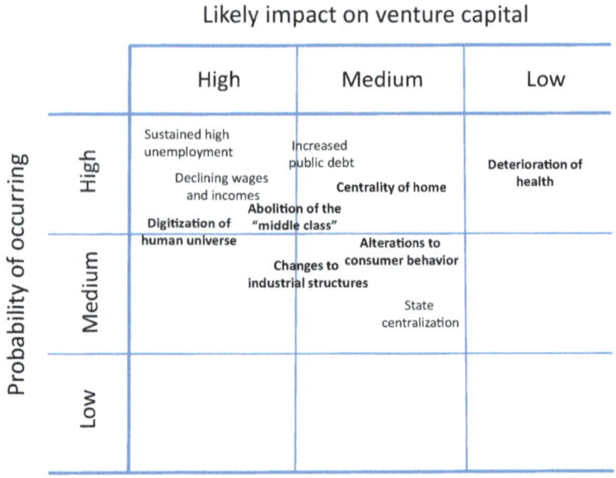

Fig. 4.1 The key undercurrents in the external environment and their impact on venture capital (*Source* Adopted from Hunger and Wheelen [2011])

The second tier of factors relates to the home becoming the center of human activity, and the increased digitization of the human universe. These factors are interconnected since home isolation relies on digitization for normal life functions, and digitization allows the home to become a hybrid configuration, simultaneously acting as a school, office, family base, gym, restaurant, entertainment center, and so on. Lockdowns, quarantine, physical distancing measures, mask wearing, and other constraints lead to rapid changes in consumer behavior; these trends also intermingle with digitization and home-centered human behavior. Figure 4.1 further identifies potential changes to various components of industrial structures which would need to be analyzed, understood, and scrutinized to fully understand their future profit potential and overall long-term sustainability.

However, the most impactful consequence of COVID-response is the decline of the middle class, which has been under assault since the mid-1960s. Due to its comparatively strong economic standing, secure employment, entrepreneurial orientation, and asset ownership, the middle class is comprised of the most independent, free, and unencumbered individuals in any society; they generally do not rely on the state. Lastly, as noted throughout this book, COVID-response leads to a significant deterioration of mental and physical health. Although this factor may not impact the venture capital industry to a high degree, it is nevertheless significant that researchers estimate considerable increases in excess deaths resulting from the previously detailed state-led restrictions.

Changes to Global Industrial Structures

As stated in Chapter 2, governments around the world have exhibited an unprecedented propensity for the centralization of political power post COVID-response. Under these redefined political configurations, and with increased regulations and restrictions, the state consequently became a major stakeholder in many industrial structures; the state may be the driver or disruptor of revenue growth, profitability, and innovation. This global disruption has occurred at a moment when some states, like the United States (U.S.), were aiming to bring their manufacturing capabilities back onshore. One of the major structural changes that affects a vast number of industries is the distortion of global supply chain configurations: manufacturers, intermediaries, wholesalers, and retailers have experienced a major interference in the delivery of goods. This has primarily impacted businesses aiming for leaner operations, a reduction of costs and cash flow, and optimized systems. Thus, for firms maintaining small inventories and relying on just-in-time delivery systems, manufacturing came to a complete halt. Evidence from previous recessions suggests that it would likely take these businesses years to return to pre COVID-response output and trading levels.

Such massive distortions and dislocations to the global supply chain have many practical implications for established supplier networks. Firstly, when possible, corporations and small firms are likely to seek new relationships with local suppliers, even if these suppliers are somewhat more expensive or if their products are of lesser quality. It is also anticipated that firms will have a variety of back-up suppliers in addition to their main supplier. These measures would ensure that firms no longer experience unwanted stockouts, frustrated customers, or foregone revenue. Secondly, firms would likely review the efficiency and practicality of maintaining their current management systems (i.e., just-in-time, six sigma, etc.) in light of new systems that rely on more reasonable levels of local inventory stockpiles. Thirdly, since the traditional methods of delivery through rail and road are less likely to be subject to restrictions and disruptions, more capacity will likely be added to these modes of local and global transportation. Conversely, there may be a decreased reliance on ocean and airfreight transportation because of additional regulations and restrictions.

As we observe throughout this book, the politically led COVID-response resulted in significant adjustments to the fundamental building blocks of many industries. Industrial redefinition relates to concepts such as economies of scale, which may no longer convert into a competitive advantage; product differentiation, where differences between products or services may be either diluted or amplified; selective access to normal distribution channels, which may disrupt production, the accessibility of products, and availability of raw materials, ultimately resulting in increased bargaining power of suppliers; the number, and diversity, of competitors in the marketplace; the rate of industry growth, which may be accelerated or decelerated in relation to its traditional growth trajectories; and the capacity of the industry to provide products and services adjusted to actual market demand (note that some industries are likely to have excess capacity, which is unlikely to be absorbed in the near future). It is unclear whether governments have fully accounted for these economic and human costs when implementing their COVID-response restrictions.

One of the key areas of analysis for most industries is to re-imagine, re-discover, re-define, or re-design their existing mode of operations or business model. A business model, which is an operational framework that a firm employs to conduct its business, captures how the business works and how its various components fit together and contribute to the firm's success. Business models, which have been improved and enhanced over many years, determine revenue growth potential, investment levels, profitability, value creation, cash flow generation, and investment requirements. As discussed previously, the hardest-hit businesses are retailers, many of whom are expected to close the doors to their traditional brick-and-mortar operations because of the severe financial distress caused by government restrictions; continued stay-at-home appeals have forced consumers to shift toward online shopping. In view of these changes, the retail industry aims to re-imagine and re-define its interaction with clients through the hyper-personalization of products, live-streams, virtual interactions, and digital outlets. These new digital modes of operation are expected to augment reality when touching, feeling, and trying on items in-person are more difficult to achieve. However, it is challenging to ascertain what final model of operation will emerge as successful.

Other industries deeply affected and left decimated post COVID-response are tourism and travel; these sectors include many economic sub-segments such as airports, airlines, hotels, and cruise lines. The tourism industry and its various related sectors are likely to struggle in the foreseeable future since there is a need to address physical distancing restrictions, accommodate testing and quarantine requirements, and deal with continuous sanitation issues. Additionally, retailers such as grocery stores and restaurants are in the process of resolving their last-mile delivery arrangements as they near destruction. In 2020, the restaurant industry struggled to replace its regular revenue with curbside pickups, home deliveries, and other means. In the meantime, concepts of centralized kitchens begin to emerge. However, while many industries have been negatively impacted post COVID-response, there are some that have thrived. A prime example is fintech, which now offers branchless banking, mobile banking, investment management, credit assessment, tax preparation, and digital payment platforms; these services are developed on the basis of a consumer preference for digital banking. Another related area, insure-tech, is similarly prospering under increasingly digital consumer services and interactions.

There are three key trends influencing industrial structures around the world.[1] The first of these trends relates to global labor-based de-industrialization, which likewise affects developed countries and emerging markets. In the past, traditional modes of economic development were based on a continual shift of manufacturing from developed to developing nations; this transition offered cheaper means of production. Consequently, developing countries have received a substantial share of foreign direct investment and global capital flows. However, such a scheme required complex and costly arrangements in supply chain networks. Through the application of automation, robotics, and artificial intelligence (AI), manufacturing now requires less labor, so the comparative advantage of emerging markets has greatly diminished. In addition, there is a growing trend for producing and delivering locally with a higher degree of market customization. The second key trend that naturally flows from increased localized production is de-globalization. Evidence suggests that global capital flows have declined to about 50% of their historical levels. The rise of tariffs, regulations, and other measures has negatively impacted global trade, although this trend of de-globalization is also driven by increased waves of protectionism. The last global trend affecting industrial structures relates to increased labor migration from developing to developed countries. While some immigrants seek improvements in their economic wellbeing, others are simply displaced by wars, civil unrest, and military conflicts. Significantly, an increase in unemployment in many developed nations is likely to give rise to anti-immigration sentiments.

Lastly, it is important to emphasize that entire industries are likely to be reshaped in ways which may be difficult to predict. There may also be strong undercurrents leading to industrial monopolization. As noted in Chapter 2, the early 1900s saw a significant wave of industrial consolidations and the emergence of monopolists. For many industries, it is unclear what new risks, key success drivers, customer responses, supply chain solutions, or profit potential may emerge. A prime example of an industry where major concerns still exist today is the airline industry.

Alterations to Consumer Behavior

COVID-response, which has resulted in lockdowns, movement limitations, travel restrictions, and various other constraints, has had a major impact on consumer behaviors, attitudes, and purchasing practices. And yet, it is unclear at this moment whether these changes and shifts will be permanent or temporary. There is evidence to suggest that consumers aim to incorporate at least some of their newly acquired behavioral consumption patterns into the future. As observed in Chapter 2, the net result of constant fear-based messaging in the media is that roughly 50% of people wish to work from home, restrict outings, avoid using public transportation, and physically distance from friends and even family.

There are numerous consequences of these new behavioral patterns on both a personal and an economic level, such as the exponential growth of e-commerce evidenced in many countries. This trend has even influenced older consumers who were unlikely to begin online shopping prior to state-imposed restrictions. Trading on major e-commerce platforms such as Amazon increased its net sales from $280.5 billion in 2019 to $386.1 billion in 2020, which represents a 37.6% increase. Beyond altering their method of shopping, consumers have also exhibited changes in their purchasing orientation. One of the most significant changes is a focus on essential products and services that offer a clear and uncomplicated value proposition; in other words, price considerations, frugality, and saving accumulation have become vital. This trend of reduced consumption is driven by a fear of further layoffs, sustained unemployment, and declining incomes. Newly prioritized essential items include non-perishable groceries, household and cleaning supplies, pharmaceutical products, frozen goods, perishable grocery items, pet care products, and personal care. Consequently, there has been a visible restraint in discretionary spending on clothing, shoes, jewelry, and electronics. Evidence also suggests that consumption driven by status, brand image, self-concepts, and other personal considerations has also declined. There have similarly been delays in purchasing bigger-ticket items such as automobiles, large household items (i.e., white goods), luxury items, and home decorations, as well as spending on vacations and holidays.

Moreover, a fear of contagion has resulted in consumers aiming to be more protective of their health by shopping closer to home and reducing their frequency of shopping visits. Consumers may also rely on home delivery or curbside pick-up services to further reduce their contact with others. Although some evidence points to consumers being willing to try new products, services, or solutions, there is also a preference for tried and trusted brand names. This resistance to try new things may reflect the fact that consumers are unable to have direct exposure to new products through physical contact, touch, feel, and experience. There is also a simultaneous propensity to buy local, the most significant consequence of which is the reversal of globalization trends. These new and evolving consumer behavioral trends are likely to give rise to new fields related to behavioral analytics, crowd examination, behavioral stimulation, and data management.

Digitization of the Human Universe

One of the most profound changes post COVID-response has been the digitization of many aspects of human life, including healthcare, education, and socialization. There has been a mass adoption of online and digital solutions, although digitization has been most visible in e-commerce. Disruptive technologies, innovations, inventions, and new applications of existing technologies may initiate the development of new products and services, which have either not been offered before or were offered on a smaller scale. Examples of these services include digital medicine, education, learning, counseling, and pharmaceutical consultations. The acceleration of these trends has been astonishing as they normally take decades rather than months to implement and embrace.

However, the growth in digitization is likely to require more telecommunication infrastructure, equipment, and service solutions to continue offering stable connectivity (i.e., bandwidth). In terms of education, for example, although some observers are actively promoting and encouraging the transfer of in-person and classroom-based experiences to virtual platforms, this transition is likely to compromise teaching outcomes and generate a less educated and work-ready workforce. Similarly, negative outcomes are also anticipated to emerge in healthcare, public services, the judicial system, and other newly digitized services.

One of the key concepts in the area of digitization is the "Internet of Things" (IoT). The term was initially coined in the earlys 1980 and refers to a comprehensive and connected network of physical objects or things. This networking of things has been enhanced with the usage of digital sensors and devices, software applications, and other digital technologies, all of which are connected by the Internet. The aim of this intertwined connection is real-time data exchange, automation, and organization in the areas of home, health, energy management, environmental monitoring, healthcare, manufacturing, agriculture, supply chain management, and consumerism, to name a few industries. The main objective behind these applications is allegedly increased efficiency, cost reduction, and control.

Home as the Center of Human Gravity

Human responses to state-led restrictions, lockdowns, quarantines, and stay-at-home orders have resulted in profound changes to normal patterns of human life. This, in turn, has led to a broad array of developments which may vary from country-to-country. For some countries, such as the U.S., a negative consequence of excessive home nesting has been a strain on marriage, resulting in increased divorce rates. However, in other countries like the United Kingdom, there is evidence that marriages have been strengthened by increased time at home. In Canada, family issues are one of the top concerns, followed by worries related to access to necessities and the maintenance of personal freedoms. Elsewhere, massive layoffs of women resulted in a rapid resurgence of children rearing, family expansion, and stay-at-home motherhood. Evidence also suggests that it is likely to take years for family and individual incomes to return to pre-COVID levels.

One of the key areas of change is home life, as the home has increasingly become the center of gravity for the family. Due to fear of contagion, a heightened perception of risk, state restrictions, and social distancing measures, people spend increasingly more time away from their previously natural social settings. Home has been re-formed into a personal coffee shop, restaurant, gym, office, fitness center, and beauty salon, while for children and young adults, home became a digital classroom, playground, recreation facility, and music practice auditorium. However, this new model of home as a hybrid structure has blurred the delicate line between work, rest, and play for the entire household, and may prevail for some time. In terms of working from home, evidence from the U.S. suggests that up to 50% of the workforce may be encouraged or choose to work from home. These work arrangements are enabled through multiple digital platforms. While some employers may be excited to introduce flexible working arrangements by having their employees work from home and on an as-needed basis (thereby potentially savings some cost), these blended models often result in an initial improvement in productivity, followed by its decline, and will ultimately lead to a staff that is less efficient, innovative, dedicated, and loyal.

Furthermore, home has become a center for family entertainment, as nearly 50% of people prefer not to go to arenas, stadiums, concerts, theatres, and other live performance. The consequence of home nesting is that individuals turn to television, social media, live-streams, and gaming; evidence from different countries confirms a 15–25% increase in time dedicated to these media. The prominence of home entertainment is likely to stay post-COVID because these media formats are often regarded as sticky and can quickly become a part of one's regular life. This, in turn, would cause changes to the allocation of advertising budgets, which would be increasingly directed to popular media formats.

Accelerated Deterioration of Physical and Mental Health

A sudden arrival of social distancing, quarantine, self-isolation, a lack of socialization, community disengagement, economic and financial uncertainty, limited travel and vacations, and inadequate downtime has had a profound impact on the physical and mental health of many individuals. As observed in Chapter 2, there is already evidence of excess deaths due to poor screening, delayed or cancelled appointments, and the acceleration of various diseases due to chronic stress. Despite widespread fears about the healthcare systems being overwhelmed by COVID-19 patients, hospitals have stayed below their operating capacity. In fact, many hospitals were empty, reduced their operations, and even terminated employment contracts.

The healthcare system has been one the fastest changing industries. Hospitals, for example, needed to change their internal structures (i.e., new units, staffing, safety, etc.), develop plans for a potential patient overflow, address increased risk of infectious disease, and deal with personnel burnout. Evidence suggests that these alterations placed significant operational and financial burdens on hospitals, thereby decreasing their efficiency in the public sector and profitability in the private sector. Outside of hospitals, the healthcare system attempted to shift to telemedicine, such as in countries like Canada, where medical professionals discouraged in-person clinic visits. Evidence from the U.S. also suggests that post COVID-response, nearly half of medical visits occurred through virtual means (this is in compared to about 20% a year earlier).

However, patients are not only remotely diagnosed, but are now treated virtually. It appears that home-oriented healthcare is likely to persist in the future, especially if medical corporations find this to be a more efficient mode of service delivery. This trend of remote healthcare is likely to be supplemented by a more intense application of at-home diagnostics, monitoring, testing devices, novel diagnostic methods, and robotic care. Chronic conditions are expected to be monitored through tracking systems, digital therapeutic systems, cameras, sensors, and electronic devices, which would be able to monitor vital signs (i.e., heart rate, oxygen saturation, respiration, etc.) and perform rapid tests. These modifications are at least partially driven by medical professionals' anxiety about contagion and the subsequent need for quarantine, which, in turn, has negative financial implications; financial worries may be more pronounced for doctors when they are the only income provider in their family. There is also the possibility the healthcare industry could be restructured with respect to the partial or full disintermediation of local doctors by distant or foreign doctors.

Moreover, seniors have been unduly affected by the coronavirus as an especially vulnerable part of the healthcare system, particularly those residing in long-term care facilities. However, senior care is an area of healthcare where digital solutions and innovations are unlikely to be widely or quickly adopted. Isolation, separation, social distancing, visitation restrictions, loneliness, and depression have also unduly affected seniors more so than other areas of the population.

Abolition of the Middle Class in Developed Countries

The social, economic, and political trends that have emerged post COVID-response are essentially negative for many individuals. While single wealthy individuals have financially benefited from this period, the majority has incurred significant economic, physical, and mental distress. One such group that has been overwhelming affected by COVID-response in a detrimental way is the middle class. Although a definition of the middle class is elusive and somewhat abstract, it can be defined in terms of economic, social, educational, and occupational parameters and characteristics. Among these definitional orientations, the economic characterization of the middle class is the one most commonly accepted. However, the middle class can also be defined on an individual, household, or familial basis, and the way in which the middle class is understood varies country-to-country and even region-to-region within the same country.

In terms of economic-driven descriptions, the most common understanding of the middle class is related to income. One characterization of the middle class is the group of people generating income who fall between the demarcations of poor and rich. In this case, a middle-class income simply resides in the middle of income distribution. Another way in which the middle class can be defined economically is as the middle third quintile of income distribution, or sometimes the middle fifth. Alternative conceptualizations of the middle class may relate to people who do not belong to the bottom or top 20%, or who earn between certain percentages of the median household income after tax; however, in the latter case, the percentage range is often defined so broadly that it becomes impractical or even useless to define the middle class. Moreover, because this spread can vary from country-to-country, Canada, for example, defines middle class in the income band of 75 and 200% of the median income. If such a definition is adopted, households generating income between $45,000 and $120,000 fall within the middle class; this is an enormous income band. Another commonly used income band is between 50 and 150% of the median income. And yet, it is clear from an objective observer's standpoint that the households at both ends of this spectrum are likely to have a completely different lifestyle, experience, and existence.

For practical terms, the middle class will be understood as the group generating income in excess of $100,000 on a household or family basis. The middle class is thus defined as a group of individuals who can comfortably afford to implement their unique lifestyles, have job security, have a reasonable amount of discretionary income, sustain savings, have access to comfortable housing, and have decent prospects for retirement. In terms of occupational preparation, the middle class may be a professional managerial class (i.e., lower-level managers), owners of small and medium-sized businesses, salaried workers (i.e., teachers, social workers, engineers, nurses, and administrators), skilled craftsmen, or people in technical positions, among other employment possibilities. Since the middle class often represents a desirable social outcome, many people define themselves as belonging to this class; everyone wishes to be a part of this social strata. For example, 70% of Canadians view themselves as middle class, while in the United States, this number is equal to 60%. In the United Kingdom, about 40% consider themselves middle class. Because of these percentages, politicians spend a disproportionate amount of time on various pretentious efforts to advance and promote the middle class.

However, another group of individuals residing in developed countries who have experienced drastic consequences of COVID-response are young adults and graduates. Evidence indicates that young adults are likely to be worse off than their parents, which is a historically unprecedented trend. These young adults are expected to have problems beginning careers and earning reasonable wages, even with a strong educational background and preparation, and are furthermore anticipated to directly experience wage deterioration. Young but less educated adults are similarly projected to see a downward pressure on wages throughout most of their adult lives. Although education is normally correlated with higher wages, a four-year bachelor's degree is no longer a guarantor of higher and increasing wages, stable employment, or a secure career. In short, young adults are likely to experience difficulties joining the middle class.

It is evident that the middle class has been badly affected by COVID-response, experiencing impacts that are both wide and multidirectional.

These effects include the stagnation of the hourly wage, downward pressure on salaries, the rise of unemployment, a decline in labor force participation, poor housing affordability, limited savings, and enormous personal debt (i.e., student loans, consumer debt, and mortgages). The impact of COVID-response will be demonstrated by examining the cases of the U.S. and Canada, although similar trends can also be observed in other countries, with few exceptions.

The Squeeze of the Middle Class in the United States

Prior to COVID-response, there were about 36.2 million Americans, or roughly 12% of the U.S. population, who relied on food stamps and donations for basic survival, 8.6 million individuals who earned incomes below the poverty line, and approximately 17.8% of the population lived in poverty. Furthermore, 62% of Americans did not have $1,000 or more in cash savings, around 27.5 million Americans did not have health insurance, and 43.3 million Americans were not able to afford medical expenses. Due to COVID-response, the vast majority of these statistics worsened and reached new highs in 2020; they are expected to degenerate further in subsequent years.

Americans have struggled in terms of wages and family incomes over the last fifty years, especially considering that, when adjusted for inflation, real wages in the U.S. remained flat between 1978 and 2018. Real wages, expressed in 1982–1984 constant dollars, declined from $9.0 in 1978 to $7.6 in 1995, which represents a 17-year period of decline, followed by a 23-year period of slow increase back to the $9.1 level in 2018. Thus, U.S. labor has been playing catch-up for nearly half of the last 40 years of effectively flat wages. The fact that real wages have been flat is particularly disappointing since local labor has generated significant productivity gains over this period. Moreover, the median family income in the U.S. has increased from $6,957 in 1965 to $78,464 in 2018 (in comparison to a median household income equal to $63,179), which represents an annual increase of 4.2% in nominal terms. However, expressed on an inflation-adjusted basis, median family incomes increased at just 0.8% in real terms. Declining incomes and worsening wages have strained family finances since the onset of COVID-response, as now over 60% of Americans live paycheck-to-paycheck. Beyond these issues with wage and income, the American family has been subject to a number of other negative trends in the last 50 years, including expensive housing, healthcare, and education.

A further negative consequence of COVID-response is the massive job losses seen in the U.S. In May 2020 alone, over thirty million people filed for unemployment assistance in the U.S., which caused the unemployment rate to increase from 3.5% in 2019 to 14.8% in 2020, subsequently declining to 6.9% by yearend. The average rate of unemployment in the U.S. during the last 50 years was equal to 6.0%, with persistent and stubborn periods of excessively high unemployment. The highest rates of unemployment occurred during the tenures of Barack Obama (7.4%) and Ronald Reagan (7.5%). Of course, it is important to note that these unemployment figures do not describe the full negative impact of high unemployment, since these statistics hide U.S. workers' inability to generate employment as reflected in the labor force participation rate, which has been consistently low in the U.S. with an average of 64.0%.

Another issue in the U.S. is related to the quality, rather than the quantity, of jobs. There has been a visible increase in precarious employment, which is often presented to labor as an advantage. However, this leads to problems with employers terminating higher-paid workers in favor of lower paid, dispensable workers who are frequently exploited immigrants or temporary visa workers. These employment substitution tactics not only occur in low-end jobs, but are similarly present in professional, managerial, high-skill manufacturing, research, product development, and engineering jobs; these positions alike have been threatened by termination due to offshoring or outsourcing. Subsequently, terminated employees who were unable to replace their previous jobs in the local market may only be able to substitute their past employment with low-pay service positions as waiters or waitresses, bartenders, taxi drivers, retail associates, or ambulatory health care workers, to name a few. Corporate strategies to eliminate higher-paid positions often culminate in negative financial implications for the middle class, a deterioration of the high-skill labor pool, and a disengagement with professional associations, including labor foregoing professional accreditations, among other adverse effects.

All of the previously described trends have a negative impact on consumption and economic growth for the middle class, of which only four are noted here. The first and most detrimental implication of the decline in the standard of living is the inability for a significant portion of the population to pay for basic necessities, such as food, shelter, medication, education, and healthcare. Secondly, reduced family economics is likely to directly translate into increased poverty rates. Thirdly, poorer families are unlikely to engage in other activities which are required for maintaining well-rounded human development. Poor economics can also negatively affect a child's potential to engage with sports, music lessons, hobbies, and other extracurricular events. Finally, a poor economic standard of living may lead to the loss of interpersonal relationships and connections due to high travel costs, and will especially impact those who were required to travel from their home cities to secure employment.

The Economic Distress of the Middle Class in Canada

In the last 50 years, Canada has seen a persistently high level of unemployment equal on average to 7.4%. The highest levels of unemployment occurred during the periods between 1982 to 1985 and 1991 to 1994 when unemployment exceeded ten percent. Higher quality, stable, and higher wage production employment have increasingly disappeared as lower pay, part-time, and precarious employment have been made more readily available. The deterioration of the quality of employment in Canada has brought multiple issues for labor and the family. The first issue, which has impacted the quality of employment, is that the availability of part-time and precarious jobs in Canada has grown faster than full-time employment. Secondly, there has been slow growth in high paying jobs, while low and mid-paying jobs have grown substantially. In the last 30 years, there has also been a widespread substitution of high-paying employment opportunities for lower-paying ones in Canada. This is related to the persistent disappearance of manufacturing in Canada, meaning that, simply, Canada has been de-industrialized. The lack of available jobs in the marketplace has moreover forced individuals to seek self-employment opportunities, which tend to pay less than salaried positions and do not offer any benefits. Finally, similar to what has occurred in the U.S., young adults also struggle to find employment in Canada. The unemployment rates for young adults are at least double the average unemployment statistics for the entire country and have not dipped below the ten percent mark since 1976.

Canadian labor has seen an average annual increase in nominal wages equal to 4.9%, however, when adjusted for inflation, there has actually been a stagnating level of wages in real terms. There were two distinct phases in the evolution of real wages in Canada, with the first period between 1965 and 1977 seeing an average increase in real wages by 3.3%. This period coincided with a strong average growth of the economy and better than average labor productivity increases in Canada. However, real wages remained basically flat at a minimal increase of 0.02% per annum during the second period between 1978 and 2018. These two periods represent four decades during which Canadian labor was not able to improve its purchasing power in any meaningful way. The length of stagnation is similar to that experienced in the U.S., as real wages initially declined and subsequently took over 20 years to recover. Stagnating purchasing power manifested in declining real wages is an economic issue that has profoundly affected the Canadian family. The median family income has, consistent with real wages, also stagnated in the last 50 years, as the average growth in real median family income over this period was equal to 0.6%. The family income declined by 0.2% during the first phase between 1965 and 1993, which was followed by a 1.2% increase in the phase between 1994 and 2018.

Persistent unemployment and stagnation in purchasing power for the Canadian family do not occur without social consequences. For example, in 2019, 46% of Canadians were $200 away from financial insolvency, 31% did not have enough to cover their expenses (including debt payments), 51% were likely to struggle with mortgage payments when interest rates increased, and 45% were anticipated to fall into more debt to cover ongoing living expenses. Therefore, Canadians were not able to reduce their level of debt while experiencing continuous financial difficulties. Other evidence suggests that over 40% of working Canadians report it would be difficult to meet their financial obligations if their paycheck was delayed by even a week. Additionally, about two million individuals in Canada, which equals seven percent of the population, struggle to fulfill their basic food needs. The rate of poverty in Canada was equal to 8.7% in 2018, with poverty affecting about three million Canadians and half a million children.

Another issue negatively affecting the economics of the Canadian family is the extraordinary increases in housing costs. While home ownership has increased, Canadian households have spent exceedingly higher amounts of their income to cover home ownership costs, which include mortgage payments, property taxes, and utility costs. In fact, evidence confirms that the average share of household income in Canada required to cover house ownership was equal to 51.9% at the end of 2018. In other words, half of Canadians' household income was dedicated to fulfilling the "Canadian dream" of house ownership. The highest percentages of income required to cover housing costs in 2018 were 84.7% in Vancouver,

66.1% in Toronto, and 44.5% in Montreal; unsurprisingly, house ownership has become extremely difficult to attain for the average Canadian family in these cities. The average house cost about four years of labor-time in Canada during the 1970s, while in 2016, this number was equal to eight years. These high housing costs further impacted Canadians' level of indebtedness, as, in 2018, the average level of debt to disposable income in Canada reached 1.8 times; this exceeds the average level of debt in the U.S., which is equal to only 1.1 times.

Like the U.S., Canada's unemployment rate increased to 13.5% in 2020, with over 3 million Canadians applying for unemployment benefits. Although unemployment has subsequently declined to about 9.8% by yearend, it is still 1.4% higher when compared to the 50-year average. Job losses have affected roughly one out of two households, resulting in nearly 6 million Canadians applying for emergency protection. About 376,000 businesses closed between January and July 2020, and only half of these businesses were able to open by the end of July. These consequences of COVID-response have left 41% of Canadians feeling that they are in a worse financial position in comparison to pre COVID-response, and 31% confirm that they have not yet recovered from their financial distress.

The Rise of the Middle Class in Emerging Markets

On the other hand, the decline of the middle class in developed countries may be offset on a global scale by the emergence of such a class in emerging markets.[1] Evidence suggests that the largest addition to the global middle class, which is estimated to be equal to about 150 million, is likely to come from emerging markets, especially South East Asia, Asia, Latin America, the Middle East, and South Africa. The two major countries driving increased middle-class consumption in emerging markets are China and India. Developing nations already account for more than 40% of global consumption, the value of which is nearing $20 trillion annually; rising wages and incomes, increased education, a strong propensity for entrepreneurship, innovation and invention, and the dissemination of modern technologies contribute to this trend. Members of the middle class in emerging markets are successful entrepreneurs, well-paid executives of prominent locally owned firms, managers and directors of major international corporations, and leading officials of international organizations and institutions. These newly appearing consumers in emerging markets are now more likely to be the driving force behind high-end, luxury products and trends in fashion, technology, travel, fitness, and other lifestyles.

Sectoral Orientation of Venture Capital in the Future

There may be various ways to examine future investment opportunities for the venture capital industry post COVID-response. The first analytical approach relates to examining potential investment opportunities in specific sectors, divisions, niches, windows of opportunity, and segments of the economy. These opportunities are likely to be influenced by the six major themes outlined earlier in this chapter, although it should be stated that many of these trends and resulting investment opportunities are not discrete; they are interrelated, interconnected, and symbiotic. The second approach in investigating these opportunities relates to the types of available transactions, their origins, and the transaction values. Buyouts are likely to continue their prominent role among mid-size and larger venture capital transactions, since these types of transactions already account for the vast majority of deals. These available transaction opportunities could arise from either the private or public sectors, but nevertheless, evidence suggests that deal values are on the rise.

It is also important to note that an initial reaction from the venture capital industry to COVID-response was a general and widespread pull-back of investment from many sectors of the economy. This occurred without much reflection, but this over-reaction by the industry was grounded in the perception of heightened levels of economic uncertainty, business risks, ambiguity over consumer reactions, and doubt regarding the expected timespan of government restrictions.

The Future of Venture Capital Investment Opportunities in Specific Segments

In the opening section of this chapter, we identified six major undercurrents in the external environment. In this section, the objective is to elaborate on these specific investment opportunities that will be available to venture capital in the future. Table 4.1 illuminates these opportunities in more detail.

Table 4.1 Structural and individual undercurrents post COVID-response

Key themes	*Main areas of impact*	*Areas of investment opportunities for venture capital*
Changes to industrial structures	• Distortions of global supply chain; de-personalization of relationships • Importance of road and rail transportation • Previous efficiency and optimization methods may no longer work well • Revisions to value chain and profitability • Massive dislocations of many industries • Difficulty in predicting what industrial demand curves are likely to look like in the future • Modifications to existing business models • More monopolists are likely to emerge across various industries • Potential for new disruptions in many industries • Potential for de-globalization and de-industrialization • Increased localization of business operations	• Negative impact on many industries, including travel, tourism, hospitality, entertainment, airlines, retail, transportation, leisure, food and beverage, commercial real estate, consumer goods, event organization, infrastructure, etc • It will likely take a number of years for struggling industries to return to pre COVID-response levels • New opportunities to invest in fintech, cyber security, digital platforms (i.e., work, education, public services, etc.), pharmaceuticals and associated solutions, data monitoring and analysis, education technology, solar technologies, biotechnology, medical technologies (see below), logistics services, marketing technologies, renewable energy, etc • New market segments that emerge will increasingly rely on digitization • Unique delivery solutions and applications • New supply chain efficiency and optimization solutions • Minimal labor-content manufacturing

(continued)

Table 4.1 (continued)

Key themes	*Main areas of impact*	*Areas of investment opportunities for venture capital*
Alterations to consumer behavior	• Change in consumer habits, attitudes, and purchasing behavior; unclear whether these new behavioral patterns are sustainable • Consumers avoid leaving home, using public transportation, and interactions with friends and family • Focus on essential products and services • Reduction of discretionary spending • Some consumers are likely to experiment with new products; evidence of strong loyalty to tested and known brands • Consumers shop locally • Retailers offer blended customer delivery models	• Exponential growth in e-commerce across various segments of the economy • The use of artificial intelligence (AI) to analyze and match consumer needs to market solutions • Two-sided seller-buyer interactive solutions • Online groceries and delivery services • Hygiene and wellness products and services • Provision of essential goods • Last-mile delivery and courier services • Local shops and retailers, where limited foot traffic exists
Mass digitization of human universe	• Mass adoption of digitization; unclear whether sustainable in the long-term • Digitization to affect most spheres of human life • Likely emergence of disruptive technologies, innovations, and inventions • Increased usage of AI • Potential for unwanted monitoring and surveillance	• New technologies and applications in existing industries • Digitization to affect medicine, education, public facilities, and other services • Voice-activated technologies • Cyber-security services • Telecommunication infrastructure; Increased demand for bandwidth

Key themes	*Main areas of impact*	*Areas of investment opportunities for venture capital*
Home as the center of human gravity	• Disruption of normal patterns of life • Reformation and redefinition of home life • Availability of excess spare time • Ability to develop personal hobbies and interests • More time to prepare home meals • Fitness at home for the entire family • A need for more frequent communication with family members and friends • More dedication to household duties	• Digital entertainment (TV, movie streaming, games, e-sports, etc.) • Music, books, arts, reading, photography, gardening, etc • Self-improvement courses (i.e., cooking and baking, hobbies, etc.) • Exercise equipment and online fitness on demand • Other physical outdoor activities: trampolines, bicycles, swimming pools, ski or winter equipment, etc • Sport apparel • Social networking platforms, video connectedness • Possible increase in social media consumption • Remote learning • Headsets, speakers, and various telecommunication devices • Educational online solutions and management tools for students, teachers, and parents • Supplies and fixtures for home improvement

(continued)

Table 4.1 (continued)

Key themes	*Main areas of impact*	*Areas of investment opportunities for venture capital*
		• Home-based office facilitator solutions (i.e., furniture, lightening, quiet space, management, etc.) • Online platforms to improve productivity and efficiency • Various work-related solutions (i.e., task managers, work boards and sharing, productivity tools, etc.)
Public health	• Isolation, social distancing, and separation due to fear of contagion leads to deterioration of physical and mental health (i.e., excess deaths) • Fear of contagion forces a decline of in-person medical appointments • Healthcare system may be under pressure, but no such evidence in 2020 and early 2021 • Medical profession resists having in-person consultations and appointments • Major issues to resolve for the elderly population, especially those living in long-term care facilities	• Telemedicine; online consultations and mental wellness • E-counseling • Online medical platforms • Centralization of clinics to reduce cost (i.e., local monopolization) • Online health screening • Home testing and diagnostic testing kits • Online monitoring systems • Contact tracing and surveillance technologies • Increased demand for natural and organically-grown products • Age technological solutions for seniors

Key themes	*Main areas of impact*	*Areas of investment opportunities for venture capital*
Abolition of the middle class	• Wide squeeze of the middle class • Stagnation of hourly wages and salaries • Rise of unemployment • Changes to the quality of employment and emergence of precarious jobs • Likely decline in the economic standard of living • Potential for exploitation of immigrant and temporary workers • Increased offshoring and outsourcing • Poor housing affordability • Decreased savings • Increased levels of personal debt • Diminished propensity for business development • Increased failure rates for entrepreneurial firms and decreased rates of business survival • Significant economic challenges for young adults	• Online discount stores and discount retailers • Demand for inexpensive products and services across various industries (i.e., automotive, leisure, travel, entertainment) • Increased price sensitivity of consumers, which may lead to increased export activities from countries with low labor costs • Temporary agencies • Rental housing due to decreased affordability of house ownership • Affordable housing solutions • Demand for additional education and training

Various surveys from the industry suggest that venture capitalists try to remain optimistic regarding the general prospects of the asset class post COVID-response. Venture capitalists therefore believe that new disruptive ideas, industrial dislocations, structural adjustments, and the redefinition of business models may generate new investment choices, good return potential, and strong exit opportunities. However, venture capitalists are also aware that examining these opportunities is likely to take some time; spotting winners and deciding on selective investment themes may be more difficult than in the past. Furthermore, in spite of this positive mindset, reports from the industry point to a vast range of fundamental challenges in the venture capital ecosystem which are likely to impact all stages of the venture capital investment process, from deal generation to exit. Venture capitalists will require a significant amount of time to fully understand the impact of COVID-response on their portfolios and strategize about priorities and future deal flow.

Table 4.1 presents specific opportunities with respect to the key themes outlined in this chapter. In terms of changes to global industrial structures, there are opportunities to invest in sectors such as digital communication platforms, cyber-security, fintech, data monitoring, pharmaceutical, biotechnology, and renewable energy. With regard to the alteration of consumer behavior, there are multiple areas of opportunities related to e-commerce in various segments of the market, especially in those sectors that do not rely on in-person interaction. Evidence suggests that the most attractive areas of e-commerce are connected to the provision of essential goods, hygiene and wellness products, and courier and delivery services. The most profound change in consumer behavior relates to the mode of grocery acquisition, which has grown exponentially post COVID-response. Another critical area where strong investment prospects are likely to emerge is the mass digitization of many areas of human life. The key areas where digitization is likely to make a profound impact are medicine, education, and the provision of public services.

Furthermore, the disruption of normal patterns of life and the effective redefinition of home life could result in attractive investment picks arising in relation to digital home-based entertainment (i.e., TV, movie streaming, games, e-sports), the development of hobbies, and home improvement solutions. Lastly, public health issues will likely re-emerge as one of the central themes post COVID-response. Mental health issues, especially will negatively affect people across various industries, including those working in the venture capital industry. Strong investment opportunities are likely to emerge in the delivery of health services, monitoring, and surveillance, while a unique category of investment would relate to senior care specifically.

Lastly, it may be difficult to imagine the existence of investment opportunities for the venture capital industry based on the diminishing role of the middle class, since this trend has largely negative consequences on economic activity, particularly consumption. And of course, the diminishing or outright abolition of the middle class would translate into poor GDP growth prospects for the future of a wide range of industries because increased consumption and small business ownership is a significant part of the economic prosperity in many countries; these challenges would also have negative consequences for the venture capital industry. Nevertheless, the weakening economic wellbeing of the middle class is likely to translate into an elevated demand for discount retailers (both online and in-person), inexpensive goods and services across a wide range of industries, and further educational and training opportunities.

Sources of Venture Capital Transactions Post COVID-Response

Having discussed specific investment opportunities for venture capital, it is worthwhile to examine some of the potential sources and origins of future deal flow (note that some of these prospects have been previously mentioned in Chapter 2). There are four major sources of deals, namely corporate disposals, privatizations, inter-generational auctions, and deal "recycling", that are likely to arise in relation to COVID-response.

One of the most prevalent sources of deals for the venture capital industry is expected to be large multinationals. Post COVID-response, many corporations were forced to re-assess their market strategies, profitability, and cash flow. A consequence of these internal evaluations is that many corporations have identified business divisions which may not fit their strategic plans for the future and will be subsequently sold to raise cash for other parts of the business. Such disposals may include unwanted resources and assets, marginal businesses, privately held firms, or public concerns. A prime example of such a recent disposal is the Advent-led acquisition of the elevator business from Thyssen Krupp.

Pressure to reduce public expenditure, avoid printing more money, and incur additional debt may lead the state to privatize state assets, which could include crown corporations, natural resources, entire sectors of the economy (i.e., healthcare, education, and social assistance), or infrastructure (i.e., roads and highways, airports, seaports, parks, and railways). Venture capital (especially mega-funds) would be excited about this type of investment opportunity that consists of a stable "captive audience" of clients. One of the most significant benefits of this prospect is that these "defensive" sectors, which may include water, energy, waste management, recycling, and other utilities, are less likely to be affected by economic cycles. As noted in Chapter 2, many of these state-owned investment opportunities would be available to well-connected venture capital firms that have former heads of state on their boards of directors with strong political affiliations.

The third major source of deals, which has provided a strong deal flow to venture capitalists in the past, may be founders of entrepreneurial firms who have built their businesses over the last two or three decades. These founders may have notable apprehensions and nervousness about the future prospects of their firms post COVID-response. Despite lower-business valuations, these business owners may now feel sufficiently incentivized to dispose of their firms in massive amounts.

Finally, during periods when generating deals is problematic, venture capital firms are likely to resort to another tested tactic for deal generation and investment, namely "recycling" deals between each other. Together, these four sources of deals constitute the future of venture capital post COVID-response.

Note

1. Joseph Quinlan describes these concepts in more detail in his essay "Promise and peril in the age of turbulence in emerging markets: Implications for private equity investors" included in an edited collection by Klonowski (2020).

Bibliography

Alini, Erica. 2017. Are you earning a middle-class income? Here's what it takes in Canada, based on where you live. November 6. www.globalnews.ca.

Berkowitz, Jeff. 2020. Covid-19 and the trajectory of U.S. venture capital and technology innovation. December 3. www.csis.org.

Camarena, Ana. 2020. How will COVID-19 impact each industry? 9 experts share their views. April 23. www.plugandplaytechcenter.com

Ernst & Young. 2020. How the COVID-19 pandemic is changing consumer behaviors in Canada. July 29. www.ey.com.

Fraser Institute. 2020. Ottawa has a middle-class definition problem. March 18. www.fraserinstitute.org.

Greenwald, Michelle. 2020. How Covid has impacted startups' ability to raise VC money and thrive: 9 global experts weigh in. October 7. www.forbes.com.

Hogan, Stephanie. 2019. Who is Canada's middle class? October 13. www.cbc.ca.

Hunger, David J. and Thomas L. Wheelen. 2011. *Essentials of strategic management*. Upper Saddle River: Prentice Hall.

IBIS. 2020. Five industries set to outperform due to COVID-19. April 13. www.ibisworld.com.

Kharas, Homi. 2017. *The unprecedented expansion of the global middle class*. Washington, DC: Brookings Institute.

Klonowski, Darek (ed.). 2020. *Entrepreneurial finance in emerging markets: Exploring tools, techniques, and innovative technologies*. New York: Palgrave McMillan.

Lee, Peter. 2020. Private equity can be the big winner from Covid-19 sell-off. April 20. www.euromoney.com.

McKinsey & Company. 2020. Consumer sentiment and behavior continue to reflect the uncertainty of the COVID-19 crisis. October 26. www.mckinsey.com.

McKinsey & Company. 2020. How COVID-19 is changing consumer behavior—Now and forever. July 30. www.mckinsey.com.

Mehta, Seema, Tanjul Saxena, and Neetu Purohit. 2020. The new consumer behavior paradigm amid COVID-19: Permanent or transient? *Journal of Health Management*, 22: 291–301.

Netzky, Brian and Gregory Healy. 2020. 12 industry channels expected to thrive post-COVID-19. April 28. www.knowledge-leaders.colliers.com.

OECD. 2019. Under pressure: The squeezed middle class. How does Canada compare? May 1. www.oecd.org.

Powell, Chris. 2020. COVID-19 will lead to long-lasting changes in consumer behavior: Accenture. May 20. www.canadiangrocer.com.

Puttaiah, Mahesh, Askash K. Raverkar, and Evangelos Avramakis. 2020. All change: how COVID-19 is transforming consumer behavior. December 10. www.swissre.com.

PWC. 2020. Evolving priorities: COVID-19 rapidly reshapes consumer behavior. www.pwc.com.

Reeves, Richard V., Katherine Guyot, and Eleanor Krause. 2018. *Defining the middle class, credentials, or culture*. Washington, DC: Bookings Institute.

Sagie, Itay. 2020. How COVID-19 changed the VC investment landscape in the U.S. July 23. www.crunchbase.com.
Stackhouse, John. 2020. After the crisis: 8 ways COVID will transform the economy and disrupt every business. September 24. www.thoughtleadership.rbc.com.

CHAPTER 5

The Venture Capital Investment Process Redefined

Previous chapters have outlined how COVID-response has significantly contributed to mental health issues in society as a whole, with a particularly detrimental impact on the elderly. However, the venture capital community has been similarly affected, as evidence confirms that venture capitalists have been under excessive duress since the onset of COVID-response; for example, the normal patterns of their daily operations, deal processing routines, regular habits of communication, and other tacit behaviors have been disrupted. COVID-response has been an extraordinarily intensive period for venture capitalists, many of whom have not had sufficient time to decompress, de-stress, switch off, or reflect because they have been overwhelmed with their portfolio firms, deal flow, fundraising, and communication with main stakeholders in the venture capital ecosystem such as limited partners (LPs), portfolio firms, external consultants, and others. Furthermore, while some venture capitalists have found that COVID-response was adequate and reasonable, others strongly concluded that the social, economic, mental, and physical damage it caused has not been proportional to the actual threat posed by the coronavirus; in other words, this second group of venture capitalists perhaps directly experienced the colossal damage of COVID-response.

COVID-response has affected the venture capital community differently from country-to-country, so although it is difficult to generalize, venture capital firms predominantly encouraged their staff to work

D. Klonowski, *Venture Capital Redefined*,
https://doi.org/10.1007/978-3-030-83387-9_5

Fig. 5.1 The five major phases of the venture capital investment process

remotely beginning in early March and April of 2020, initiating a retreat-and-hide mode throughout the industry. The situation in most countries was improved enough in June that venture capitalists were urged to return to work on a more regular basis, although many restrictions were continued (i.e., limited face-to-face meetings, in-person interactions only when absolutely required, restrictions on the number of people coming into the office, implementing shift work, splitting the investment team in different ways, and so on). However, it was evident by the fall when even more strict COVID-responses emerged in many countries that the venture capital community would no longer be able to engage in its normal and customary processes for the foreseeable future.

The successful completion of a venture capital deal is contingent upon its progression through a multi-stage process. Some venture capitalists do not rely on formal and orchestrated processes, which, of course, does not imply that no process actually guides investment activities, but rather that the process is navigated by tacit knowledge and a transfer of the art of venture capital deal making from one employee to another through active interaction. However, other venture capital firms have perfected the venture capital deal process into a near-science, with distinct stages and rules that are strictly adhered to and described in investment manuals. In any case, whether the process is formal, casual, or tacit, the venture capital investment process is typically understood to be a five-stage progression model involving deal generation, screening and evaluation, financial contracting, monitoring, and exiting (see Fig. 5.1); the function of each structure within the general framework of the venture capital investment process will be the focus of this chapter.

There are additional observations regarding the venture capital investment process that should be made at the outset of this chapter. Firstly, venture capital firms rely on formally established internal approval bodies, such as investment committees or supervisory boards, when processing deals; venture capitalists must effectively subject their actions to these decision-making units at every step of the process. Secondly, the venture capital investment process relies on a significant number of internal documents, including preliminary, investment, monitoring, and exit memorandum. During the course of the investment, a venture capitalist may produce as many as ten documents with varying levels of analysis, length, and detail.

As initially stated, the normal patterns of the venture capital deal process have been increasingly dislocated due to COVID-response. Each phase of the process has seen unexpected disruptions and challenges, and it will likely be a while before new and effective modes of operation are discovered, tested, and established. An obvious consequence of this disruption is the lengthening of the investment process, as venture capital surveys have already confirmed that venture capitalists not only struggle with the process, but also with its key parameters, such as valuations, exits, and deal flow. These parameters represent the most fundamental building blocks of venture capital investing, and their deterioration would adversely affect the entire industry.

Before each stage of the investment process is comprehensively discussed, it is important to understand the business valuation of entrepreneurial firms, which is one of the most critical parameters of venture capital. It is becoming apparent that COVID-response significantly impacts venture capital at both ends of the investment process, namely at entry and exit; these effects can be both positive and negative. In relation to entry valuations, evidence suggests that, on average, business valuations have fallen between 20 and 40% compared to 2019 levels. Thus, the historical levels of valuation that are based on 12 times the historical EBITDA (earnings before interest, taxes, depreciation, and amortization) are no longer applicable. This has resulted in downgraded entry valuations of mature firms with a track record of revenue growth, profitability, and stable cash flow due to questions surrounding the firms' ability to sustain their historical financial trends. The entry valuations of younger ventures have been similarly impacted and reflect perceptions of higher risks and uncertainty about their financial performance, including cash burn rate, cash requirements, and cash flow.

Various uncertainties have also led to adjustments of valuations by founders, who frequently look for an equity partner who can provide a capital increase and therefore hold a meaningful ownership stake in the venture. Alternatively, business owners can seek a partner to either buy a majority interest in the firm, or buy the entire firm outright. Of course, entrepreneurs have a third option, namely, to put their decisions on hold for a period of 18–24 months or so until trading and EBITDA performance returns to pre-COVID-response levels. This option could be a possibility if firms have sufficient financial resources to sustain themselves in the interim period, but unfortunately many firms face critical cash flow problems or insolvency issues that do not allow them to wait for potential valuation increases in the future. Other considerations, such as intergenerational changes, death, divorce, or additional unexpected circumstances can also influence entrepreneurial behavior. And yet, in spite of these downward pressures on valuation, venture capitalists have experienced problems securing subsequent rounds of financing for their portfolio firms; venture capitalists' unrealistic expectations and terms may be to blame for this issue.

Reduced business valuation has critically impacted the venture capital industry in a number of ways, including causing substantial markdowns in business valuations within existing portfolio firms. The velocity at which business valuations have fallen is similarly distressing to the venture capital industry. Additionally, the period post COVID-response may create investment opportunities which the industry has not previously seen, provided that it can effectively deal with the many uncertainties it is currently facing. As it stands now, however, the most attractive deals are over-priced and are often well in excess of the average EV/EBITDA (enterprise value to earnings before interest, taxation, depreciation, and depreciation) multiples of 12 times. Finally, beyond entry issues with downward pressures, these valuations are equally problematic for venture capitalists seeking exits.

The main objective of this chapter is to describe the key elements of the venture capital investment process and the challenges that impact each of its stages post COVID-response, beginning with deal generation. Table 5.1 describes the details of the key changes in each stage of the venture capital investment process post COVID-response.

Disrupted Deal Generation

Access to the highest quality and most attractive investment opportunities, otherwise known as deal flow, is crucial to venture capital. A strong pipeline of deals is likely to be converted into strong returns, so deal flow is therefore not only critical to venture capital firms' current operations, but also for their future fundraising initiatives. It is likewise important to LPs that the venture capital firm confirms its access to a proprietary

Table 5.1 The key changes to the venture capital investment process post COVID-response

Stage of the process	*Main impact*
Deal generation	• Considerable decline in deal pipeline • Prolonged and sustained imbalance between fundraising and investment opportunities • Limited new deal flow due to restrictions in face-to-face interactions • Deal pipelines would take some time for replenishment • Competition for deals likely to continue to be fierce • GPs are selective in deal search; higher quality deals may only be pursued • GPs may overlook sectors of the economy affected by COVID-response, which may create less opportunities for proper sector diversification • GPs may increasingly focus on flight-to-quality and flight-to-safety • Limited cross-border deals
Screening and evaluation	• Lack of in-person interactions creates multiple problems in due diligence • GPs likely to continue to take shortcuts in due diligence • Inability to properly assess founders and management • Screening and evaluation takes significantly more time, negatively influencing venture capitalists' ability to process deals in a timely manner • Due diligence over video conferencing is confirmed to be suboptimal • Hiring external advisors proves to be difficult; their assessment may be compromised • Compromised due diligence may lead to poor investment selection and decisions • More problems in ***adverse selection*** for venture capital

(continued)

Table 5.1 (continued)

Stage of the process	*Main impact*
Financial contracting	• Focus on reasonable entry valuations and downside protections • Valuation reflects normalized revenue growth, EBITDA, and cash flow • Deal terms are less entrepreneur-friendly; terms aim to strengthen rights and provisions • In expansion deals, changes in terms include liquidation preferences, anti-dilution protections, and stronger operational controls • For buyout deals, changes to deal terms include more usage of earnouts, equity rollovers, and other performance-based mechanisms; other terms may include stricter operational controls • Fierce competition for some deals is likely to lead to excessive entry valuations, poorly structured deals, and weak legal protections • Less experienced GPs may increasingly crowd-out others, thereby unduly depressing returns for the entire industry
Monitoring	• COVID-response unduly tests the entire venture capital industry • Adding value to investee firms would become a hallmark of successful GPs • A significant percentage of portfolio firms have been affected by COVID-response • GPs focus on "triaging" and stabilizing portfolios firms • GPs react in different ways to challenges for investee firms; while many became more involved, others barely increase their time commitment • Key focal points for investee firms include liquidity, cost reduction, burn rate, contingency planning, and operational support • Investee firms are likely to resist GPs' generic advice for professionalization • Investee firms would quickly be able to distinguish between value-adding and non-productive GPs; this would also be more apparent to LPs • GPs' lack of operating experience is likely to create more conflict with founders and management • GPs' over-bureaucratization is likely to diminish investee firms' operational agility and flexibility

Stage of the process	*Main impact*
Exit	• Deal volume significantly decreases, prolonging a trend of continued decline • In 2020, exits were driven by public listing, trade sales, and deal recycling • GPs expect further problems with exits post COVID-response • Lower realization may negatively impact LPs • GPs may excessively focus on premature exits, engaging in more "pump-and-dump" tactics

Abbreviations: *GPs* general partners, *LPs* limited partners deal flow. Some of the most common deal origination techniques include self-generation, where capital demanders directly approach venture capital firms, and direct marketing, in which case venture capital firms focus on identifying deals in specific industries, stages of development, or valuation ranges. New deals can also come from established long-term relationships with bankers, lawyers, accountants, consultants, advisory firms, and brokerage houses.

The most successful deal generators rely on an active deal generation approach that is grounded in a bottom-up analysis of socioeconomic trends, including the examination of key tendencies, demographic shifts, consumer behavior drifts, and business cycles; an identification of key industries which would benefit from these socioeconomic trends; a detailed marketing plan; internal deal identification systems (i.e., contract registries and systems); and execution (i.e., attending networking events, making cold calls, participating in conferences, and attending trade). Active deal generators may commit time to visiting entrepreneurial firms, even if these firms are not immediate investment prospects. The most successful venture capital firms aim to gain a competitive advantage over their competitors by approaching high-quality firms first; this first-mover advantage allows venture capitalists to develop strong interpersonal rapport with founders and management, conduct slow and deliberate due diligence, and negotiate acceptable deal terms without undue pressures.

Significantly, the development of proper deal generation is grounded in three interrelated components: the amount of capital under management, portfolio diversification strategies, and deal orientation. For example, the amount of capital under management determines the number of human resources required to generate, processes, monitor, and exit deals. Therefore, a small investment team is unlikely to process a large amount of deals or pursue deals with a significant amount of hands-on involvement, both of which are highly time-consuming. The size of the fund also drives the number of investee businesses that the firm can optimally pursue to achieve proper diversification. Competitive considerations must furthermore be taken into account, for if a venture capital firm chooses to focus on a highly competitive segment of the market where more skillful, experienced, and reputable venture capital firms operate, the competitive dynamics will create higher entry valuations and less optimal legal deal protections. In these situations, venture capitalists may need to identify new and unique niches of the industry that they can successfully pursue, rather than overwhelm the already saturated market.

When pursuing deal generation strategies, venture capitalists look for investment opportunities with special characteristics. Venture capitalists will primarily pursue firms that are capable of embracing an accelerated model of business development and value creation. This strategy to engage in faster value creation is grounded in time constraints (i.e., funds are established for a period of ten years) and a belief that growth acceleration may be lost if investee firms' decisions are delayed. Therefore, venture capitalists assume that revenue growth is likely to convert into sustainable cash flow and enhanced profitability. Venture capitalists are also attracted to investing with market leaders, which is again grounded in the belief that, at the time of exit, strategic investors, financial institutions, and public equities markets may be more willing to place premium valuation in the frontrunners. Additionally, when pursuing investment opportunities, venture capitalists prefer to invest in firms with complete management teams rather than solo entrepreneurs. There are also multiple other commercial considerations which will be discussed in relation to screening and evaluation in the next section.

Weak Deal Generation Post COVID-Response

It may be concluded that venture capitalists have found it difficult to connect with successful entrepreneurs post COVID-response due to cancelled networking events, suspended company visits, and limited face-to-face interactions with business contacts. Although more active deal origination activities were taking place by the end of 2020, venture capitalists understand that it will take a significant amount of time to replenish deal flow. Conversely, many entrepreneurs recognize that their ventures have not performed well compared to the past, since COVID-response has negatively impacted the vast majority of industries, especially the small and medium-sized enterprise (SME) sector. Therefore, entrepreneurs have been forced to re-assess the impact of COVID-response on their ventures and their timeframe of recovery to 2019 levels prior to contemplating the sale of their venture or inviting an equity partner. As evidence suggests, entrepreneurs are aware that most active buyers may only be looking for bargain prices at this time.

Evidence also substantiates the idea that venture capital firms increasingly consider deals, which they perceive as high-quality investments, in pre-selected sectors of the economy. Other sectors that have been profoundly affected by COVID-response are simply overlooked, while deals which may be viewed as marginal are ignored. On the other hand, investment opportunities which are thought to be of high quality receive disproportionate attention from many different types of financiers, such as venture capitalists, investment bankers, strategic investors, and other sponsors. One obvious consequence of such flight-to-quality or flight-to-safety tendencies is an increase in valuation for these opportunities, while a further implication of such behavior is that early-stage firms may have fewer chances to obtain external finance, including venture capital. Many of these early-stage entrepreneurial firms are perceived as too risky in the era of COVID-response, with the exception of selected segments of the economy; this is in line with venture capitalists' current focus on more conservative, cautious, and risk-averse investment opportunities.

Additional evidence suggests that venture capitalists may be advertising their willingness to accept new investment prospects but are not actively investing. Instead, many venture capitalists have adopted a wait-and-see approach to investing in spite of significant cash reserves, which would contribute to the further accumulation of dry powder; in other words, they have been stalling deal completion post COVID-response. Studies confirm that two-thirds of venture capital firms have limited their investing, resulting in a decrease in deal volume by between 25 and 40% compared to the global 2019 levels. For example, the volume of global buyout transactions fell from about 4,100 deals to 3,100 deals between 2019 and 2020, which represents a 24.4% decline. The segments of the economy most affected by these venture capital trends were retail, consumer, entertainment, transportation, media, and telecommunications. The average deal size over this period increased by 23.6% from the 2019 level (i.e., $628 million), compensating for the decline in deal volume. This trend was underpinned by leverage, which was more freely available for larger transactions than for smaller deals. Globally, buyouts declined by 85% in the U.S., 69% in Europe, and only 27% in Asia–Pacific. Another obvious consequence of travel restrictions is the reduction of cross-border investment activities and an increased focus on domestic transactions.

Compromised Deal Screening and Evaluation

A significant part of venture capitalists' daily activities relates to reviewing business plans, receiving investment pitches, and meeting with entrepreneurs. Less than 5% of these submissions, presentations, and meetings convert into an actual investment, so in order to filter through the vast majority of proposals, venture capitalists rely on the screening and evaluation process. The screening process, or the first form of venture capital's due diligence, is an attempt to eliminate from consideration those proposals that do not meet the venture capital firm's specific investment criteria, seem unpromising, have an incomplete management team, or are unsuitable due to certain restrictions (e.g., funds may be restricted from investing into sectors such as military equipment and weapons, alcohol and alcoholic beverages, or tobacco). These strict conditions mean that the vast majority of proposals are rejected at this stage of the process.

Once a proposal passes the initial screening stage, it is more heavily scrutinized, as it is important to gain a complete and thorough understanding of all the aspects of the potential investee business at this stage of due diligence. There are numerous critical aspects of such detailed evaluation, the first of which is the identification of any potential "deal breakers" that could prevent venture capitalists from going ahead with the deal. Identifying a "deal breaker" issue early eliminates the need to dedicate financial and human resources to deals which are unlikely to be consummated.

Another form of examination that normally occurs during this screening stage relates to ascertaining the likelihood of closing a deal. This exploration involves preliminary discussions of legal terms, provisions, rights, and requirements that venture capitalists expect. The key areas of discussion include exit provisions (including involuntary exit), business valuation, corporate governance, related party transactions, approvals and veto rights, and any conditions or events which may lead to changes in control of the venture. If these discussions are constructive, venture capitalists draft a relatively short, non-binding document called a term sheet, heads of terms, or letter of intent to outline important areas of agreement. This milestone document, which summarizes the understanding of both parties, is the basis on which venture capitalists and entrepreneurs proceed to conclude the deal on the best effort basis. While this short agreement acts as a framework of future co-operation for entrepreneurs and venture capitalists, it purposes to address fundamental operational, financial, implementation, and execution risks in the deal. In other words, the terms sheet is an integral step in the screening process that represents a set of deal-specific protections for venture capitalists.

Venture capitalists will also investigate the commercial attractiveness of the potential investee firm, with an emphasis on the firm's commercial proposition and financial aspects. This secondary assessment is performed on the basis of information available from the firm, or in other words, no external consultants or advisors are brought into the transaction at this stage of the process. The most critical areas of evaluation include management, products and services, market dynamics, competition, and historical financials. The investigation also focuses on financial projections, business valuation, and an estimation of financial returns. This evaluation stage takes weeks or even months of intensive face-to-face interactions, during which venture capitalists, in addition to analyzing the numbers, learn about the strengths and weaknesses of the founders and management. Furthermore, these interactions allow valuable time for both sides to consider alternative business development scenarios, different strategic options, expansion and execution plans, financing choices, and additions to management. This rigorous evaluation process may be one of the most creative and intense phases of the venture capitalist-entrepreneur interaction.

Once the proposed deal has obtained internal approval from the investment committee, another expensive form of evaluation involving the participation of external consultants occurs. The basic assumption behind the use of external advisors is to examine various facets of the entrepreneurial firm's activities, including accounting, legal, and environmental matters. During this additional stage of evaluation, external advisors have an opportunity to uncover any unknown factors or circumstances about the business, including quantifying potential liabilities (such as tax or environmental liabilities), discovering any "skeletons in the closet", and performing negative screening. External advisors are typically involved in due diligence through active interaction with founders and management over four to six weeks, and their involvement often ceases upon submission of a final report, with the exception of lawyers, who, in addition to conducting legal due diligence, are also frequently involved in preparing final legal documentation. However, the scope of this external investigation is likely to differ from firm-to-firm, depending on the unique characteristics of the business, its size (i.e., revenue), the extent of commercial relationships, its financial characteristics, and the nature of the contemplated transaction (i.e., expansion, buyout, and so on).

Although not strictly necessary, there may be some benefits to the utilization of external advisors, the foremost of which is their ability to provide an independent analysis and assessment of the potential investee firm. This fresh look at the venture allows for the identification of new areas of risk that may have been previously overlooked or unknown. The advisors' report may help outline areas of potential improvements within the venture, therefore allowing venture capitalists to better prepare for the post-transaction period. Finally, external advisors can also provide greater certainty about the firm's capabilities to achieve its planned financial and non-financial goals.

Compromised Due Diligence in Venture Capital

A lack of face-to-face interactions during due diligence is likely to create multiple problems for venture capitalists, some of which were already mentioned in Chapter 2. Firstly, and most importantly, venture capitalists continue to struggle with the proper assessment of entrepreneurs' values, motivations, ambitions, aspirations, and goals. Deal teams have less understanding of the entrepreneur's weaknesses and vulnerabilities due to a lack of interaction with founders, which can lead to a compromised or inappropriate assessment of important behavioral aspects that make the biggest difference in entrepreneurial performance. Venture capitalists may have problems differentiating between long-term builders of sustainable organizations and those who are short-term arbitrageurs of a single concept or idea.

Secondly, venture capitalists are less likely to conduct comprehensive evaluations of management; while they intuitively recognize that value creation is grounded in a complete management team, venture capitalists often disregard this principle in practice. Venture capitalists furthermore avoid looking "beyond the surface" of human resources to investigate issues such as staff turnover, employee training and development, and internal promotions. Thirdly, the most effective form of due diligence is dependent upon the key assets of each individual firm. When firms have fixed assets, a proper inspection may be more difficult to do, in which case due diligence necessitates in-person investigations of production lines, other fixed assets, inventory, and distribution facilities. However, if the key assets are intellectual property (i.e., software, digital solutions, media, digital platforms, and so on), evaluations could be done online.

The already challenging nature of the screening and evaluation process has been compounded by two additional fundamental changes to due diligence that were not previously evident. The first major change relates to timing, as beginning in March and April of 2020, the general avoidance of person-to-person interactions proved frustrating for venture capitalists and their advisors who were attempting to engage with the screening and evaluation process. Venture capital firms became more active and willing to engage in face-to-face meetings in June and July and even agreed to fly domestically for meetings that were deemed essential, although they still avoided international travel. Remaining meetings that were determined to be non-essential or were difficult to have in-person due to gathering or transportation limitations occurred through video conferencing. However, the level of these due diligence interactions was still below what venture capitalists would consider as ideal. This poor interaction negatively influenced venture capitalists' relations with management, since venture capitalists typically would not close a deal without meeting management a few times and particularly during buyout situations where existing management is such a critical element of investing. To compensate for a lack of in-person interactions, venture capitalists attempted to perform more reference checks, Zoom calls, and desk research, although it is currently questionable whether these extra online efforts will convert into better decision-making now, and in the future.

The second key area of issue relates to venture capitalists' inability to successfully deal with significant uncertainty surrounding the potential investee firm's operations, reliability of supply chain structures, market demand, revenue trajectory, and consumer behavior (i.e., loyalty or resumption of purchase). Consequently, venture capitalists are unable to reliably predict the future financial performance (i.e., especially EBITDA) and value creation potential of ventures. This uncertainty has also created a hesitance to rely on historical financials to establish proper business valuation, as well as substantial challenges in establishing normalized levels of financial performance. The venture capital industry has not faced such adverse circumstances in its due diligence over the last 50 years.

Virtual due diligence is not a novel concept in the venture capital industry, as this mode of evaluation, based on virtual data room, has been around for at least the last 20 years. However, there is of course a difference between performing proper due diligence, which includes human interactions, and the mere verification of key data. Evidence confirms that some venture capitalists may also be experiencing fatigue with the amount and duration of their now required online interactions.

Another area of evaluation that has experienced challenges post COVID-response is related to the involvement of external advisors.

Venture capitalists have faced difficulty when retaining lawyers, accountants, and other consultants to conduct due diligence because these consultancy outfits have placed significant restrictions on staff. In many cases, consultants have simply refused to perform the service or have promised major delays in engagement. Of course, these consultants rely on in-person visits to the investee firm to properly execute their services, and it appears that the level of staff restrictions at the advisory firms was proportionate to their size. In other words, the larger and more reputable the consultancy firm, the more restrictions they had in place. As substitutes, venture capitalists could resort to the use of smaller consultancy firms or independent advisors. Although these problems were somewhat reduced in the second half of 2020, external due diligence has continued to take more time than usual.

Therefore, it is evident that the screening and evaluation stage has been significantly lengthened post COVID-response. In practical terms, meetings with management, performing site visitations, and conducting reference checks were prolonged. Furthermore, interactions with employees, external advisors, underwriters, insurance agents, government officials (in cases where certain approvals or permits are required), and financial institutions may be problematic and lengthy. For venture capitalists, this additional time could have been used to arrange the external debt financing required for buyout deals, which has become increasingly challenging post COVID-response because financial institutions are more cautious.

Due diligence thus appears to be the most negatively affected aspect of the venture capital investment process post COVID-response. Missed and incomplete analyses, suboptimal assessments of the founders and the entire management team, misappraisal of entrepreneurial firms' commercial propositions, and the compromised ability of external advisors to perform their duties is likely to convert into progressively suboptimal investment decisions. Even though venture capital firms could theoretically resort to personality tests and psychological assessments for management, which have been previously utilized in other industries, it is unclear how these tools would function in the venture capital industry. In any case, the suboptimal evaluation of founders and management may lead to analytical errors on the part of venture capitalists, who will thereby proceed with inadvisable deals. Therefore, venture capitalist would not be able to overcompensate for poor investment decisions even with the best intentions, dedication, and commitment throughout other stages of the process. Inferior investment decisions with seemingly strong downside protections are also unlikely to help if the investment underperforms, goes bankrupt, or is liquidated; in other words, the initial damage from poor deal evaluation is likely to be perpetual.

More Adverse Selection Problems in Venture Capital
It is important to raise the problem of adverse selection, which, as academics commonly acknowledge, was an issue already plaguing the venture capital industry prior to COVID-response. While the topic of adverse selection is normally discussed in the context of financial contracting, it is likely to arise much earlier in the venture capital investment process post COVID-response.

There are two unique selection problems in venture capital, with the first being that venture capitalists are likely to face issues related to the rejection of more promising deals post COVID-response. Thus, with reduced interactions, limited face-to-face meetings, and extended teleconferencing, venture capitalists are anticipated to experience increasing problems recognizing and ascertaining good investment prospects and value. The list of wrongly rejected deals includes some of the most prominent firms today, such as Apple, Dell, Cisco, eBay, Fedex, Fitbit, Intel, PayPal, Skype, and Twitter. Interestingly, while some venture capital firms failed to recognize the value creation potential of these innovative firms, others did choose to invest in them; this phenomenon of misappraisal is likely to continue in the future as screening and evaluation processes are increasingly compromised. On the other hand, the reverse problem will also continue to arise, as past experience confirms that advisors often question venture capitalists and their decisions to reject transactions. Advisors find both that venture capitalists may not have been able to spend sufficient time and resources in understanding the fundamental strengths of rejected deals, and that they are often over-fixated on certain investment cues including market sectors, "hot" industries, specific types of investment opportunities (i.e., market consolidation plays), or forms of transaction. The problem of rejecting valuable deals, and conversely, the second-guessing of rejected deals are both issues in the deal selection process that are anticipated to be more pronounced in the future.

A further complication of venture capitalists' inability to do proper due diligence is that venture capitalists would likely continue to approach deals with relatively undistinguishable valuations, deal terms, and return expectations. With a compromised ability to perform these necessary functions, this generic approach to the marketplace will result in many superior investments being overlooked, thereby pushing superior firms to acquire other sources of capital or perhaps abandon their search for equity partners altogether. Consequently, the next generation of venture capital firms may end up with a disproportionate number of "lemon" investments and poor returns in their portfolio. On a positive note, however, evidence suggests that some venture capitalists continue to engage in exceptional levels of scope, breadth, and detail in the screening and evaluation process to fully appreciate the impact of COVID-response on all commercial and financial aspects of their potential investee firms' operations. Of course, more in-depth due diligence can only mean higher chances of improved returns.

Complexities in Financial Contracting in Venture Capital

If the due diligence stage confirms the underlying commercial, operational, and financial strengths of the potential investee firm and no deal breakers are identified in the process, venture capitalists proceed to conclude the deal through the conversion of a short deal agreement into lengthy, detailed, and comprehensive legal documentation. This legal package is normally comprised of the shareholders', subscription, and option agreements, as well as any amendments to the constitutional documents of the firm (i.e., articles of association, charters, statutes, or deeds). The legal documentation functions to guide the relationship between the two sides for the duration of the deal and only ends with the venture capitalists' final exit from the investee firm.

Financial contracting between entrepreneurs and venture capitalists is inherently complex and is comprised of three fundamental areas: deal pricing, security types, and various provisions. Business valuation, often called entry valuation, is a critical first step in establishing the percentage ownership for venture capitalists or, in other words, determining how much equity entrepreneurs should surrender in exchange for capital contribution. Establishing the entry valuation of the business may be difficult because entrepreneurs and venture capitalists may differ in their understanding of the firm's strengths and weaknesses, particularly at the beginning of their interaction; for example, although venture capitalists generally have less information, the information asymmetry is moderated as venture capitalists become more familiar with the affairs of the venture.

However, entrepreneurs and venture capitalists alike are often emotionally attached to the valuation figure, which is an initial hurdle that must be overcome.

Entrepreneurs are generally optimistic about the future of their venture that they have nurtured and developed over time. By the time entrepreneurs discuss the issue of valuation with venture capitalists, they may have already determined the value of their venture. One of the most common ways for entrepreneurs to discover the value of their business is through discussions with strategic investors, who often approach successful firms. Owners can also obtain confirmation of valuation from investment bankers if the firm contemplates going public, or from external consultants who entrepreneurs may employ specifically to establish the business's value. Entrepreneurs can also perform valuation on their own, which is a relatively simple method once a set of financial projections is developed. On the other hand, the establishment of an entry valuation by venture capitalists may be a more complex process, as they not only need to consider the appropriate level of entry valuation, but they also must evaluate exit valuation and calculate the anticipated rate of return. Therefore, venture capitalists will offer a business valuation that makes the most financial sense and will meet their return expectations.

Another critical component of contracting relates to the type of security acquired by venture capitalists, which may include common shares, preferred shares, convertible shares, or even convertible debt. However, the most popular security type by far is the convertible preferred share because it yields a number of benefits to venture capitalists, including repayment priority in the case of business windup or liquidation and realization (i.e., venture capitalists will receive their capital first before any proceeds are distributed to entrepreneurs). Venture capitalists may also receive common shares issued at low nominal values, which allow them to maintain their economic and voting interest in the venture.

Once the deal is completed, the next concern for venture capitalists is whether the business performs in accordance with the business plan and if the exit timing can occur as anticipated. Because any deviation from these two objectives would negative influence returns, a wide range of rights and provisions are included in the legal documentation for the purpose of addressing these two issues. It is important to differentiate that some rights are symmetric, and are thus offered to both parties, while others are asymmetric and are held by venture capitalists only. The most common symmetric rights include pre-emptive rights (i.e., protection against dilution), rights-of-first refusal (i.e., protection against uncontrolled share disposal), and piggyback rights (i.e., protection against uncontrolled sale of shares). Rights and provisions that are more asymmetric include lock-in rights (i.e., protection against sale of shares before venture capitalist complete the exit); voting flip-over events or change of control provisions (i.e., ability to assume full control of the venture); drag-along rights (i.e., right to sell the entire venture to a willing buyer); share adjustment or "ratchet" mechanism (i.e., a mechanism which allows adjustment to entry valuation in follow-on rounds and exit); inspection and information rights (i.e., access to information); representations and warranties (i.e., confirmation of legal and financial status of the firm); related party transactions (i.e., assurance of arm's length transactions in the firm); and approval and veto rights (i.e., commonly related to the appointment of auditors, acquisitions or disposals, issue of debt, modification of management compensation, and approval of share options program).

In addition to the general terms described above, there are additional mechanisms used in venture capital to address gaps in valuation expectation between the business owner and venture capitalists, tie valuation (and cash consideration) to the actual financial performance of the venture, reduce the risk of overpaying for the venture, diminish the initial investment, and extend the allocated period of time to pay for the venture (here, venture capitalists may be able to offer higher bids). These mechanisms also allocate more risk to the seller, in part because they are typically paired with liquidation preferences accruing to venture capitalists, in which case the seller does not receive any proceeds until venture capitalists recoup their initial investment.

One of these deferral mechanisms is an earnout, which may be defined as additional compensation provided to the seller of the venture once it achieves certain objectives. Specifically, an earnout is a payout structure where the selling founder agrees to receive a part of the price in contingent payments. These outlays may be regarded as performance incentives or postponed gratifications to the selling founder, who will stay in the business for a pre-defined period of time post-acquisition (note that earnout clauses may extend for a period of up to five years). The key parameters that are used in determining earnouts are grounded in financial (i.e., achieving certain revenue, gross margin, EBITDA targets), strategic (i.e., attaining specific market share, closing a major contract, launching a new product), and operational (i.e., completing a production facility, developing a distribution structure) milestones; of course, venture capitalists prefer using EBITDA targets. This earnout mechanism has been utilized in about 60% of deals in the life science industry and about 20% of transactions within other sectors of the economy.

Another mechanism used to address problems with financial uncertainties is an equity rollover, in which case rollover participants take a percentage of agreed consideration in the form of equity in a special purpose vehicle (SPV) established by venture capitalists to purchase the firm. These rollovers are offered to founders, other shareholders, and management, all of whom are expected to work with the venture capitalists' firm in effort to increase the value of the underlying asset. This arrangement is popular in venture capital since it reduces the amount of cash required for the deal (shares in the underlying asset are exchanged for shares in the SPV). Rollover shares are liquidated at the final exit.

Deal negotiations regarding these critical terms of rights and provisions occur throughout various stages between entrepreneurs and venture capitalists. The early interactions focus on general principles, key terms, and the role of the venture capitalists in the firm, while subsequent interactions encompass detailed legal procedures and mechanisms. Of course, these interactions often lead to multiple points of disagreement and contention. Entrepreneurs are often concerned about operating freedoms and business valuation, as they worry venture capitalists' various impositions, restrictions, and approvals may negatively impact the decision-making process, the speed of project implementation, and operating agility. Venture capitalists, on the other hand, are sensitive to achieving a liquidity event (i.e., exit), making sure the business develops according to the plan, and avoiding overpaying for the venture. Thus, face-to-face interactions are critical to resolve these complex issues and address many other sensitivities on both sides. These contentious matters are often resolved informally over tea or coffee, dinners, sporting events, golf, or other casual settings, which simultaneously test whether the two sides are likely to work well together in the future.

Finally, there is evidence to suggest that venture capitalists seek disproportionate and one-sided protections in contracts with entrepreneurs. Some of the most draconian clauses in venture capital include founder dismissal rights, the ability to sell the entire firm to a willing buyer (even if venture capitalists hold a relatively small ownership), the capacity to assume full control of the venture, and the right to retrospectively adjust the entry valuation. Of course, these mechanisms do not accrue to owners, who are left unable to dismiss venture capitalists or reduce their influence on the firm if they prove to be incompetent or operationally obstructive. The only possible recourse for entrepreneurs is forms of non-compliance or legal action. It may be easily argued that the aim of venture capital contracts is to overcompensate for venture capitalists' inabilities to properly size up various business risks, their lack of expertise, and poor hands-on involvement. However, contractual asymmetries are normally reduced once venture capitalists become more knowledgeable about the venture, which they seek to financially support.

Additional Lopsided Agreements in Venture Capital Contracting

In broad terms, the increased perception of risk, operational uncertainty, and the possibility of financial distress may cause venture capitalists to offer less favorable terms to entrepreneurs. Research confirms that because venture capitalists aim to strengthen their contractual arrangements post COIVID-response, deal terms may be less entrepreneur-friendly. Within expansion transactions, these deal changes include firming up liquidation preferences (between 1.25 and 2 times of invested capital), re-introducing full ratchet anti-dilution protections (in comparison with weighted average protections, which protect against valuation mark-downs), attaching cumulative dividends to preference shares, including redemption rights, solidifying operational controls, toughening veto powers and approval rights, instilling pay-to-play provisions to penalize investors for not participating in new rounds of financing, introducing IPO protections (setting a minimum price at floatation), including provisions for investor control of the board, and toughening exit provisions (uncompromised drag-along rights). In simple terms, venture capitalists are increasingly seeking to de-risk investments through legal documentation and a focus on downside protections. However, and as stated previously, these protections would not be effective for venture capital investments in the face of compromised screening and evaluation.

Therefore, business valuation continues to be one of the most contentious issues in financial contracts. The key questions with respect to business valuation relate to the sustainable levels of revenue growth, EBITDA profitability, and cash flow; the significant uncertainty surrounding these three parameters determines valuation and, hence, the severity and extent of downside protections.

Substantial Contractual Amendments to Buyout Transactions
In the last two decades, buyout transactions have become one of the most vibrant sectors of the venture capital industry. In these deals, venture capitalists normally acquire control of a venture, which can occur through its outright purchase or acquisition of a controlling interest in it, through a combination of equity and debt. The most well-known types of buyouts, any of which may be supported by venture capitalists, include management buyouts (i.e., existing management buys the firm), management buy-ins (i.e., management team is assembled), and institutional buyouts (i.e., institutional investors, like venture capital, buy the firm and assemble a management team post-transaction to manage it for extra compensation). Founders may be contractually obligated to stay in the business for a transitional period, a longer period of time, or until the final realization in some of these arrangements.

COVID-response has necessitated significant changes to venture capital contracting in buyout deals, which, as observed previously, was due to a number of uncertainties. For example, buyouts were especially vulnerable because venture capital firms pay to acquire the entire firm, or a controlling stake, for substantial consideration. Therefore, paying for a venture with uncertain prospects in cash or borrowed funds elevates the risk of buyout deals to levels the industry may not have experienced before. One change occasioned by COVID-response has meant that venture capitalists are no longer able to offer valuations equal to 11–12 times EBITDA. The new range may be equal to eight to nine times projected (rather than historic) EBITDA; valuations may be even lower in sectors more severely affected by COVID-response. Secondly, with regard to the amount of cash paid at closing, venture capitalists paid EBITDA multiples of ten times and settled the vast majority of consideration when closing pre-COVID-response. However, in the period post COVID-response, venture capitalists may now only pay 50 or 60% of total consideration, with the payment for the remaining share subject to various deferral arrangements such as earnouts or equity rollovers. There is also an increased use of these deferral payment mechanisms, with earnouts currently representing 40 or even 50% of agreed consideration. Moreover, evidence suggests that there is a trend of extending earnout lengths for a considerable period of time (beyond the previously common one-year period), and even indefinitely, in the face of operational and financial uncertainties post COVID-response. Venture capitalists are also focusing on the confirmation and re-confirmation of warranties and representations at various points in the transaction, while there may be a return to the more frequent utilization of escrow arrangements to cover arising indemnification issues. Lastly, there is evidence to suggest that venture capitalists are strengthening operating covenants, in which case the selling shareholder continues to be involved in the venture.

Challenging Value-Addition to Investee Firms

The venture capital industry often prides itself on their active and hands-on involvement in entrepreneurial firms, the close monitoring of financial performance, and timely interventions when modifications are needed or when deviations from the plan arise. Capable and experienced venture capitalists who sit on the board of directors of investee firms, especially those with practical industry experience, can add significant value to portfolio firms by improving the firm's operational and financial performance, reducing various business risks, and preventing failures. Thus, once the transaction is completed, venture capitalists begin to focus on three singular, yet interconnected, considerations: achieving key financial milestones (i.e., revenue, EBITDA, cash flow), accomplishing strategic goals (i.e., market share, market leadership), and confirming exit timing. The attainment of strategic objectives, such as securing market leadership and commanding market share, directly coverts into premium profits and cash flows, which, in turn, allow extra financial resources to defend the market position. These intentions are realized through the development of new products and services, business expansion, and the employment of capable managers. Of course, attaining these objectives will also eventually translate into a profitable exit.

Venture capitalists' contributions to entrepreneurial firms may arise from fulfilling a variety of roles, including serving as valuable sources of industry knowledge and information, which may become the foundation for future strategic decision-making. Venture capitalists can also effectively optimize a firm's resources and are frequently adept at finding value creation, generation, and perpetuation. Thirdly, venture capitalists can help in identifying management gaps and building well-rounded management teams. Under special circumstances and conditions, which can arise as a consequence of triggering voting flip-over event provisions, venture capitalists can even assume leadership roles in investee firms to solve certain operational, business, or financial problems.

With regard to monitoring activities, venture capitalists generally participate in board meetings and selective committees, appoint senior management, and approve strategic plans. Board participation also involves the receiving and reviewing of information packs by venture capitalists, which normally consist of financial and operational summaries, financial statements, and any other pertinent information (i.e., new clients, new projects, new competition, expansion execution, changes to the distribution structure, pricing changes, drawn financial facilities, and so on). Most importantly, however, board packs focus on the venture's vital signs. In terms of the frequency of interaction, venture capitalists commonly insist on regular reporting from younger firms or those facing operational and financial challenges; for more mature ventures, they rely on quarterly meetings supplemented by more frequent informal interactions.

There are various ways to measure a venture capitalist's performance, such as by ascertaining the number of successful, or non-successful, investments in their portfolio. Most venture capitalist firms follow a two-six-two formula: two superior deals, six single-digit returns or no return investments, and two complete write-offs. However, no matter what their ultimate performance record, venture capitalists are likely to experience significant underperformance, distress, and complete meltdowns in their portfolios. While the underlying causes of these problems may vary from firm-to-firm, they generally relate to poor management, sluggish market growth, unwise expansions or acquisitions, poor cash flow management, below-average profitability, severe competition, disruption to an existing business model, excessive debt, lawsuits, and unfavorable partnerships.

Once deals become problematic, venture capitalists can consider a number of alternatives, including attempting to pursue a turnaround strategy. In instances of severe financial and operational underperformance, venture capitalists may resort to hiring an external consultant to develop a turnaround strategy, which may involve CEO dismissal and a change in management. Existing board directors serve as interim CEO in these instances. Venture capitalists may also resort to one of the most difficult decisions they are required to make, namely providing an unanticipated follow-on round of financing. Moreover, in situations when the financial performance of the firm is challenging but there is no immediate loss of liquidity, venture capitalists may attempt to sell the firm through a "fire sale" (i.e., low valuation), which may involve a partial write-off of the venture capitalists' investment. Because venture capitalists typically maintain sufficient legal power to affect such a sale, they can sell the business to strategic buyers, incoming managers, existing management, or the founder. The final option, which is enacted when the investee firm faces an imminent financial decline, is to simply "pull the plug" and proceed to liquidation; this is considered a complete write-off.

As noted previously in Chapter 1, there is a broadly held public assumption that venture capitalists provide significant value-added contribution to investee firms. Academics commonly produce long laundry lists of areas where venture capitalists claim to be helpful to investee firms, but these lists are often inconsistent, general, and incoherent. The most commonly quoted accolades of venture capitalists include aiding firms in the hiring of senior management, assisting in strategic planning, populating boards of directors with knowledgeable members, helping to secure additional financing, and assisting in executing acquisitions. And yet, as observed in Chapter 3, venture capitalists tend to oversell and underdeliver, typically resulting from a lack of operating experience, which less than 15% of all professionals working in the industry may possess. In fact, there is evidence that suggests venture capitalists may actually impede entrepreneurial development by providing flawed operational advice, ill-founded tactical guidance, and inappropriate input with regard to decision-making. They may also impose unrealistic operational and financial goals that can magnify risks rather than seek to moderate them as venture capitalists likely intend. In fact, their short-term determinism may result in less investment toward long-term research and development, innovation, and commercialization, in addition to the further negative consequences their erroneous attempts to professionalize firms may generate. However, the most intrusive of these professionalization initiatives is undoubtedly founder dismissal. Lastly, there is evidence to suggest that venture capitalists do not cause innovation in entrepreneurial firms, but rather follow it; in the best-case scenario, venture capitalists may perpetuate innovation that already exists.

Difficulties in Working with Portfolio Firms

The period post COVID-response represents one of the most challenging acid tests the venture capital industry has faced over the last 50 years. It is increasingly evident that only the most unique and dedicated venture capital firms, that have performed a robust bottom-up industry analysis, built strong operations and special-task value-creation teams (in addition to deal teams), developed proprietary deal flow, dedicated resources to the digitization of their own and investee firms, and developed more statistical-based approaches to deal evaluation, are likely to emerge from the COVID-response era victorious. These firms are anticipated to become the future leaders and consolidators of the venture capital industry and are therefore likely to secure a disproportionate amount of future fundraising activity. The reactions of venture capital firms to COVID-response may be one of the most significant differentiators in financial performance and, subsequently, fundraising in the post COVID-response era, with the hallmark of strong performers being an avoidance of a substantial number of losers and fatalities.

It is estimated that between 40 and 50% of portfolio firms were substantially or severely affected by COVID-response, with between 10 and 20% of firms experiencing outright disaster. And yet, evidence suggests that a further deterioration of portfolio firms is still expected by venture capitalists. Firms operating in industries that relied on in-person interactions or were unduly impacted by COVID restrictions were the most affected and saw the most significant decline in revenue. The financial fortunes of these ventures are not yet determined and will depend on the extent of further restrictions. Other firms that were substantially affected had to reschedule or revise capital expenditure programs and postpone major strategic decisions in order to conserve cash. In many cases, venture capitalists were required to support their portfolio firms with additional rounds of financing, more active involvement, operational handholding, and frequent interactions. The key areas of focus for portfolio firms were slowing down the deployment of capital, cost reduction (i.e., management, products, operations, and so on), and an emphasis on liquidity (i.e., drawing down available financial facilities, arranging new financing), while the main objective was to provide sufficient cash runway for these firms. In other situations where cash was tight, but firms did not require additional financing, studies confirm that a significant effort toward strategic advice and reducing cash burn rate was still necessary. However, it is estimated that about 20–30% of firms have benefited from COVID-response, which include firms that operate in telehealth, online education, video streaming, or online pharmacies. And yet, it appears that venture capitalists were nonetheless required to spend significant time in portfolio "triaging" and firm stabilization sessions.

In post COVID-response, the top priority for many venture capital firms became the maintenance of existing portfolio firms, with a focus on a combination of postponement, prioritization, and delay tactics. It was necessary for the appraisal of existing firms to be done quickly in order to determine their financial and operational status, ascertain capital needs, and establish turnaround, restructuring, or rescue plans. Because cash was tight in most situations, some venture capital firms focused on capital efficiency and profitability rather than growth. However, other firms proceeded to hire additional professionals to assist with key operational activities occurring in portfolio firms, including stress-testing liquidity and updating strategic plans.

While some venture capital firms greatly increased their involvement in, and commitment to, their portfolio firms, other venture capital firms barely strengthened their dedication to their ventures. In fact, evidence suggests that some venture capitalists only increased their commitment to portfolio firms by about one hour out of their sixty-hour workweek, which is surprisingly low given the number of underperforming portfolio firms. There may be numerous explanations for this uncommitted behavior, including the possibility that venture capitalists have not yet performed a detailed analysis of their portfolio firms and are thus unaware of the severity of the problems. In this case, the minimal increase in time commitment is proportional to their limited perception of the depth of their portfolio's issues. It is also plausible that venture capitalists were able to recognize the challenges in their portfolio firms but were unable to provide the necessary aid; in other words, venture capitalists simply determined that they did not have the skill set required to deliver the required operational assistance. This would be consistent with evidence verifying that only a small pool of venture capitalists are able to effectively assist firms, which is due to their hands-on practical experience from previous careers. In fact, research also confirms that venture capital performance has been driven by multiple expansion and revenue growth opportunities, rather than operational improvements. A more positive interpretation of this evidence could be that venture capitalists, recognizing their shortcomings, were able to secure external assistance for firms through the appointment of experienced board members, external advisors, industry specialists, and consultants.

Additionally, there is evidence to support the idea that venture capitalists, potentially at the expense of interacting with portfolio forms, have actually increased the time spent interacting with LPs. In these instances, venture capitalists intuitively recognize that because their planned fundraising could be in jeopardy, the dedication of additional time responding to LPs' concerns could pragmatically lead to successful fundraising initiatives in the future, even if the current financial performance is suboptimal; research evidence confirms that the number of funds being raised has declined since 2016. However, this decrease in funds could simply account for the trade-off in time spent by venture capital firms on LPs versus portfolio firms. For example, if about 50% of existing LPs continue to successor funds on average, any problems with existing LP relationships would almost certainly destroy all prospects for a new fund.

It is also possible that venture capitalists indicated their willingness to help portfolio forms in surveys but chose to behave differently in practice. This bias is not uncommon in research where respondents wish to present themselves in a most positive light. There is further evidence to suggest that venture capitalists may quickly lose interest in their underperforming firms, to the disappointment and outrage of the ventures' founders. It is well known that venture capitalists pursue a "batting average" approach to portfolio firms, so it may be conceivable that venture capitalists consciously chose to ignore their underperformers and instead dedicate their attention to firms with the strongest financial prospects and new deal flow. If indeed this is the case, venture capitalists effectively broke one of the most fundamental promises made at the onset of their relationship to entrepreneurs regarding their commitment to hands-on involvement and active partnership.

However, it is important to reiterate that some venture capital firms have weathered the period of COVID-response well. In such cases, portfolio firms were minimally disrupted, recovered quickly, and did not require any new rounds of financing. The saving grace of these successful venture capital firms appears to be the diversification of their portfolio firms across various industries and the maintenance of prudent amounts of leverage.

Exiting in Venture Capital

At some point in their relationship with entrepreneurs, venture capitalists begin to shift their attention toward exiting, which is an orchestrated manner of cashing out of the investment. This fundamental stage in the venture capital investment process is understood to be the monetization of illiquid investments into cash, which can be subsequently returned, with profit, to LPs. If the investee firm has developed according to the original business plan, achieved a considerable market share, secured high brand awareness, developed a strong and loyal customer base, and maintained a solid business outlook for the future, a successful exit may be achieved relatively easily because the investee firm may attract a wide range of interest (i.e., financiers, strategic investors, underwriters, and so on). However, if the investee firm has not developed according to plan, the range of profitable exit options may diminish significantly. In the most difficult and critical situations, the firm may be liquidated, and venture capitalists would effectively write off their investment. Evidence suggests that venture capitalists commonly resist navigating through the exit process on their own, instead relying on external consultants for this purpose.

There are many exit routes available for venture capitalists to pursue, including trade sales, IPOs, sales to financial investors, buybacks and buyouts, asset sales, mergers, and liquidations. Venture capitalists aim to maximize value and liquidity in a successful exit, although there are tradeoffs between these two components. The two most preferred exit routes for venture capitalists are IPOs and trade sales, each of which have their own advantages, disadvantages, and consequences. An important advantage of an IPO, for example, is that it yields the highest amount of value; there is also an additional certification premium that may accrue to venture capital-backed firms. This option is also attractive to management who may wish to stay with the firm for some period of time, as well as other shareholders who may want to time their own exit. Additionally, there is no need to provide warranties to buyers in public markets. Disadvantages to an IPO include the potential for a rapid decline in price, additional restrictions on the sale of shares (especially when venture capitalists are on the board of directors), the high cost of achieving and maintaining listings, pressure to achieve regular profits and pay dividends, and a potential for liability under securities regulations. IPOs also do not guarantee a conclusion to the venture capitalists' relationship with the investee firm. Trade sales, on the other hand, are relatively straightforward and inexpensive, with the potential to achieve a premium price if the buyer is particularly interested in specific characteristics of the firm. This form of monetization, in contrast to an IPO, represents a complete and full exit. Disadvantages may include confidentiality issues (i.e., buyers request access to sensitive information), resistance from management and shareholders, warranties and representation, and an escrow arrangement

Menghi, Jason, Bhuvanesh Abrol, and Eric Savoy. 2020. Opportunities for private equity post-COVID-19: How can private equity firms help reverse the economic damage? www.deloitte.com.

Pryzant, Paul. 2020. An M&A guidebook for a post-pandemic world: Creative ways to bridge the gaps between buyers and sellers after the COVID-19 pandemic. July 4. www.seyfarth.com.

Pryzant, Paul, Suzanne L. Saxman, and Andrew Noble. 2020. Anatomy of an earnout in the era of COVID-19: Best practices for designing earnouts to avoid disputes. August 19. www.seyfarth.com.

Riley, Duncan. 2021. Startup exits, deal values and venture capital raised hit record highs in 2020. January 14. www.siliconangle.com.

Robinson, Mark, Jamie McLaren, and Matthew Wentz. 2020. Pressure points: Venture capital in Southeast Asia post-COVID-19. June 24. www.herbertsmithfreehills.com.

Sagie, Itay. 2020. How COVID-19 changed the VC investment landscape in the U.S. July 23. www.crunchbase.com.

Thorne, James and Priyamvada Mathur. 2020. Coronavirus forced venture capitalists to adopt new script on fundraising. June 2. www.pitchbook.com.

Tse, Byron, Bryan Haynes, Ian Michael, and Annie Tonken. 2020. The impact of COVID-19 on M&A dealflow. May 20. www.bennettjones.com.

Wiens, Al and Troy Pocaluyko. 2017. Structuring earn-outs in M&A transactions. April 25. www.wildlaw.ca.

Woodward, Isabel. 2020. Covid has put VCs under the spotlight, and exposed their vulnerabilities. November 6. www.sifted.eu.

Unruch, Ryan, Marko Trivun, Brook Wong, and Josh Teichman. 2020. Potential impact of COVID-19 on Canadian venture capital deal terms. September 23. www.torys.com.

Yehezkel, Ariel and Allison Wu Troianos. 2020. The impact of COVID-19 on M&A transactions—Part II. Deal terms. July 27. www.corporatesecuritieslawblog.com.

CHAPTER 6

Degeneration of Future Venture Capital Performance

The first chapter of this book provided an in-depth analysis of venture capital performance, which outlined that even prior to COVID-response, the venture capital industry struggled on multiple fronts, including financial performance. There has also been a widening disparity in performance between top performers and the remaining market participants, which will likely continue to drive industry consolidation in the future. While it has been previously observed that venture capital performance was subject to increasing deterioration even in the absence of COVID-response, this chapter will extrapolate the future of venture capital performance, as impacted by COVID-response.

Of course, determining the industry's future performance is no easy task as there are a plethora of moving parts in the venture capital ecosystem that may impact returns. The current changes plaguing the venture capital industry are significant, leading to uncertainty if and how the industry can establish a new comfort zone. These changes appear to affect every component of the investment process and challenge the role of all critical stakeholders within the venture capital model, including general partners (GPs), limited partners (LPs), and investee firms. The objective of this chapter is to revisit the investment process one more time for the purpose of guiding a discussion of venture capital performance. Analysis in this chapter will begin with a discussion of the impact

D. Klonowski, *Venture Capital Redefined*,
https://doi.org/10.1007/978-3-030-83387-9_6

of fundraising and fund formation on venture capital performance, which has been omitted from analysis in previous chapters.

Fund Formation and Venture Capital Performance

Fund formation is one of the foundational activities in venture capital, as without the provision of capital from LPs, the venture capital ecosystem seizes to exist. However, LPs can have both positive and negative impacts on this ecosystem. In terms of a positive impact, LPs provide capital to the ecosystem, which is subsequently directed to entrepreneurial firms. Even though the contribution of venture capital to the overall development of these firms is relatively small, a complete lack of capital may negatively impact the firm's ability to develop and grow, as at least some entrepreneurial firms may not be able to raise capital from any other financing sources. Another positive LP contribution may relate to the introduction of proper governance structures in the financial industry to entrepreneurial firms.

And yet, LPs may also have a significant number of destructive impacts on the venture capital ecosystem. For example, a study conducted by the Kauffman Foundation produced evidence to confirm that one of the most profound "enemies" of the venture capital system, who also contribute to low returns, are actually LPs themselves. Moreover, the report outlined that LPs' excessive allocation of capital toward GPs is one of the most significant destroyers of value in the entire ecosystem; LPs' permissive behavior in this respect allows, perpetuates, and encourages the malfunctioning of the venture capital model. This disruption to, and destruction of, the venture capital model can occur through multiple interconnected channels, such as in the event of a significant disconnect between fundraising and the venture capital firms' ability to locate suitable investment opportunities. An over-allocation of excessive amounts of capital in the venture capital ecosystem can lead to a substantial accumulation of dry powder, which in turn creates a snowballing effect that can result in compromised returns and an inability of the industry to meet the minimum illiquidity premiums expected by LPs. Given that the average annual global fundraising is equal to about $400 billion per annum, the misallocation may be severe. As argued in Chapter one, the optimal size of global fundraising should be substantially lower than the current amount.

Furthermore, LPs continue to be enticed by the venture capital industry in spite of their history of poor returns. This inherent attraction toward the venture capital industry may be explained by the strong interpersonal and business relations that form between LPs and GPs, the fear of losing out on potentially high returns (which have not been delivered since the 1990s), and the inability to locate alternative investments opportunities. LPs also fail to perform thorough due diligence on GPs, which may reflect their lack of experience, know-how, and expertise. Thus, LPs may be driven to allocate capital to the investment schemes they perceive to be most attractive without properly understanding GPs' operational characteristics, such as robustness of internal decision-making processes, human resources, ability to provide hands-on assistance, and capability to generate strong deal flow. A failure to properly comprehend these operational matters leaves LPs unequipped to distinguish between inferior and superior GPs, which causes LPs to supply capital to underperforming GPs, therefore permitting these GPs to raise even larger funds to financially support suboptimal segments of the market. LPs must also unduly tolerate poor access to information regarding fund performance and internal GP operations, including team stability, carried interest allocation, and GP succession issues.

Although LPs intuitively recognize that the current LP-GP compensation structures create multiple areas of misalignment, incongruence, and conflicts of interest, they have not been able to practically address these critical issues thus far. In essence, a fear of making the right decisions, and potentially destroying valuable personal and professional relationships in the process, prevents LPs from fixing many fundamental issues in the venture capital ecosystem. It is therefore evident that LPs are unable, or perhaps even unwilling, to negotiate sufficient rights in their LP-GP agreements that would allow them to properly, responsibly, and effectively monitor GPs' activities throughout the entire life of the fund.

Finally, there are significant behavioral issues in venture capital management that may hurt the industry as a whole. For example, professionals working for LPs are unlikely to admit to GPs' obvious underperformance, since admissions of this kind would tend to eliminate their own employment if LPs' exposure to this asset segment was limited or avoided entirely. These same professionals are also hesitant to admit that billions of dollars in carried interest are economically justified as payment for returns which are in line with those generated in public equities markets or even lower.

In view of the issues previously raised, many LPs have spent considerable time contemplating their involvement in the venture capital industry;

some have even decided to leave the venture capital ecosystem altogether in pursuit of other investment opportunities. Other LPs understand the potentially strong role venture capital has in the creation of a well-diversified investment portfolio while simultaneously pursuing their own internal operations. Still more groups of LPs may see value in venture capital and desire to secure careful exposure to the asset class. LPs may also selectively invest in some funds managed by a specific GP, but not in others, which is becoming a more common practice.

The Cost of Venture Capital Services

Critical to the consideration of venture capital performance is the cost to LPs for the provision of financial services by GPs. This is an important topic since it illuminates that the largest beneficiaries of the venture capital ecosystem are GPs themselves. The high cost of providing venture capital services is manifested in the vast difference between the gross returns declared, and often promoted, by GPs in comparison with the net returns that eventually flow to LPs. This difference may be as high as ten percent (note that net returns account for all costs of procuring venture capital).

The venture capital process is inherently expensive, due in part to the high salaries and bonus payments claimed by GPs' personnel, who include founding partners, partners, managing directors, vice presidents, and associates. In addition to these direct payments, GPs rely on a wide selection of advisors, investment bankers, financiers, lawyers, accountants, consultants, and other intermediaries; these "supplementary" or "substitute" venture capitalists perform duties that LPs would typically expect to be performed by GPs. The list of these subcontracted jobs is long and involves the execution of acquisitions and disposals, the provision of operational and strategic advice when investee firms underperform, conducting due diligence and background investigation, and the resolution of any other issues GPs may experience. Consequently, what GPs actually do, and the significance of their role in the venture capital firm, may be increasingly unclear.

Moreover, GPs progressively utilize external firms for fund administration, the cost of which is often charged against the fund to prevent the reduction of GPs' management fees. Bankers, who are other critical stakeholders in the venture capital ecosystem, also employ their own advisors, consultants, and lawyers to perform due diligence on the investee firm and prepare legal documentation; this represents yet another layer of cost duplication within the venture capital ecosystem. LPs likewise hire their own teams of lawyers, placement agents, accountants, intermediaries, gatekeepers, and other various advisors. Of course, it is questionable whether the extensive involvement of external consultants in the venture capital process converts into value creation for LPs, although these consultants are nonetheless happy to charge fees and actively promote a positive image of venture capital and its alleged above-average financial performance. For example, one researcher estimated that private equity "funds charge at least $50bn to invest $200bn" over a ten-year period (Phalippou 2020, p. 2). This appears to be excessive.

One of the most expensive and contentious arrangements within the venture capital investment process is GP compensation, which is understood as a 2/20 scheme (i.e., a two percent fixed fee and a 20% performance-based reward called carried interest, or simply, "carry"). This payment structure represents the most profitable and lucrative compensation in the entire financial industry. Evidence furthermore concludes that GPs are addicted to these guaranteed fees, which, as academics confirm, may represent as much as two-thirds of GPs' overall compensation. GPs charge such substantial fees due to their erroneous promise of excess returns, and subsequently live comfortably and even flourish through protracted economic downturns and slowdowns in investment activities due to these same excessive fees. Of course, the general public is often led to believe that venture capitalists are rewarded on the basis of pure performance; this public perception is false and is rarely corrected.

LPs do occasionally require that GPs provide their own capital to the fund. However, in these instances, LPs will provide 99% of capital to the partnership and GPs are only responsible for one percent. While LPs believe that GPs' one percent contribution assures their "skin in the game", GPs treat it as the cost of securing a ten-year management contract. For example, in the case of a one billion fund, GPs are expected to contribute $10 million into the partnership structure. Given that they can charge two percent in fees, they would be able to generate about $200 million with their $10 million contribution (although this may be subject to some reduction after the investment period). This arrangement does not produce any significant form of financial alignment between LPs and GPs since, in reality, GPs' one percent contribution rarely comes from their own pocket, but instead from management fees (which are often set at excessively high levels when compared to the actual cost of running a fund), fees charged to portfolio firms, salaries and bonuses (also paid by

LPs), and early distributions of carried interest. As a last resort, this one percent contribution may even be borrowed.

Carried Interest: Friend or Foe?

It is generally believed that LPs must provide an appropriate incentive structure to GPs to encourage them to achieve above average returns. Carried interest, or carry, is defined as a financial arrangement, under the terms of which LPs receive 80% of profit generated by the limited partnership and GPs receive the remaining 20%. In this case, profits are defined as the difference between the net realizable value of the fund and the value of the initial LP contribution to the partnership. Within these agreements, significant value accrues to GPs only because LPs place their capital at substantial risk in the ironic pursuit of GPs' own financial windfall.

It is often deceptively advertised that paying for performance (or carried interest) reflects GPs' efficiency in generating above-average returns. This claim is often misleading, as there are in fact numerous problems with carried interest. Firstly, if LPs invest in a portfolio of GPs, they may pay carried interest to some GPs, but not to others. LPs can easily pay significant carried interest while generating losses or substandard returns from investing into venture capital on an entire portfolio basis. Evidence suggests that in the period between 2006 and 2015, for example, GPs charged about $230 billion in carried interest while delivering returns that were predominantly in line with those achieved by public equities markets. Secondly, LPs are substandard at keeping track of the amount of cash paid out in carried interest, especially when they have capital commitments to numerous GPs (i.e., CalPERS, for example, has investments in more than one hundred GPs). Additionally, LPs may not verify the monetary distributions they receive from GPs, due in part to the fact that these distributions are presented to them as the net of carried interest. LPs are also somewhat dismissive of carried interest because, in their view, paying carried interest confirms to the general public that they made a profit, which acts as a tangible confirmation of investment success and their appropriate allocation of capital among different asset classes. Thus, LPs often prefer not to remember the historical record of GPs they choose to fund and may simply view carried interest as the cost of doing business.

Carried interest arises because it is paid as a percentage of absolute nominal profits rather than relative performance. In other words, GPs may charge 20% carried interest whether or not they actually generate returns higher than those found in public equities markets. Looking at returns on a comparative and absolute basis should be critical for LPs because of the high cost of accessing venture capital. Additionally, carried interest schemes are often poorly structured and lacking precision and clarity in partnership agreements, which is valuable for GPs, but problematic for LPs. For example, a significant amount of value can be captured by GPs through "catch up" provisions. Under such an arrangement, the initial return equal to the amount of invested capital is returned to LPs, who then may receive preferential returns (if any). The remaining proceeds are directed toward GPs until the value of all distributions is equal to 20%, and it is only after reaching this point that the remaining proceeds are split 80/20 between LPs and GPs. Therefore, it is easy to comprehend how such an arrangement effectively circumvents the 80/20 compensation scheme. There are also other arrangements which effectively incentivize GPs to focus on investments yielding lucrative financial returns to themselves while ignoring their lesser performing portfolio firms.

Value-Chain Analysis of Venture Capital Performance

One of the most fundamental evaluations of the profit potential of the firm, and the entire venture capital industry, is the value-chain analysis. This form of assessment analyzes the most critical activities in the firm, examines the linkages between these activities, and determines the most important value-generating components. A thorough analysis of the firm's value-chain involves examining each product or service line's value chain activities (i.e., understanding the underlying strengths and weaknesses behind these activities), analyzing linkages between different activities that go into each product or service line (i.e., establishing how different activities fit together in terms of cost, benefit, and efficiencies, as well as how these activities cross-influence each other), and finding synergies between different product and service lines, business units, or divisions (i.e., achieving optimization, efficiency, and cross-sharing of resources).

The firm's key activities may be divided along different planes of analysis, as, for example, one method of investigation is Michael Porter's division between primary (i.e., inbound logistics, operations, outbound logistics, marketing and sales, and services) and secondary (i.e., management, human resources management, technology, and procurement) activities. Another approach may be a division into upstream and downstream activities, which is commonly used in the petroleum industry.

Although Chapter five examined the venture capital investment process, which consists of five basic stages (i.e., deal generation, screening and evaluation, financial contracting, monitoring, and exiting), an even more detailed breakdown of venture capital activities could be imagined. In broad terms, however, the venture capital investment process represents the value-chain for the venture capital industry, as it is along this process that value is either created or lost. In other words, this value-chain determines whether a venture capital firm, or the entire industry, is capable of generating strong and sustainable returns.

In the case of the venture capital industry, each stage of the investment process can be examined to determine whether that stage creates or destroys value and financial returns. It is through this detailed descriptive analysis that one can decipher if each small component of the process works optimally, breaks down, or completely malfunctions. Similar to the petroleum industry, where the value-chain is complex, multi-dimensional, and intricate, the value-chain analysis of venture capital may also be split into two main sets of activities, namely pre-deal completion and post-deal execution; it is along this pre-and post-deal demarcation line that value may be lost or created. In a pre-deal completion step, venture capitalists prepare for future co-operation with investee firms by accessing the right investment opportunities, properly ascertaining the underlying strengths and weaknesses of investee firms, and devising the most optimal set of financial contracting legal protections. In the post-deal execution stage, venture capitalists' value-creation activities commence. However, there is no more important determinant of financial performance than venture capitalists' abilities to provide pragmatic, practical, experienced-based, and hands-on value-enhancing assistance to investee firms; many GPs are unfortunately not prepared for this job. This ability of GPs to assist investee firms is critical because, as one experienced venture capitalist noted, "over 80 percent of Domain's successful portfolio companies owe their success to products that were either not in the original business plan, or were to be a minor part of the company".[1] It is only through a combination of the dynamic nature of entrepreneurial development, the provision of capital, and active hands-on assistance that value may be created.

While the two major sub-components of the value-chain analysis, specifically pre-deal completion and post-deal execution, are connected and intertwined, they are also disconnected in the sense that efficiencies, with which deals are located, processed, and negotiated, may be completely detached from the regular weekly or monthly grind of working with investee firms. Put simply, processing deals in a pre-completion stage may prove to be futile if venture capitalists are unable to provide value to investee firms, as it is during this intense and interactive process that the most significant value-added contribution can be made. Therefore, even the best efforts during the information- and document-driven (i.e., financial contracts) stage of the investment process may not be transformative for investee firms if operational, strategic, and financial matters begin to fail alongside entrepreneurial development. As one famous investor noted, "it is only when the tide goes out do you discover who's been swimming naked"; working with portfolio firms is the venture capital industry's "swim-naked" test.[2]

Venture Capital Performance: History and Future

Historical evidence indicates that venture capitalists have a poor performance record of generating strong and persistent returns. Although GPs were able to generate significant returns in the 1980s and 1990s, their inability to do so in the last 30 years is problematic. In fact, the value-chain analysis detailed further in the chapter confirms that the venture capital industry may actually destroy value throughout the various phases of the venture capital investment process. This section of the chapter revisits the historical performance of venture capital and discusses its future performance in the context of the simplified value-chain analysis (as outlined above).

Another Look at the Historical Performance of Venture Capital

Chapter one provided some historical evidence regarding global venture capital performance, of which there were five main conclusions. Primarily, academic studies dispute venture capital's ability to generate above average returns, which is especially evident when venture capital returns are compared to those available from public equities markets. Historical evidence confirms the reality of strong excess returns in the 1990s, although contemporary research evidence from major public pension funds in the United Sates (U.S.) indicate that venture capital currently provides cash-on-cash returns equal to about 1.5 times net of fees, which is equal to annual returns of about 10%, assuming an investment period of four years; this return is in line with returns from public equities markets (i.e., S&P 500 index). Of course, this level of cash-on-cash returns would generate lower annual percentage returns if the longer investment-holding period were assumed.

Additionally, financial performance has been declining across different forms of private direct investing, including venture capital, private equity, and buyouts. Research evidence clearly identifies this deterioration as beginning in the mid-1990s and perpetuating over time (1995 to 1999—31%; 2000 to 2004—28%; 2005 to 2009—13%; 2010 to 2013—12%). Based on data from the U.S., venture capital performance further declined to 11.6% during the period of 2014–2020. Other research confirms that returns have declined by an additional 1.6% in 2020. While this percentage decline may appear to be relatively small, it may mean the difference between positive and negative illiquidity premiums, and surveys have indicated that over 40% of GPs expect a further deterioration of returns in the future. A third conclusion to be drawn is that venture capital financial performance is no longer persistent, meaning that GPs are not able to produce consistent results from one fund to another. This lack of dependable performance affects the most prominent funds, including Apollo, KKR, Blackstone, CVC, and TPG, and consequently creates suboptimal capital allocation for LPs. There is also a substantial return variance in performance between quartiles, as the drop-off between the top and second quartile may be as high as 20%. Lastly, there is evidence to confirm that returns are inversely related to industry size.

In addition to an overview of the historical evidence discussed in Chapter one, this chapter will also provide further research evidence as a prelude to a consideration of the venture capital industry's future performance. Figure 6.1 presents a numerical analysis of financial performance with respect to different classes of private equity-based investing (i.e., private equity, buyout, growth equity, and venture capital) and geographic orientation (i.e., global, U.S.-based, and global excluding U.S. performance). For the purposes of this discussion, private equity is defined as financing more mature firms, buyouts as buying firms outright, growth equity as investing in expansion opportunities, and venture capital as capitalizing younger entrepreneurial firms. Figure 6.1 also demonstrates illiquidity premiums calculated on the basis of data

Classes of equity investing

Geographic orientation	Private equity	Buyout	Growth equity	Venture capital
Global	0.16%	0.18%	0.12%	
U.S.	1.60%	**2.09% - Small cap** 1.92% - Mega cap 1.35% 0.92% - Large cap (0.15%) - Mid cap	**2.70%**	**2.31% - Early stage** 1.16% 0.30% - Late & expansion stage (0.42%) - Multi-stage
Global, excluding U.S.	(1.93%)	(1.58%)	(3.26%)	

Fig. 6.1 Illiquidity premiums across various classes of equity investing and geographies (*Source* Developed on the basis of data from Cambridge Associates [2020]. S&P 500 ten-year index is used as a benchmark [nominal return of 14.0% as quoted by Cambridge Associates])

provided by Cambridge Associates (June 30, 2020) and return values from the S&P 500 index. As noted in Chapter one, achieving an illiquidity premium in excess of three percent is important because LPs expect to be compensated for prolonged periods of illiquidity and other underlying risks.

Moreover, Fig. 6.1 confirms that none of the cross-sectional numbers have been able to exceed the three percent threshold expected by LPs on a ten-year basis. Overall, returns from global equity-driven investing are marginal, and illiquidity premiums are close to zero. And yet, the U.S. illiquidity premiums consistently exceed the S&P 500 average by one to two percent. The investment category with the highest illiquidity premium, which is equal to 2.7%, is growth equity, followed by private equity, and then buyouts. Among buyout opportunities, the category with the highest returns and an illiquidity premium of 2.09% is buying out firms that have relatively small capitalization (i.e., "small cap"). The worst record accrues to investee firms operating in the "mid cap" market segment (−0.15%). Furthermore, the illiquidity premiums from global markets excluding the U.S. market are disappointing.

Figure 6.2 presents another analysis of venture capital performance, in the form of buyout transactions, which are provided on the basis of gross cash-on-cash returns and are frequently misleading to the general public when only the raw data is presented. It is only when gross returns are adjusted for the cost of venture capital (i.e., management fees, carried interest, and other expenses) and compared to returns from public equities markets that illiquidity premiums may be calculated. The difference between gross and net returns is assumed to equal seven percent in these calculations (although it may be as high as ten percent, as evidenced by major public LPs in the U.S.), while returns from public equities markets are equal to ten percent (note that the ten-year average from the S&P index was equal to about 14.0%). A further expectation when calculating illiquidity premiums is that the average holding period for GPs was equal to five years, a number which is likely to increase in the future. Under these basic but reasonable assumptions, the average illiquidity premium was equal to 0.2% for the period between 2005 and 2020, which thoroughly eradicates the venture capital industry's widely promoted claims of strong and persistent excess returns. In fact, seven periods out of the 16-year time horizon are outright negative, which represents 44% of observations (we provide a zero-percent return reference line in the graph

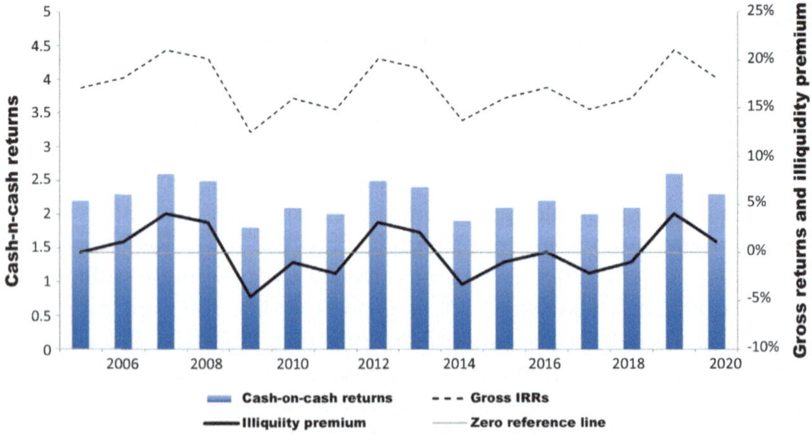

Fig. 6.2 Conversion from gross returns to illiquidity premiums (*Source* Developed and adjusted on the basis of data as reported by Bain and Company [2021, p. 25])

for better visibility). Furthermore, the ten-year average is equal to 0.1% and the illiquidity premium in the five-year period following the 2008 financial crisis was negative and equal to 0.5%; these historical precedents suggest what investors can expect for the foreseeable future post COVID-response.

There are further extrapolations which can be made regarding future venture capital performance. For example, an optimistic, although less realistic, assumption for the average GP would be a five percent difference between gross net returns with a holding period equal to four years. The average cash-on-cash returns of 2.2 times over the same period converts into net returns equal to 22.0% and an illiquidity premium equal to about seven percent. Coincidentally, these returns correspond to the level of returns achieved by GPs situated in the top quartile, but do not accurately reflect the performance of an average GP in the industry.

Based on the ongoing trends demonstrated in Fig. 6.2, there are additional observations that can be made regarding the impact of COVID-response on venture capital performance. One of these trends is an increase in deal size while the overall number of deals has declined, which represents a growth in mega deals. However, the direction of massive amounts of capital toward mega deals is likely to reduce returns. Another trend may relate to the shift in the negotiating power vis-à-vis entrepreneurs, which occurs due to lower capital flow into the entrepreneurial ecosystem. GPs furthermore indicate that they expect to outperform public equities markets, but given their performance history in the last two or more decades, such optimism may be unfounded; and yet, these claims do serve as a useful promotion strategy for the industry. The impact of COVID-response has also led to decreased global flow and foreign direct investment (FDI), resulting in fewer exits through trade sales.

Moreover, significant problems with existing portfolio firms are likely to decrease returns for recently established GPs who committed capital to the sectors primarily affected by COVID-response. While some research indicates that the proportion of portfolio firms impacted by COVID-response is minimal and equal to about ten percent, which supports claims that the industry has been affected in a negligible manner, others suggest that nearly half of portfolio firms have been affected; this may represent a pool of about thirty thousand portfolio firms, many of which operate in sectors of the economy that have been deeply impacted by COVID-response. Thus, mediocre GPs with a number of severely altered portfolio firms would be disproportionately affected and completely forced out of the market. This, in turn, can initiate an increase in returns for the remaining industry participants, thereby beginning a new phase or era in the venture capital industry's development cycle.

It is also important to consider a point, namely that of valuation, which has already been stated previously. The issue of valuation as it pertains to venture capital performance may persist within the industry for years to come. In simple terms, an increase in valuation on attractive deals, accompanied by a decrease in valuation for all other deals, would represent one of the worst-case scenarios for the venture capital industry. For example, entry valuations on deals completed in 2020 have increased, thereby exacerbating the already existing problem of excessive or even "fantasy" valuations (i.e., 20 times EBITDA [earnings before interest, taxes, depreciation, and amortization] or 10–20 times projected revenues).

Lastly, there is a penchant within the industry to misleadingly report venture capital performance by showcasing high returns, which can be accomplished in a number of ways. Most commonly, and as confirmed by academic research, venture capital performance may be presented by selecting specific benchmark indexes for evaluation purposes. In other words, GPs can choose a low value benchmark index as a reference point to demonstrate their own returns. A broadly used approach is to select a wide international index, which often includes poorly performing geographic regions. When questioned, GPs frequently claim to have significant international activity, even if only a relatively small percentage of their investment portfolio relate to global deals. Additionally, GPs often claim that really long-term returns from the asset class are favorable, which include the exceptional returns from the 1990s. As careful observers note, the influence of returns from the 1990s can be marketed by the industry and selective GPs until a new set of exceptional returns are achieved.

Longitudinal Impact and Venture Capital Performance in the Future

There are multiple ways to investigate the potential returns and performance of venture capital in the context of COVID-response, such as by analyzing its longitudinal impact; in other words, industries, segments, or sectors of the economy may be affected in a more everlasting or transient manner. The longitudinal impact of COVID-response may have both positive and negative short-term implications and long-term consequences for all industries, sectors, and segments of the economy. These changes may, in turn, impact existing or future investee firms in terms of revenue growth, profitability, and cash flow, which are metrics that directly impact GP performance and LP net returns.

Before the potential development of various industries, market segments, and sectors of the economy is considered, it is important to highlight the significant uncertainty regarding how the global economy is likely to develop post COVID-response, including the impact on small and medium-sized enterprises (SMEs) and necessary adjustments to the venture capital ecosystem. Observers have suggested that it is unclear whether the economic recovery is likely to have curvatures resembling alphabet letters like L, M, N, U, V, W, or perhaps another shape.[3] There are a plethora of challenges that represent strong headwinds for the venture capital industry, while tailwinds are limited. As previously noted, the main headwinds for venture capital may include geopolitical tensions, poor economic growth, social unrest, and so on. The venture capital industry has been historically able to find creative ways to capitalize on economic, social, and political turmoil, although the depth, scope, and breadth of issues due to COVID-response are severe. Additionally, the venture capital industry is simultaneously experiencing independent challenges with respect to its operational model, and excess of dry powder, and issues within existing portfolio firms.

Table 6.1 considers four basic scenarios with respect to the longitudinal impact of COVID-response on investee firms (both existing and perspective) and the financial performance of the venture capital industry. In the first scenario, COVD-response is estimated to have an immediate and direct short-term impact that may also creative problems with the longer-term survivability of many firms across specific sectors of the economy, including retail, leisure, entertainment, or events. Firms operating in these market segments have already endured immense shocks to revenue, although these declines are expected to progress further. While it is unclear whether these economic sectors would be able to recover over a period of time, or what changes to their operating models may be required, the damage will likely be perpetual and long-lasting. Furthermore, short- and medium-term economic losses caused by a brisk fall in demand may not be sustainable for many firms, in which case even additional financing, careful cash management, and restructuring may not assure business survival. Thus, many firms within the most impacted

Table 6.1 Longitudinal analysis and impact on future venture capital returns

	Short-term ↓, *Long-term* ↓	*Short-term* ↓, *Long-term* ↑	*Short-term* ↑, *Long-term* ↓	*Short-term* ↑, *Long-term* ↑
Revenue	• Fear of contagion negatively impacts demand in selected sectors of the economy • Demand recovery prospects uncertain • Adjustment to business models may not generate new revenue streams	• Timing of recovery unclear • Trajectory of growth difficult to predict • Business prospects may be worse than before • Revisions to business model may not be successful in revitalizing revenue growth	• Temporary spike in demand • Unclear revenue trajectory in long-term • Persistence in newly formed consumer habits unclear • Emergence of new business models for disruption of existing industries	• Strong and repeatable long-term demand • Ability to expand operations and increase market share
Profitability	• Continued losses may be unsustainable in short- and medium-term • Cost cuts and closures may not be sufficient to resolve financial issues • Success of turnaround strategies may be uncertain	• Cost reduction, restructuring, and turnaround may be viable • Sustained downward pressure on margins	• Initial high profit potential may not be sustainable • Premium pricing likely to enhance profit margins • Successful ventures may pivot to other profitable business segments	• Premium profit potential • New ways to achieve optimization and efficiency

	Short-term ↓, *Long-term* ↓	*Short-term* ↓, *Long-term* ↑	*Short-term* ↑, *Long-term* ↓	*Short-term* ↑, *Long-term* ↑
Cash flow	• Sustained working capital issues • Careful cash flow management may not assure survival • Additional financing required; equity financing may be highly dilutive while debt may be difficult to secure • High possibility of bankruptcy, liquidation, and winding down	• Cash flow management may allow business continuity • Debt may be difficult to secure • More capital required to affect changes to operations	• Increased cash flow needs to meet growing demand • Ability to raise significant debt	• Cash flow needs commensurate with normal business development • Additional financing freely available • Ability to secure equity at premium valuations
Sectors	• Retail sector, restaurant, commercial real estate, leisure, entertainment, events organization, energy, consumer goods	• Travel, tourism, hospitality, automotive, transport, consumer goods, airlines, natural resources, industrials	• Online grocery, home fitness, media, television, online entertainment, online education, social media, delivery	• Telehealth, online pharmacy, cyber security, social media, e-commerce, work solution, Fintech, financial services, pharmaceuticals, biotechnology, business services

(continued)

Table 6.1 (continued)

	Short-term ↓, *Long-term* ↓	*Short-term* ↓, *Long-term* ↑	*Short-term* ↑, *Long-term* ↓	*Short-term* ↑, *Long-term* ↑
Return potential	• Significant number of turnaround and distressed cases in existing GP portfolios • Markdowns and write-offs in existing portfolios • Opportunistic investments may include distressed debt and acquisitions	• Achieving reasonable returns may take longer than expected • Turnaround cases may be prevalent in existing portfolios • Opportunities to buy valuable assets at depressed valuations • Opportunities to provide distressed debt and engage into distressed buyouts	• Likely markup in valuations • Return potential may depend on proper timing and choice of exit	• Markups for existing portfolio firms • Various exit choices possible • High potential for premium returns

Abbreviations: *GP* general partners
Source Based on a general "short-term, long-term" framework developed by Lino et al. (2020)

sectors of the economy may be facing bankruptcy, liquidation, or an orderly winding down of business affairs. GPs with substantial exposure to these sectors are also likely to face significant markdowns in the valuations of their portfolio firms, or complete write-offs. Future deals may focus on opportunistic investments, such as market consolidation strategies, turnarounds, restructurings, or the provision of debt. There may also be opportunities to acquire firms at low valuations in sectors that have reasonable prospects of bouncing back.

The second category of longitudinal impacts in Table 6.1 includes the situation wherein industries, sectors, and segments of the economy have seen a similarly rapid decline in trading due to COVID-response and ensued restrictions, but prospects for longer-term recovery exist. Examples of such sectors may include travel, tourism, hospitality, transport, and airlines, although it is important to note that these sectors are sensitive to COVID-response restrictions. For these segments, if these restrictions are repeated again, a significant revision of their business models may provide opportunities for revenue recovery and improved profitability, while the timing and trajectory of this growth is uncertain. Based on experience gleaned from previous economic downturns, it may take a decade or more for some of these sectors of the economy to rebound, and demand prospects still may not reach pre COVID-response revenue levels. A rapid decline in trading has also put significant pressure on margins.

Furthermore, firms may require additional capital to draw from, including either existing facilities or new lines of credit, while GPs who are exposed to firms operating in these sectors may require more time to execute turnaround, improve profitability, and enhance trading activities. This likely prolongation in the maintenance of investee firms will only further depress percentage and absolute returns. GPs without the possibility of additional time, due to fund and other restrictions, may be forced to exit at a valuation below expectations, which, in turn, may lead to partial write-offs. When pursuing new investment opportunities in tourism, hospitality, and transportation industries, GPs are likely to be selective and hunt for opportunistic investments at low pre-money valuations. Some GPs could even have the chance to provide distressed debt, which may be a new area of business for GPs, or participate in distressed buyouts and acquisitions. However, other GPs will likely focus on PIPE-type deals (i.e., private investment in public equity), which has been a growing trend in the industry.

The third category of longitudinal impact encompasses situations in which COVID-response positively impacted industries, segments, and sectors of the economy. Examples of such segments include media, television, digital platforms, social networking, movie streaming, e-sports, video connectedness, online grocery shopping, gaming, hygiene and wellness products, and work-related solutions. While COVID-response created into an immediate spike in market demand for these industries, it is unclear whether revenue growth is likely to continue in the foreseeable future due to uncertainty surrounding the permanency of novel and emergent patterns of consumer behavior. High revenue growth in these sectors has also led to excess profits, in addition to a demand for additional financing since revenue growth often necessitates further investments in working capital. GPs holding investments in these segments of the economy may also have short-term opportunities for profitable exits and strong returns. Exits are likely to be driven by demand by strategic investors, many of whom are cash rich, that are motivated to add new products or service lines to their existing portfolios.

The fourth scenario outlined in Table 6.1 relates to economic activities which have clearly benefited from COVID-response. Sectors such as telehealth, online pharmacies, online shopping, social media, biotechnology, pharmaceuticals, and e-commerce have already enjoyed strong market demand and high profitability prior to COVID-response, and these trends have only been enhanced and accelerated. Investments in these areas would generate premium valuations and returns in the long-term.

Profiling General Partners and Financial Performance

There is sufficient evidence to challenge the widely held public perception that venture capitalists provide value to investee firms, which is persistently mentioned throughout this book. Although venture capitalists have mastered their internal processes, their approach often promotes short-term economic efficiency rather than long-term value creation and enhancement. Additionally, by enforcing standardization, providing erroneous strategic and operational advice, and boxing entrepreneurial firms into standard rules of operating behavior, GPs may destroy firms' flexibility, adaptation, and experimentation, which are the core components of successful entrepreneurship and entrepreneurial perpetuation. The venture capital investment process is often designed to control, regulate, and administer rather than allow and encourage operational freedoms when establishing goals, objectives, and structures; in this respect, GPs may act like financial bureaucrats rather than value enhancers. A divergence in objectives can also result in a poor behavioral alignment between venture capitalists and entrepreneurs, which can only lead to perpetual conflict in virtually every aspect of the investee firm's operations.

Once venture capitalists negotiate an agreement with entrepreneurs, capital flows into the venture and both sides begin to co-operate; this stage of the venture capital investment process is normally termed as monitoring. GPs' value addition can potentially occur at two different levels, such as through their involvement in operational and supervisory matters. However, venture capitalists' operating experience has by far the greatest impact on the quality of the value-added contribution provided to entrepreneurial firms, the value creation process, and the likelihood of a successful exit. Significantly, it is during the monitoring stage that the most consequential decisions regarding the future success of the firm, the entrepreneurial value-creation process, and venture capital performance are made.

Of course, it may be difficult to provide a generalized description of funds in the industry, as they are different with respect to industry focus, the stage of investee firms they pursue, geographic orientation, and degree of hands-on involvement. In the book *The Venture Capital Deformation*, there is an outline of four distinct and discernable categories of GPs, which include financial propeller heads, untested promoters, entrepreneurial disconnectors, and business companions. Most entrepreneurs would readily admit that they have significant operating challenges, which is unfortunately the precise type of experience that the vast majority of venture capitalists lack.

While LPs have developed sophisticated qualitative and quantitative methods to assess GPs, they frequently dismiss the value of GPs operating experience, perhaps because most LPs lack such experience themselves. However, the most important question LPs should ask to discriminate between inferior and superior funds should be: How many years of practical hands-on experience do team members have in the industry? Intriguingly, but not surprisingly, studies confirm that more years of experience in the venture capital industry does not directly translate into superior performance. While research indicates that there are some decision-making improvements early in venture capitalists' careers, over time, and due to a combination of cognitive shortcuts and a lack of operating experience (which one is not able to make up by working in the venture capital industry), investment decisions and financial outcomes worsen.

Before the main differences between inferior and superior venture capitalists are discussed, it is worthwhile to note that both types of venture capitalists are likely to raise funds that are largely comparable to investment opportunities available in the marketplace. Thus, if given a choice for fundraising targets, GPs are often unable to resist the temptation of additional management fees that accrue from larger funds. Therefore, fund formation is generally regarded as a valuable, yet destructive, aspect of the venture capital investment process.

Table 6.2 includes a bullet-point differentiation between superior and inferior GPs, which is broadly defined through an analysis of pre-deal closing and post-deal execution sections. This discussion begins with a depiction of superior venture capitalists who have been responsible for generating financial performance in the top quartile of the venture capital industry. Beginning with an illumination of superior venture capitalists allows for the easier identification of inferior GPs.

The Superior Venture Capitalist

The left side of Table 6.2 presents the main characteristics of superior venture capitalists. Of course, the most distinguishing characteristic of superior venture capitalists is the practical experience they have gained through working at multiple industrial firms, which impacts venture capital activities in the post-deal completion stage. Venture capitalists' careers should demonstrate a progression of increasing managerial responsibility, multiplicity of assignments (including turnaround, operational improvements, products or service development, and international transfers), and even different industries. Superior venture capitalists may even have had previously successful careers in the industry as entrepreneurs themselves before become venture capitalists. Their educational background is often technical, where details, step-by-step processes, deconstructing issues, and resolving actual operating and strategic problems matter the most. Many of these superior venture capitalists have also completed undergraduate degrees (which may be supplemented with business degrees) in the sciences (i.e., biology, computer science, physics, chemistry, psychology, or even medicine) or engineering. Such experiences and educational backgrounds allow these venture capitalists to offer

Table 6.2 Types and characteristics of general partners and simplified value-chain analysis

	Types of venture capitalists	
	Superior (up to 15% of GPs)	*Inferior (remaining GPs)*
Pre-deal completion	• Focus on narrow scope of industries, sectors, and segments of the economy • Less competition for attractive deals • Founders may seek out partners with industry experience • Strong and well-rounded analytical capabilities allow the identification of strong management teams and attractive investment prospects • Ability to develop clear and implementable plans for value creation and enhancement • Ability to spot "lemon" deals quickly in due diligence • Financial contracting may not be the most critical focus; terms, rights, and provisions may be somehow suboptimal • Deal terms may assure operational flexibility and agility for investee firms	• Deal pipeline unfocused and inconsistent • Strong competition for deals (i.e., auctions) • Inability to distinguish between "lemons" and "superior" investment opportunities • Excessive focus on financial matters; poor ability to assess commercial propositions • Due diligence unfocused, long, and cumbersome • Inability to properly evaluate intellectual property • Focus on standardization and generic professionalization • "Tight" legal protections, terms, and provisions (downside protections may not result in capital protection)

(continued)

Table 6.2 (continued)

	Types of venture capitalists	
	Superior (up to 15% of GPs)	*Inferior (remaining GPs)*
Post-deal execution	• Practical experience allows significant improvement to investee firms' operational and strategic decisions • Command respect of entrepreneurs • Reduction of conflict during co-operation • Investee firms likely to flourish beyond the time of venture capital participation	• GPs unable to provide value enhancement due to lack of industry experience • Standardized (cookie-cutter) approach to value creation unlikely to work well across many industries • Provision of erroneous strategic and operational advice, which can lead to value destruction and interpersonal conflict • Excessive focus on financial monitoring • Realizations may reflect luck and timing
	• Avoidance of a standardized approach to value creation • Exit opportunities flow from strong deal selection and exceptional value creation in investee firms • Ability to build firms "to specification" of strategic investors • Preference toward exit through trade sales	
Investment process & returns	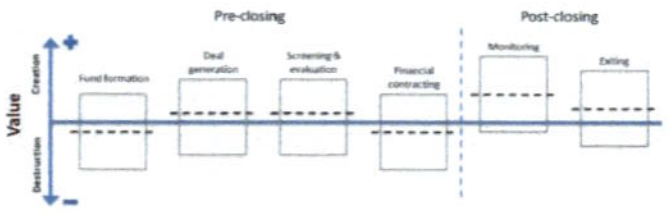	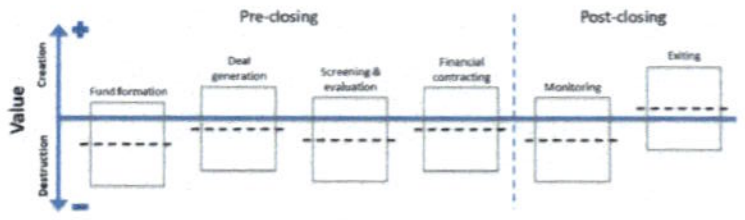

Source Graphs at the bottom of the table based on a general framework developed by Klonowski (2018)

superior strategic management advice, develop practical and hands-on solutions to real day-to-day challenges, envisage plans for value generation, and steer clear of operational problems; they are not just smart and savvy business individuals, but more importantly, they are skillful implementers of ideas.

The combination of superior practical experience, a strong educational background, and executive experience allows superior venture capitalists to quickly spot and ascertain investment opportunities in existing and newly developing industries. These venture capitalists generally focus on a narrow scope of industries and market segments that coincide with their past experience; they rarely expand outside of their comfort zone because they understand the risk this entails. Furthermore, deal flow may be easier, or even self-replenishing, for superior venture capitalists because entrepreneurs may actively pursue them. Their previous practical experience allows superior venture capitalists to assess the skill, talent, dedication, commitment, passion, and know-how of potential entrepreneurial venture with ease. Particularly, GPs are able to quickly identify entrepreneurs who have shown a strong resilience to crisis, are adaptable and flexible, and respond well to change. Rather than simplistic or generic, these venture capitalists employ a pointed form of screening and evaluation; they are concise in their due diligence questioning, which is often tailored to specific situations. Additionally, venture capitalists from this category quickly focus on attractive commercial propositions, understand an upside potential of the venture, and recognize its attractiveness to potential buyers.

Financial contracting for superior venture capitalists is not as natural as operating and commercial matters, so as a result, the extent of legal protections can at times be less sophisticated and polished. However, a GP's ability to spot commercially attractive propositions can more than compensate for their less robust legal protections and terms. Furthermore, entrepreneurs working with these venture capitalists instinctively understand that these superior venture capitalists know more about the industry than themselves. In these cases, venture capitalists may not need a vast range of rights, rules, regulations, and veto powers; their simple persuasion may be enough to initiate the success the venture. Deal terms that are implemented aim to protect the investee firms' agility, flexibility, and ability to pivot quickly without undue approval processes.

Although the monitoring phase may be challenging for entrepreneurs working with these types of venture capitalists, it is ultimately rewarding.

Because superior venture capitalists have a history of building proper organizational structures, developing robust business processes, creating and managing knowledge (including handling invention, innovation, and research and development projects), and establishing transformational business practices, they are able to assist investee firms with these difficult tasks. Moreover, conflicts between entrepreneurs and venture capitalists may be infrequent since superior venture capitalists may be regarded as experts and mentors. An additional distinctive feature of these superior venture capitalists is their primary focus on operational and strategic issues rather than finance; they may instinctively understand that value creation and strong financial performance follows operational excellence, rather than spontaneously arising from financial planning alone.

For these venture capitalists, exiting is a natural extension of their strong selection of attractive firms, development of a robust plan for value creation, signing a reasonable legal deal, and implementing the preconceived plan. Their practical experience aids them in understanding the actual strategic and operational needs of strategic investors, resulting in a natural gravitation of superior venture capitalists toward trade sales in their exit contemplations. Significantly, these venture capitalists can build companies to the specifications and requirements of potential acquirers, and they may even challenge or resist the notion of an initial public offering (IPO) as a preferred exit route.

It is estimated that only up to about 15% of all venture capitalists in the industry may belong to this unique talent pool; this still may be an optimistic figure. The graph at the bottom of Table 6.2 outlines the fact that superior venture capitalists are able to provide value at most stages of the venture capital investment process, excepting fundraising stages (these afflict most GPs and financial contracting and may be regarded as less critical factors to return generation). As stated previously, these strengths, which contribute to superior returns, flow naturally from superior venture capitalists' practical experience.

The Inferior Venture Capitalist

The inferior venture capitalist is the diametrical opposite of the superior performer. There are two distinguishing features, and fundamental weaknesses, of inferior venture capitalists that can be easy to spot and identify. The primary defining characteristic is a lack of practical and hands-on industry experience. This flaw is in spite of the fact that these venture capitalists have witnessed a number of entrepreneurial firms over their careers. The second quality, namely the undue belief in the extraordinary value of finance-orientation and financial contracting to cure poor investment decisions, may be even more damaging and detrimental to firms. Often supported by business education from top business schools, the comfort zone of inferior venture capitalists pertains to the areas of financial analysis, the preparation of financial forecasts, financed-based risk analysis, execution mergers and acquisitions, and other forms of financial-oriented preparation. Many inferior venture capitalists, who are best identified by their policies of standardization and generic professionalization, continue to erroneously believe that growing the revenue line converts into value creation.

Inferior venture capitalists are likely to experience problems when attempting to generate high-quality deal flow; since they may not specialize in specific industries or segments of the economy, their deal generation focus may be wide, undefined, and unprincipled. Moreover, these venture capitalists are likely to participate in deal auctions with many other inferior venture capitalists, which unduly rises entry valuation for many inferior investment opportunities. A lack of operating experience also causes problems when ascertaining superior commercial propositions, since inferior venture capitalists will likely be unable to distinguish between "lemon" investments and high-quality firms. They will furthermore have difficulty understanding true innovation, invention, and discovery, and may instead exhibit a strong propensity to pursue patent protection for investee firms' intellectual property when no such protection may actually be needed. The due diligence process is often long, cumbersome, and standardized because inferior venture capitalists are unable to focus on pointed questions, raise critical issues, or evaluate make-or-break decisions.

Again, a lack of operating experience influences the approach of inferior venture capitalists to financial contracting; they often believe that financial performance is secured through "tight" legal contracts. In reality, however, stringent legal terms and provisions may be onerous, entrepreneur-unfriendly, and more significantly, suffocate entrepreneurs' decision-making ability and operational flexibility. The focus on liquidation and other downside protections often proves useless if the investee firm underperforms or outright fails, although in these circumstances, the legal protections may offer limited safety. Inferior venture capitalists are also more likely to overpay for entry valuation.

In terms of the monitoring stage of the investment process, inferior venture capitalists are not able to provide any meaningful, noteworthy, or value-added insight into operational matters, capital budgeting considerations, project management, training and development, or mentorship. Although they may be skilled at procuring financial resources, including arranging for additional debt and equity, inferior venture capitalists will nonetheless experience significant problems with underperforming portfolio firms. This is in part because these venture capitalists are more focused on monitoring information than they are on real operational issues, margin improvement opportunities, and execution.

Finally, exits completed by inferior venture capitalists do not seem well thought out or pre-planned. There is a high propensity for pre-mature exits among these venture capitalists, although they do occasionally luck-out with the good timing of an IPO or trade sale. However, most phases of the venture capital investment process, when instituted by an inferior venture capitalist, contribute to value destruction in returns, which is demonstrated at the bottom of Table 6.2. Unfortunately, these inferior venture capitalists represent the vast majority of venture capitalists in the industry.

Venture Capital Performance: Conclusions

As an asset class, venture capital is likely to struggle to deliver the returns expected by LPs; this represents a simple continuation of the trends over the last 30 years. COVID-response, which has impacted a significant percentage of venture capital portfolio firms, will only accelerate the preexisting issues within and across the industry. The period post COVID-response has been exceedingly difficult for LPs, as they are required to make choices that are likely to influence their own net performance in the next decade. The process of analyzing returns, rebalancing existing portfolios, and mapping new strategies will also involve a serious consideration of LPs' fundamental stance on the venture capital industry.

The venture capital industry's silver lining has been superior venture capitalists, which represent up to 15% of the human resource pool in the industry. While it has been historically, and increasingly, difficult to separate inferior and superior GPs, the financial performance of portfolio firms, exits generated during difficult times, and investments made post

COVID-response will confirm and verify the unique qualities of superior GPs.

Notes

1. This quote comes from presentation by Brian H. Dovey made at the 23rd Annual Venture Capital Institute conference in Atlanta (U. S.), September 7–11, 1997. He has been a partner with Domain Associates since 1988.
2. This point was noted by Robert Olsen.
3. This observation was made by Peeyush Dalmia and colleagues.

Bibliography

Bain & Company. 2021. Global private equity report 2021. www.bain.com.

BDO. 2020. Runway to recovery: Laying the groundwork for post-COVID portfolio management and value creation. www.bdo.com.

Canderle, Sebastien. 2020. Myths of private equity performance: Part II. November 25. www.cfainstitute.org.

Dalmia, Peeyush, Vivek Pandit, Gary Pinshaw, and Gaurav Sharma. 2020. A rolling disruption: COVID-19's implications for private equity and portfolio companies. September 16. www.mckinsey.com.

eFront. 2020. Global private equity performance series 2020: An international comparison of major markets. www.efront.com.

Gompers, Paul, Will Gornall, Steven Kaplan, and Ilya A. Strebulaev. 2020. Venture capitalists and COVID-19. October. Working paper.

Hunger, David J. and Thomas L. Wheelen. 2011. *Essentials of strategic management*. Upper Saddle River: Prentice Hall.

Klonowski, Darek. 2018. *The venture capital deformation: Value destruction throughout the investment process*. New York: Palgrave Macmillan.

Kost, Danielle. 2020. COVID not slowing VC investment. November 30. www.hbs.edu.

Lee, Peter. 2020. Private equity can be the big winner from Covid-19 sell-off. April 20. www.euromoney.com.

Lino, Marc, Hubert Shen, Andrei Vorobyov, and Hao Zhou. 2020. Investing in a time of crisis. April 2. Bain & Company. www.bain.com.

MacArthur, Hugh, Graham Elton, and Brenda Rainey. 2020. The impact of Covid-19 on private equity. April 9. Bain & Company.

MacArthur, Hugh, Josh Lerner, and State Street Global Markets. 2020. Public vs. private equity returns: Is PE losing its advantage? February 24. Bain & Company.

Morris, Peter and Ludovic Phalippou. 2020. Thirty years after Jensen's prediction: Is private equity a superior form of ownership? *Oxford Review of Economic Policy*, 36: 291–313.

Mulcahy, Diane, Bill Weeks, and Harold S. Bradley. *We have met the enemy...and it is us: Lessons from twenty years of the Kauffman Foundation's investments in venture capital funds and the triumph of hope over experience*. Washington: Ewing Marion Kauffman Foundation. May 2012.

Murgatroyd, Grant. 2020. Private equity looks to capitalize on post-COVID economic recovery. September. www.financierworld.com.

Nesvold, Peter. 2020. The emperor has no clothes? Are investors misinformed about private equity returns? July 7. www.forbes.com.

Olsen, Robert. 2020. Post-COVID private equity: Thriving in a bifurcated world of opportunity. September. Deloitte.

Phalippou, Ludovic. 2020. An inconvenient fact: Private equity returns & billionaire factory. Oxford. July 15. Working paper.

Porter, Michael. 1998. *Competitive strategy: Techniques for analyzing industries and competitors*. New York: The Free Press.

Robertson, Benjamin. 2020. How Covid took niche private equity deals mainstream. February 6. www.bloomberg.com.

Skormas, Ewa and Larisa Whitmore. 2020. The impact of the COVID-19 pandemic on the private equity market. September 15. www.spglobal.com.

Sylla, Firmin. 2020. Analysis: Private equity in the aftermath of Covid-19. October 10. www.leadersleague.com.

PART III

Entrepreneurship Redefined Post Covid-Response

CHAPTER 7

COVID-Response and Entrepreneurship in Crisis

Traditional Entrepreneurship Defined

Entrepreneurship may be defined as a process wherein entrepreneurs convert a new or existing idea into a business venture. Although new business formation is often highlighted as a main objective, entrepreneurship also involves overseeing the journey of the entrepreneurial venture through the subsequent stages of its development. Therefore, entrepreneurship is a process of aggregating and assembling available resources for the purpose of pursuing opportunities available in the marketplace. Of course, the acceptance of various types of risks and failures, in exchange for potentially extraordinary rewards, is inherent to entrepreneurial development.

And yet, many entrepreneurs do not develop their ventures for financial rewards, power, or prestige; instead, many are driven by an altruistic desire to develop products or services that can change the world, alter the future of humanity in some meaningful fashion, address a basic yet currently unresolved problem, or optimize a preexisting method, process, or product. For the majority of entrepreneurs, this inner aspiration may come from a profound personal experience or from participating in a life changing event, although there are of course alternate drivers responsible for entrepreneurial actions. In these instances, desire can entice the entrepreneur's intellect and completely consume their heart, mind, and soul. Another critical component of true entrepreneurial development is

D. Klonowski, *Venture Capital Redefined*,
https://doi.org/10.1007/978-3-030-83387-9_7

passion, which may be defined as high-intensity and long-term feelings that are expressive of the entrepreneur and their persona, personality, and identity. A further critical component of entrepreneurial behavior may relate to the entrepreneur's personal values, which can include respect, freedom, friendship, honesty, courage, love, empathy, and religious orientation.

Evidence suggests that these values, when understood in context of each other, influence entrepreneurs' approach to business and thus their analysis, decision-making, problem solving, planning, and judgment abilities. These values frequently become an important part of the organizational fabric of the entrepreneurial venture and are manifested in its policies, procedures, processes, and mechanisms. In combination, meaning, passion, and values may translate into strong, clear, and persuasive personal goals, visions, and missions, which may act as powerful motivators of persistent business implementation and execution; this, in turn, may convert into entrepreneurial value creation and perpetuation. These three inner components of entrepreneurial behavior may also serve as foundational anchors for entrepreneurs during moments of difficulty, turbulence, stress, underperformance, self-doubt, or even failure. By enhancing the creativity, enthusiasm, persistence, motivation, and dedication of the entrepreneur, the formidable combination of meaning, passion, and values can even augment business performance.

However, while the main objective of most entrepreneurs is not monetary in nature, entrepreneurial firms nevertheless pursue, and understand the importance of, entrepreneurial value creation. The audacity of this pursuit depends on the entrepreneur's assumed level of risk, the types of rewards sought from the venture, the ease of access to finance, management style, the overall business objectives, and other critical circumstances. Differences in attitudes, approaches, and orientations toward these important components of entrepreneurial development are ultimately responsible for diverse curvatures of value creation, which will be discussed in more detail later in this chapter.

Entrepreneurship also involves the progression of a firm through distinct phases of development, which normally include five key stages: opportunity generation and evaluation, business planning and formation, resource procurement, rollout, and maturity. This process is easily recognizable as similar in nature and character to the five stages of the venture capital investment process. Many of these steps occur sequentially in entrepreneurial firms, although they may periodically overlap. Once an attractive market opportunity has been identified, the entrepreneur moves to the evaluation stage, wherein they aim to confirm the underlying feasibility of the entrepreneurial venture through formal and informal investigative and analytical means and processes. In the second step, the entrepreneur begins to translate their vision, ideas, and thought processes into a tangible business plan that will capture all operational components of the newly created business. This preparatory stage will also require a decision to be made regarding an appropriate legal structure for the business, which includes the consideration of various issues related to personal and business liability, capital requirements, financing, taxation, the types of financiers anticipated in the venture, and so on.

Following the two initial stages of planning and background analysis, the entrepreneur attempts to procure critical resources in the form of financial, human, technological, production, distribution, promotional, and other necessary operational components. Once complete, the next step in entrepreneurial development focuses on the execution and implementation of the preconceived business plan. At this stage of new venture development, the key objective is to prove the viability of the business model, as well as the venture's products and services, through its real-world application. If the business model is validated and proves to be successful on a smaller scale, the entrepreneur can then extend the proven business model and increase the scale of operations; this represents the exciting, but also nerve-wrecking, rollout and growth stage of the venture. In its final stage, known as business maturity, the venture may slow down, and revenue, profits, and cash flow will begin to level off as the venture reaches its natural plateau. Of course, to avoid maturation and business plateau, the entrepreneurial firm can re-invent itself by upgrading its products and services, developing new markets, or expanding into other product areas, among other solutions.

Entrepreneurs are normally optimistic to the point where they are excessively over-confident in their ability to succeed in business. For example, a common belief entrepreneurs hold is that if they successfully navigated through difficult situations in the past, they would continue to be successful in the future by implementing the same tried and tested solutions. However, this often proves to be an erroneous belief as there is no guarantee that measures effectively instituted in the past can assure future success. It is important to understand that different ventures require various types of efforts, initiatives, commitments, resources, skills, capabilities, and even education, to reach higher levels of development, which may be difficult for the entrepreneur to imagine. Furthermore, contrary to what entrepreneurs generally believe, research confirms that they do not always learn from past mistakes and poor judgment. Thus, entrepreneurship can be addictive because it emphasizes personal freedom in addition to promoting self-testing, chasing success, and engaging in above-average risk taking.

Finally, entrepreneurship plays a key role in shaping national economies and enhancing economic growth for a number of reasons, the first of which being that about six out of every ten jobs are created by the small business sector. As noted in Chapter 2, the broadly defined small and medium-sized enterprise (SME) sector is responsible for the majority of national private sector employment and accounts for about half of the global economy. Secondly, the entrepreneurial sector is often at the forefront of invention and innovation, thereby contributing to transformations not only in traditional industries, but also in the high technology sectors of the economy. These significant developments, in which existing patterns of production, operation, promotion, and distribution are re-imagined and re-designed, occur through creativity, imagination, and vision. The entrepreneurial sector is also frequently regarded as the most flexible and agile part of the economy because it is capable of quickly pivoting in new directions, re-directing capital and human resources toward new opportunities, and enacting necessary operational adjustments. In so doing, the entrepreneurial sector is believed to offset, and diminish the amplitude of, economic declines. Furthermore, successful business owners perpetuate entrepreneurship on a broader scale, as, over time, successful entrepreneurs may become role models for other entrepreneurs or active financial investors themselves. By developing a portfolio of their own entrepreneurial firms, successful entrepreneurs may initiate a "snow-ball" effect and cultivate a robust culture of new business creation. Lastly, the entrepreneurial sector is important because it contributes to the development of an active, independent, and well prospering middle class.

Entrepreneurship in the Age of Covid-Response

COVID-response has affected both the supply and demand side of economic development. On the supply side, there has been disruption to global supply chains, the supply of labor (which may have been dislocated due to restrictions, illness, and other reasons), and production capability (due to shortages of raw materials). The demand for products and services has similarly been reduced due to high unemployment and an increase in precarious employment, lower family incomes, declining wages, cash hoarding, and other measures which reduced overall consumption in the economy.

It is obvious that economic development post COVID-response is in critical need of vibrant, flourishing, and lively entrepreneurism. The entrepreneurial engine must be re-ignited for job creation, especially for the youngest segment of the population, which will aid in restarting the economy. Unfortunately, however, these processes are not occurring. Individuals who may have been thinking about starting a business for the first time may be rejecting such considerations in light of the currently unstable economic environment. Similarly, business owners who have recently started their entrepreneurial ventures may be convinced to cut their losses and move on to find another, perhaps more secure and stable, source of income. Furthermore, serial entrepreneurs who have previously taken successful, measured risks are now more selective and cautious with both their existing and new ventures. Surveys and business registration data also confirm this aversion to entrepreneurism, which supports the idea that new business formation is likely to suffer for the foreseeable future.

As stated in Chapter 2, the plethora of public restrictions has created significant turbulence in the entrepreneurial sector, especially with respect to smaller firms. These ventures have been disproportionately affected due to their limited operational resources (i.e., less personnel, limited network of contacts, small supplier base, and fewer customers), restricted financial protections (i.e., less cash, liquid short-term assets, limited chances to generate new revenue streams, restricted lines of credit, and reduced borrowing options), and constrained strategic management capabilities (i.e., inability to develop revised business plans quickly because of smaller human resources). However, different segments of the economy were impacted to varying degrees; for example, entrepreneurial firms operating in retail, hospitality, accommodations, food services, arts and entertainment, leisure, and recreation have been severely affected. Clear beneficiaries from COVID-response were major retail outlets, social media firms, and online shopping operators. Nonetheless, one of the most challenging aspects of COVID-response for firms was the speed and strictness of public restrictions, which effectively turned previous entrepreneurial planning, preparation, and strategizing upside-down, making it obsolete and irrelevant. It is thus evident that the impact of COVID-response is overwhelmingly detrimental to entrepreneurship on a global scale.

There are at least five areas that COVID-response has directly or indirectly impacted in the entrepreneurial ecosystem, with the first major effect being a severe decline, or even complete loss, of revenue. Revenue decline was inversely related to the size of the business, which is supported by research that has found revenue declined by more than 50% for smaller firms and about 30% for more sizeable ventures. These declines reflected smaller firms' inability to pay for capital expenditures, such as the development of new revenue streams or an online presence. There has also been a general decline in generating business leads, finding new customers, and retaining existing customers. Secondly, entrepreneurial firms have struggled to cover their fixed financial obligations, including, but not limited to, rent, mortgage payments, utilities, and personnel. While many entrepreneurial firms initially aimed to maintain staffing levels by shifting personnel between different parts of the organization, 30 to 40% of firms eventually resorted to layoffs.

The combination of both declining revenues and fixed obligations has resulted in negatively impacted profitability and cash flow generating abilities. The old entrepreneurial adage, namely that revenue falls faster than the firm's ability to reduce cost, has proven true under post COVID-response circumstances. In response, many firms were forced to engage in liquidity-based actions, which may have included selling inventory at reduced prices, disposing "unnecessary" assets, reducing wages and cutting work hours, re-prioritizing capital expenditure projects, and promoting new uses of existing products and services; these actions aimed to extend entrepreneurial firms' cash runways (i.e., the amount of time the firm is able to use its cash). If necessary, many entrepreneurs likely resorted to using personal savings and remortgaging their family assets (i.e., houses and property). During the time of COVID-response, any action related to cash preservation has been critical because it granted an opportunity to extend the life of the venture.

A fourth area that COVID-response has impacted in a major way was the redefinition or even destruction of existing business models and changed business economics for existing operations. Due to their limited protection against external shocks, business survival and the revision of business models became critical to the SME sector. Finally, after the implementation of public restrictive measures, many entrepreneurs exhausted their cash resources and completely lost any "sweat equity" built up over the years. Other entrepreneurs incurred substantial losses in business value.

Re-Evaluation of the Fundamentals for Entrepreneurial Success

Widespread research has been conducted on the critical importance of various financial and non-financial factors that contribute to the overall success of entrepreneurial firms. With regard to the financial factors that affect entrepreneurial firms, studies confirm that access to finance may be critical to build and perpetuate the entrepreneurial value creation process. In terms of non-financial matters, however, no uniform model of entrepreneurial success has been established because studies have developed a wide range of opposing conclusions on the importance of various internal and external factors. As an example, some studies have suggested that industry knowledge is critical to entrepreneurial success, while others alluded to the fact that such knowledge may actually be an impediment to the development of innovative products and services. Furthermore, certain sources indicate that entrepreneurs are risk takers, which is in opposition to the conclusions of other investigations that have identified entrepreneurs as risk averse and operating only with the assurance of background knowledge.

While it may be difficult to precisely pinpoint the key factors behind entrepreneurial success, academic research and practice identify six major interrelated components that appear to be critical to entrepreneurial success; these factors include market size and growth rates, the management team and founding entrepreneur, market share and competitive dynamics, mode of operation (i.e., business model), money management (i.e., cash flow management), and profitability (i.e., margins). These components can also be divided into two main categories, namely internal and external factors. In terms of external factors, the entrepreneur may have limited influence over business cycles and their length, the level of interest rates and inflation, and changes in consumer spending patterns and habits. On the other hand, the firm can influence the design of its products and services, the motivation of the management team and employees, and the integration of the right business model. Furthermore, the firm can also decide how to operate the business on a daily basis and the best method to prioritize cash spending.

Rather than providing detailed explanations of these six critical success factors, the objective in this section of the chapter is to identify how these critical components have changed in the period post COVID-response when compared to pre COVID-response trends (see Table 7.1 for a brief summary).

The market has traditionally been recognized as one of the major contributors to entrepreneurial success or failure. Entrepreneurs intuitively understand that it is relatively easy to succeed in market conditions where demand is significant and rapidly growing, competitive pressures are low, market entry barriers are high, and limited dominant players exist. Of course, it is possible to succeed in seemingly unattractive segments of the economy as well. Although entrepreneurs normally struggle to determine key market statistics, dynamics, and growth rates, the post COVID-response period has magnified these difficulties and created significant misunderstanding about demand, market size, and future growth rates. Additionally, entrepreneurs do not have the benefit of being able to depend on historical trends since these numbers are no longer reliable.

Beyond market considerations, business owners are also not certain about consumers and their adjusted habits, perceptions, choices, preferences, requirements, and senilities. As observed in Chapter 4, research confirms significant shifts in consumer behavior post COVID-response. One of the main consumer considerations may be price because of significant downward pressures on family incomes, wages, and existing debt obligations. This, in turn, can negatively impact available consumer choices as manufacturers and service providers may limit manufacturing and instead deliver higher quality and more expensive products and services. The challenges in properly sizing up market demand, understanding growth rates, and ascertaining changes to consumer behavior are likely to create difficulties for entrepreneurs in product and service development, operational planning, and financial forecasting. Another critical component related to uncertain market demand is broad-based interference from the state, which developed a wide range of restrictions and limitations that have proven damaging to the entrepreneurial ecosystem. While entrepreneurs are normally capable of navigating through different state actions and regulations with ease, they have not experienced state interference at such a heightened degree before, resulting in the ultimate destruction of many entrepreneurial firms.

The ideas and concepts surrounding decisions regarding what products and services to develop, which markets or market niches to pursue,

Table 7.1 Redefinition of the key components of entrepreneurial success

	Longitudinal perspectives	
	Pre COVID-response	*Post COVID-response*
Market size and growth rates	• Relative ease in determination of market size; verifiable market demand • External research can assist in verifying market and competitive dynamics • Firms can define consumer purchase preferences, decision criteria, and price consideration • Relative market stability in terms of growth patterns	• Market size difficult to determine • Growth rates uncertain • Difficulty in predicting business growth trajectory • Disruption to value creation due to unstable sales • Poor chances of new venture formation due to multiple uncertainties and risks • Consumer habits uncertain; they evolve in unexpected ways • Price considerations as critical consumer criteria • Business failure due to uncertainty about market demand • State interference leads to lower market demand and business failure

(continued)

Table 7.1 (continued)

	Longitudinal perspectives	
	Pre COVID-response	*Post COVID-response*
Founder & management team	• Strong management team critical to business success • Stability of management assures achievement of long-term goals • Employee retention, low staff turnover, and proper inventive structures contribute to revenue growth and sustained profitability • Long-term employment as the hallmark of successful firms • Stability of management and key personnel	• Problems in developing complete management teams; hiring the right people may be more challenging • Inability to retain key members of the management team due to operational disruptions • Layoffs and human resource disruptions prevent firms from returning to normal operations • Work interruptions create challenges for training, development, and mentorship • Low morale, poor teamwork, and a lack of co-operation • Inability to develop incentive performance targets • Increase in precarious employment discourages workforce commitment

	Longitudinal perspectives	
	Pre COVID-response	*Post COVID-response*
Market share & competition	• Sound business strategy critical to market success • Most common strategies relate to cost leadership and differentiation • Benchmarks for successful operations available • Opportunities for new firms to successful enter most industries	• Strong potential for market consolidation • Sustained emergence of monopolists • Declining and disrupted markets create extraordinary pressures on profitability and sustainability • Competitive advantage may be more difficult to develop • More firms are likely to compete on the basis of cost leadership; differentiation may be more difficult to achieve • Potential for monopolization of many industries due to elimination of existing competitors
Mode of operation	• Building and perfecting the right business model takes time • Limited innovations to existing business models • Disruptive technologies may change usual modes of operations; this does not occur rapidly or often • Traditional business models (i.e., brick-and-mortar) and modes of operation are important	• Adjustments to business models may not prove optimal; significant additional costs may reduce profitability • Changing business models is costly • Quick adjustments to business models may lead to failure • Disruption of existing business models may lead to massive dislocation of existing firms • Excessive digitalization of business models and modes of delivery of products and services

(continued)

Table 7.1 (continued)

	Longitudinal perspectives	
	Pre COVID-response	*Post COVID-response*
Money management	• Stability and repeatability of cash flow for more mature firms; predictable liquidity • Challenging cash flow management for young firms • Cash shortages can be managed due to revenue stability and repeatability • Various alternatives in access to finance; additional alternatives available for more developed firms • Access to external finance can easily smooth out cash flow challenges	• Unpredictable demand causes significant cash flow issues • Cash flow management (especially working capital control) becomes difficult, but critical to business survival • Difficult access to finance • Cash flow problems lead to more business failure • Limits to business growth due to poor access to finance • Disruption to value creation • Business fragility and instability due to liquidity problems • Difficult access to finance may thwart business growth • Cash flow problems may decrease business valuation
Profitability	• Predictable profitability for industries • Limited variance in profitability from year-to-year • A clear path from losses to profit normally exists for entrepreneurial firms	• Uncertain profitability due to fluctuating demand and unpredictable cost structure • Longer periods of sustained losses may discourage business formation, development, and growth • Inability for entrepreneurs to engage in long-term planning • Losses negatively impact business valuation

what optimal business model to adopt, and how to design and implement a strong competitive strategy, are all generated by people. Thus, the presence of a management team comprised of well-trained, creative, and innovative members with complementary skill sets is a vital component of business success. Of course, superior management teams are not self-built and are instead the result of a visionary leader who has the foresight to build powerful internal systems, long-lasting organizational structures, and strong human resources that can generate repeatable market and financial results. However, the general disruptions to entrepreneurial firms caused by COVID-response, including temporary closures, significant slowdowns in business operations, and multiple restrictions and limitations, have not created conditions conducive to the development of stable management teams and key personnel in production, marketing and sales, supply chain management, or other functional departments. In simple terms, talented managers and non-managerial personnel may not respond well to frequent layoffs, on/off work schedules, and other employment disruptions during periods of uncertain family incomes and pressures to repay family debt. While business owners are likely unable to invest in talent recruitment and retention post COVID-response, capable managers and personnel may be looking for the income stability and employment certainty that entrepreneurial firms are unfortunately no longer able to offer. These managers and personnel may instead gravitate toward employment in the public sector or large corporations, thereby entirely omitting entrepreneurial ventures from consideration.

Such disruptions may create perpetual problems for business owners in retaining the managerial cadre and personnel as the business seeks to return to normal operations. Furthermore, continued disruptions in business continuity, periods of layoffs and rehires (associated with an increase in precarious employment), and state interference may contribute to low employee morale, the destruction of teamwork and positive team dynamics (due to fear of contagion), the devastation of internal culture (developed over a long period of time), a lack of personal commitment to the firm, and a general reduction in performance. On an individual level, the stress caused by COVID-response, as well as a concern for oneself, the immediate household, and more distant family members is another way in which the quality of employee performance can be affected. Operational disruptions are also likely to halt training, development, and mentorship programs, which are critical components in the development of entrepreneurial firms. Frequent interruptions can also be damaging to normal hiring processes in which the "right people", as opposed to suboptimal individuals, are properly evaluated and employed. The ability to appraise and reward performance has similarly been stilted by COVID-response because limited reference points, such as budgets, operational plans, and marketing targets, are difficult to establish.

Market share, which is the single most important figure in marketing because it illuminates the firm's performance relative to its competitors, describes the firm's competitive stance in the marketplace when expressed in absolute terms. Market share is calculated by dividing the firm's revenue by the total estimated market value (i.e., revenue for all firms competing in a specific segment of the market), which captures the percentage of the total market which the firm's products or services command. It is evident that COVID-response, which has been grounded in restrictions, limitations, bans, mandates, and wide-ranging public orders, is likely to continue the process of temporarily or permanently eliminating smaller entrepreneurial firms from the marketplace; this is already borne out in research. However, while COVID-response has been predominantly destructive to smaller market players, it has benefitted large retail operations, online commerce, and other sectors of the economy.

Although there is not yet confirmation of the ensuing market consolidations likely occurring in many segments of the economy, the fact that the revenue of smaller firms declined more significantly than that of larger firms may serve as an indirect validation of the loss of smaller competitors' market shares. If continued in the foreseeable future, this process would lead to a massive wave of consolidations in various segments of the economy, thereby allowing strong and unchallenged market leaders or monopolists to either emerge or further solidify their already strong market positions. This would also result in massive closures within the SME sector. The persistent entrenchment of monopolists would place further pressure on existing participants, slowly and deliberately leading to their elimination from competition, in addition to acting as an effective deterrent to new potential entrants. Perpetual consolidations will also provide an advantage to larger corporations due to economies of scale. Finally, and as already noted, price is likely to emerge as one of the permanent features of competition in the marketplace, at least until such time that the "unwanted" competition is eliminated.

It is commonly understood that securing a sustainable competitive advantage in the marketplace is grounded in a firm's unique business model or mode of operations, which may be defined as a framework that the firm employs to conduct its business processes and operations. This business model functions as the firm's internal architecture to describe the complexities of the business, the different aspects that must cooperate to create a uniform unit, and how each of these segments ultimately contribute to profitability, cash generation, and value creation. However, business models may change and evolve; it often takes a significant number of years for the firm to perfect its mode of operation. The perpetual improvement of the business model is normally achieved through a continuous process of operational maneuvering, modification, re-adjustment, and benchmarking.

There is no doubt that COVID-response has either completely destroyed, or at the very least significantly amended, existing business models in many industries. While this "creative destruction" is often romanticized by academic literature, it can lead to the destruction of many firms and the possible emergence of only a few new ones. As noted continually throughout this book, the segments of the economy most affected by COVID-response have been the retail, hospitality, and entertainment sectors, to name a few. These segments were given weeks or even days to alter the mode of operations that they may honed to perfection over a number of years, which is a definitively unrealistic expectation. In fact, the severity and speed with which COVID-response measures were enacted left many entrepreneurial firms with no true opportunity to adjust their operations.

While the majority of firms did attempt to adjust their operations, they often lacked the financial, operational, technological, and human resources to affect the necessary changes. Some firms did successfully shift their modes of operations (i.e., to online ordering, curb-side pickups, and delivery), only to realize that the business model they created overnight may not be sustainable even in the medium-term. Thus, entrepreneurs made the quick decision, which in some cases was the only viable choice, to make costly adjustments to their modes of operation that may actually lead to their ultimate demise and outright failure in the long-term. The annihilation of existing business models and structures (along with associated financial challenges) due to COVID-response may be the most critical reason for future failure of entrepreneurial firms on a massive scale. The shift in existing modes of operation to digitization, which is frequently promoted by the media and various experts as a viable and preferred solution for service and product delivery, may not work for the many firms that rely on in-person contact, are labor-intensive, and thus completely unsuitable for digitization. Moreover, digitization may not be the form of business that entrepreneurs envisaged when setting up their ventures.

Another critical component to the success of entrepreneurial firms, which is responsible for a business's survival, development, and perpetuation, is money (or cash flow) management. Cash is the lifeline of any entrepreneurial venture, although the most significant aspect of cash flow is working capital (i.e., management of inventory, accounts receivable, and accounts payable). Cash flow, which is defined as the flow of cash into and out of the firm, also involves the firm's capital expenditure program (i.e., acquisition of machinery, equipment, land, and intangible assets) and the firm's ability to procure external finance (i.e., forms of debt or equity). By capturing whether the firm is adding to its cash resources or eroding them, cash flow is thereby the most comprehensive measure of the management team's ability to manage the business. Although cash flow was a perpetual issue for smaller firms pre COVID-response (i.e., small firms struggle in this area by definition), many firms would normally develop methods to achieve stability and repeatability in cash flow over time; entrepreneurs understood temporary cash flow interruptions and, barring unexpected circumstances, could manage liquidity issues. Management of cash flow is possible when entrepreneurs can rely on relative stability of incoming revenue even if available cash resources can only cover a few weeks or months of expenses.

Of course, cash flow management has become fundamentally more difficult post COVID-response because entrepreneurs must contend with both increased uncertainty regarding the future of the venture and cash shortages for longer periods of time. Declining revenue and fixed costs have pushed many entrepreneurial firms to the brink of bankruptcy due to cash flow difficulties and liquidity challenges. Research from the United States (U.S.), for example, confirms that the vast majority of small business owners had cash resources equal to less than two months of expenses in the period post COVID-response. Therefore, it is understandable that many entrepreneurs resorted to fallback tactics in desperation, including arranging or extending new debt facilities, seeking equity contributions from any willing partners, drawing on personal savings and lines of credit, selling business assets, and mortgaging personal assets. Under COVID-response conditions, the management of working capital became even more critical as firms required credit term extensions to generate revenue at a time when suppliers became increasingly unwilling to compromise on financial terms. Working capital management was especially problematic for retailers, and particularly for SME manufacturers, because they normally tie up significant cash in inventory. Due to the combination of seasonal inventory and periods of increased restrictions, and thus limited sales, in specific parts of the year, retailers were stuck with unsold inventory for a full year without the ability to achieve liquidity. In such cases, one of the only options was to sell inventory at a significant discount. Financial institutions have also been hoarding cash because they have experienced their own difficulties with underperforming portfolios of business loans. Therefore, the "valley of death" (i.e., the divergence between profits and cash flow) became an even more formidable financial trap to many entrepreneurial firms post COVID-response.

The final critical factor to entrepreneurial success is profitability (i.e., profit margins), which demonstrates the relationship between revenue and cost. Expressed as a percentage of revenue, this financial measure illustrates the efficiency with which the management team manages the venture. The most common measures of profitability are gross profit margins, operating profit margins or EBIT (earnings before interest and taxes), EBITDA (earnings before interest, taxes, depreciation, and amortization), and net profit margins. Evidence suggests that profitability and margins have declined in a wide range of industries and segments of the economy post COVID-response. The most significant profitability declines occurred in sectors related to real estate, metals and mining, gas distribution, entertainment, trucking, and various retail operations.[1] Furthermore, many segments were also forced to incur the additional costs of complying with safety protocols, hygiene requirements, plexiglass installations, and individual safety protection (i.e., masks, gloves, outfits, face shields), among other expenses; these operational modifications and changes were substantial expenditures for the SME sector in particular, which already struggled financially. Restaurant operators, for example, had to incur the additional costs of packaging while forgoing the sale of high profit margins such as entrées, desserts, and alcohol. At the same time that these alterations were being implemented to safely accommodate in-person customers, firms were required to limit the number of patrons on premises, which further exacerbated problems with profitability.

In addition to these challenges, entrepreneurs will likely experience difficulty in gauging the efficiency with which they could operate their ventures, as even prior to COVID-response nearly a third of firms operated at a loss or broke-even. Thus, firms were already vulnerable to any external shocks, additional risks, and uncertainties; their balance sheet did not have any flexibility in terms of extra financial resources. Cash flow management with continued losses requires significant mental effort from business owners because it can be discouraging. Losses are similarly not well tolerated by financial institutions and banks. Moreover, issues with continuous operational uncertainties caused by revenue generation and cost structure are also likely to create problems with long-term financial planning, budgeting, and strategizing. Of course, sustained low margins at EBIT (earnings before interest, and taxes) and EBITDA (earnings before interest, taxes, depreciation, and amortization) levels would negatively impact business valuation.

However, despite the role of these different components in the success of an entrepreneurial venture, an important distinction should be made between net profit and cash flow. While the firm can be profitable, it can become bankrupt if it does not have sufficient cash. In this case, an increase in cash needs for working capital purposes may arise from the necessity of supporting rapidly growing revenue. On the other hand, the firm could be operating at a loss but manage its cash in such a manner that it can survive for long periods of time. This divergence between growing net profit and decreasing cash flow, which tricks entrepreneurs into a false sense of financial security, is called a liquidity trap.

Magnification of Entrepreneurial Risks: The State

Business risk refers to the uncertainty which the entrepreneurial firm has with regard to various facets of its operations. In simple terms, the more uncertainty there is about aspects of the operation, the more business risk the firm faces. Historically, entrepreneurs were cognizant of the different levels of risk they assumed when embarking on an entrepreneurial venture and were able to devise some, albeit often imperfect, protections against these risks. While some risks could be expected, such as facing more formidable competition, experiencing financial difficulties, or losing major accounts, key clients, or essential personnel, entrepreneurs could count on a relatively stable external environment. Similarly, entrepreneurs could also rely on the stability of decisions made by the political system and apparatus, the relative constancy of taxes (with some possibility of improvement under different political regimes), the reliability of business laws and regulations, and the permanence of business models (which, of course, could be disrupted with new technologies, but its slow implementation process allowed entrepreneurs time to react). However, the stability of the external environment in which entrepreneurial firms operate has been severely disrupted post COVID-response. Under state restrictions, bans, and limitations, entrepreneurs are likely to face continuous, unpredictable, and evolving levels of external risks that initiate difficult predicaments on a wide range of operational and financial fronts.

One of the most fundamental question marks for entrepreneurs relates to how the decisions made by local politicians, municipal or county authorities, and the state will impact their ventures. Evidence from the so-called second and third waves of the coronavirus confirms that public authorities and political leaders have enacted policies and restrictions without proper consideration of the impact these decisions have on the entrepreneurial ecosystem, or society at large. In fact, these actions are often taken without the consideration of a proper cost/benefit analysis or understanding of potential long-term economic and human consequences. It is therefore clear that post COVID-response, the state is quickly emerging as one of the most unstable components of the external environment for entrepreneurial firms, who, as observed by many, do not need more subsidies or public assistance programs; they need sales. Entrepreneurs are unable to survive subsequent closures since they have already operated in the near loss territory prior to COVID-response, as many barely recovered from the 2008 financial crisis.

State decisions have evidently "broken the back" of entrepreneurialism in the majority of countries around the globe, with some notable regional exceptions (for instance, in some U.S. states). Not only are existing entrepreneurs impacted, but so are business owners of the future; for example, evidence from Canada confirms that most individuals do not intend to start a business. This propensity toward anti-entrepreneurialism is likely to be sustained in the long-term, leaving entrepreneurial firms more fragile and unstable than ever. Most critically, they can no longer rely on a stable migration from small to medium-sized enterprises. This migratory pattern, which has been one of the focal points of the entrepreneurial ecosystem, appears to be completely dislocated.

Disruption of Relations in the Entrepreneurial Ecosystem

As mentioned in Chapter 2, relations are critical in business, and there are numerous important relationships within the entrepreneurial ecosystem. Significantly, evidence confirms that relationships have changed post COVID-response for the majority of firms.

The first and most important relationship for entrepreneurs is the customer, and in the experience of many entrepreneurial firms post COVID-response, customer interactions have been disrupted or even completely severed. For instance, entrepreneurial firms within some segments of the economy have been required by the state or local authorities to disengage with customers. This disruption is likely to negatively affect customer relations, particularly in the case of relationships that have been nurtured over a long period of time. In the short-term, such a disconnect between the firm and its customers may only lead to revenue decline. In the long-term, however, a lack of regular interaction may result in a misunderstanding of the customer's needs, preferences, and habits, which, in turn, can translate into a loss of the customer's loyalty, commitment, and locality. These consequences can lead to consumer shifts toward large corporations (which may be perceived as more stable and reliable), thus resulting in revenue loss and outright business failure. Although some entrepreneurs have maintained a level of proximity to customers via teleconferencing, the efficacy of this mode of communication is still unclear.

The next critical interaction for entrepreneurs is valuable communication and the formation of positive relationships with the members of their management team and personnel. In cases of labor-intensive industries (i.e., manufacturing, healthcare, retail, and so on), normal operational routines and employee engagement were profoundly impacted by COVID-response; these limitations are likely to negatively influence teamwork, innovation, problem solving, and decision-making. A lack of in-person communication may also influence managers' and senior personnel's ability to mentor new employees. Furthermore, offsite interactions (i.e., picnics, drinks, sporting events, charity work, voluntarism, and informal gatherings) were limited due to fear of contagion, which is especially disastrous for entrepreneurial firms that strive to develop a family-like atmosphere in their business.

In situations where offsite work was practical (perhaps in more white-collar sectors of the economy, but also in some other labor-intensive services that can be done from home), employees either chose or were encouraged to pursue work-from-home arrangements. However, engagement with online modes of operation often required a significant redesign of workflow procedures, management processes, and quality control structures; it is unclear whether these arrangements are proving successful. Although this shift required a moderate investment to upgrade technological infrastructure, Internet services, and teleconferencing services, online work nevertheless became the new model of managing operations, liaising with customers, and interacting with employees for many entrepreneurial firms. No matter whether employment was blue-collar or white-collar, entrepreneurs had to navigate through new ways of communication to preserve employee morale and to maintain active workplace engagement. Work-from-home arrangements undoubtedly have both advantages and disadvantages, but the key questions surrounding this shift to online relations relate to the impact of such measures on work ethic, creativity, innovation, and financial performance.

Entrepreneurs' relationships with suppliers have also been impacted, primarily because supply chain management has been one of the areas most affected by COVID-response for both small and large firms. Generally, the disruption of global supply chains has led to severe interference in manufacturing processes and product distribution. Some segments of the economy were less affected since they relied on local supply chain structures, while other segments, which relied on offshore supplier arrangements and needed to obtain deliveries by sea, air, and road, were greatly disturbed. Although there is some evidence of increased flexibility in supplier relationships, there is also confirmation of significant changes to supplier arrangements. Therefore, evidence suggests that in order to maintain production, it was necessary for about one-quarter of firms to change their suppliers; it is unclear whether these arrangements would be as effective, productive, and profitable as past contracts. The development of new and effective relationships between entrepreneurs and suppliers is also likely to take a significant period of time.

Lastly, entrepreneurs interact with various capital providers, which can include financial institutions (i.e., banks and credit unions), equity investors (i.e., individual investors, institutional investors, and business angels), and other types of financiers (i.e., family-and-friends, crowdfunding, state support programs, and incubators). There is evidence to indicate that post COVID-response, these suppliers of capital insist on more frequent updates and conference calls to cover operational, financial, and market performance issues to compensate for a lack of in-person meetings. While nurturing existing relations may be possible over online platforms, establishing new relations may be more difficult with online interactions.

Changes to Entrepreneurial Value Creation

One of the key processes in entrepreneurial development is value creation; although value creation may be a quick process for some entrepreneurs, for others it represents a more protracted, measured, and calibrated activity. With respect to the dynamics of value creation, variable value creation patterns may be observed in cases of different entrepreneurial profile types, including the "average" entrepreneur, the family-oriented entrepreneur, the female entrepreneur, and the serial entrepreneur.

Figure 7.1 illustrates a comparison between the different patterns of value creation with regard to pre and post COVID-response situations. The curvature of value creation can be divided into three separate phases, namely value uncertainty, value development, and value perpetuation. As Fig. 7.1 outlines, value creation does not occur from the moment of new business formation because there is an initial period of uncertainty that can be characterized by excessive business risks, operational challenges, complications in access to finance, constant cash "starvation", staffing problems, and incomplete management teams. The extent of these issues can be severe, although any one of them alone can be detrimental to business survival and continuation. In the second phase of value creation (i.e., value development), the entrepreneurial venture has been able to properly establish its business model and begins to "mushroom" its development. This phase is characterized by a more stable and loyal customer base, a distinct competitive position, improved product and service offerings, increased commitment to capital expenditure, a more complete management team, a stable personnel base, increasing profitability, steady cash flow, and commitment to future growth. Of course, these features describe the idealized and best-case scenario of value development.

In the pre COVID-response period, entrepreneurs were allowed the opportunity to embark on a mission of systematic value creation. Thus, many entrepreneurs initiated their ventures with the development of a solid management team (although numerous firms developed their teams over time), the establishment of superb organizational structures and

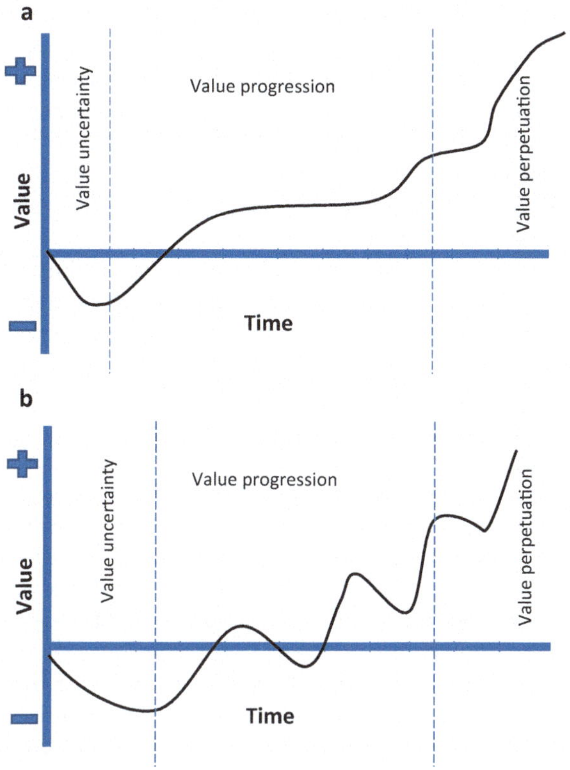

Fig. 7.1 Value creation in the entrepreneurial venture (**a**). Value creation pre COVID-response (**b**). Value creation post COVID-response (*Source* Developed on the basis of Klonowski [2018])

internal architecture, and a focus on a unique part of the market or market niche. While both young and even more mature entrepreneurial firms struggled to access capital, there were multiple alternatives, such as various "bootstrapping" techniques, that could be pursued in the pre COVID-response business environment to allow for the continual development of the venture. Additionally, the stability of market demand allowed entrepreneurs to focus on long-term innovation and experimentation with products and services in order to obtain the right commercial mix of value and quality for their customers, as well as mushrooming on the periphery of their commercial propositions. Thus, in pre COVID-response conditions, entrepreneurial firms aimed to balance the goals of growth, profit, cash flow, and value generation; external means of expansion (i.e., growth by mergers and acquisitions) were generally avoided as preference was instead given to internal growth.

The generalized depiction of the curvature of value creation pre COVID-response is depicted in Fig. 7.1a. Significantly, this curvature does not represent a hockey stick pattern in which the entrepreneurial firm continuously creates value once the initial uncertainty phase passes. As shown in Fig. 7.1, the value creation curvature instead declines, flattens out, and then stabilizes in the decline at some point in the firm's development. The preliminary phase of value development reflects the period of business experimentation, testing, and continuous improvement in virtually every part of the business. This is a stressful time for founders, the management team, staff, and investors alike, since the business's survival is unknown for an indeterminate, and often prolonged, period of time. Eventually, however, the venture will begin to gain some traction in the marketplace and the organization will proceed with the development of its normal operational rhythms, initiating a slow rise in the value creation curvature that resembles a stepwise configuration. This stepwise pattern is characteristic of entrepreneurial firms that continuously improve their business model, expand commercial offers, and enhance internal operations. While value growth is slow at the curvature's initial rise, the growth reaches a point of stability that resembles a plateau as the firm improves its value creation, which affords the required time to integrate any improvements, novelties, and enhancements. It also provides the firm additional time to secure the financial and human resources necessary for expansion. The entrepreneurial firm continues to enhance its value creation with this step-by-step process until such time when it reaches a more seamless patterns of development, thus continuing the process of value perpetuation.

Of course, there may be periods of time when the firm encounters operational or financial problems that halt, temporarily stall, or outright destroy the process of value creation. Such instances of value destruction can occur at any point of the entrepreneurial development process.

As depicted in Fig. 7.1b, the curvature of value creation is likely to look different for entrepreneurial firms under post COVID-response conditions. Differing from their normal patterns of development, newly created entrepreneurial firms may experience a more protracted first phase of the value creation process due to multiple and simultaneous market, operational, and financial risks. Moreover, additional time will likely be required to assess the market, develop the right product or service, combine all the necessary non-financial resources, and secure the requisite financial means to develop the venture. The prolonged nature of uncertainty, the amplitude of risks, and an inability to effectively resolve problems during this first phase may be discouraging to entrepreneurs, staff, and financiers alike. However, once the organizational fundamentals are established, the firm would eventually move to pursue its value creation. Unfortunately, value creation is projected to be interrupted by frequent periods of value reduction or destruction, which may be transient or more permanent; the actions, restrictions, and limitations of the state also contribute to entrepreneurial value destruction. The period of value reduction may be followed by another (albeit limited) phase of value creation, which would reach a brief plateau, and again be followed by value correction. This zigzag pattern of value creation may represent the new manner in which entrepreneurial firms will be developed and nurtured.

Should these new patterns of entrepreneurial development materialize in practice, entrepreneurs will experience many associated difficulties, including an obvious issue related to access to finance. Financiers, whether banks or equity providers, will likely be skeptical about financing entrepreneurial firms with a mixed track record of profitability, cash flow generation, and value creation/destruction; in short, a zigzag pattern of value creation will discourage financiers. Secondly, there is an issue of staffing stability, in terms of both members of the management team and other personnel. The weave pattern of revenue, profits, and cash flow would frequently necessitate cost reduction, including temporary or permanent layoffs, which, in turn, would result in more training, limited innovation, and poor employee and employee-management co-operation. Many entrepreneurial firms will be stalled due to such stop-and-start entrepreneurial development. Furthermore, the combination of these two factors may translate into unbearable levels of frustration, stress, and anxiety for entrepreneurs, which will be difficult to manage with even the most effective personal support structures. If such consequences of COVID-response continue, they may begin to adversely affect and irreparably alter the entire entrepreneurial ecosystem.

Entrepreneurial Survivability in the Age of COVID-Response

Statistics regarding business survival under normal entrepreneurial conditions are not optimistic. In the U.S., for example, research indicates that over 90% of newly formed ventures fail, while less than 50% survive beyond the five-year mark. Furthermore, only about one-third of newly created entrepreneurial firms will reach ten years of operation, and merely ten percent of entrepreneurial firms survive in the long-term. Most importantly, evidence suggests that continuing operations over the years does not assure business survival, or in other words, more entrepreneurial experience does not improve the odds of business survival. The most common reason for business failure relates to the broadly defined category of financial mismanagement, which may include an inability to generate adequate levels of revenue, problems with managing working capital, excessive costs, a high cash burn rate, and other cash flow problems. Non-financial reasons for business failure pertain to inadequate market demand, an incomplete and weak management team, and entrepreneurs' inability to develop their business venture in a systematic, orchestrated, and deliberate manner.

Despite already underwhelming statistics regarding business survival for entrepreneurial firms, they are likely to worsen as a consequence of COVID-response. In addition to a combination of the reasons previously discussed, the most predominant causes of business failure are market demand uncertainty, worsened access to finance, problems with developing an optimal business model, and continued mental stress. While entrepreneurs may be able to withstand a number of these adverse conditions when they occur over a long period of time, entrepreneurial firms are unlikely to survive a series of simultaneous difficulties compacted within a short time frame.

Although no precise estimates of long-term survival rates exist at the moment, business closures may provide some indication of this metric's evolution in the future. For example, the Organization for Economic Co-operation and Development (OECD) estimates a 20 to 40% increase in small business insolvencies compared to previous years. In the U.S., for instance, various estimates confirm that there were between 500 and 1,500 business closures per day in the initial stages of COVID-response, most of which were permanent. In comparison, business closures in Canada averaged 1,300 per day between January and March; this increased to an average of over 2,900 per day in April.

Canadian evidence furthermore suggests that one out of every five or six entrepreneurial firms is at the risk of permanent closure, which translates into roughly 180,000 to 220,000 firms. Additionally, the rate of business closures in the hardest hit segments of the economy may be as high as one-third, resulting in a loss of 2.4 million Canadian jobs, or 20% of private sector employment. The Canadian provinces most affected by business closures were Newfoundland and Labrador, Alberta, and Ontario. Although there is very limited hope of immediate recovery, these adverse statistics are anticipated to improve in the next two or three years.

Conclusions

It may be concluded that COVID-response has left deep scars on the entrepreneurial psyche that are not likely to heal quickly after recent experiences. For entrepreneurs, internal operations and the external business environment have become significantly more complex, uncertain, and risky. In addition to addressing the basic operational, financial, and strategic matters, entrepreneurs are now forced to consider new business models, understand unit economics, imagine new ways of generating revenues streams, establish novel behaviors for competing in an increasingly uneven marketplace, deal with fluctuating revenue, and address choppy value creation processes. Moreover, many entrepreneurs experienced difficulty in imagining a clear path to profitability and business sustainability.

In addition to business issues, entrepreneurs are also required to deal with elevated levels of personal uncertainties, fears, anxieties, and self-doubts. During COVID-response, many entrepreneurs struggled with social support because they were adjusting to working from home and were disconnected from employees, family members, business networks, and other social circles. While it is difficult to continue operating a business under such adverse conditions, it is even more challenging to start a new venture. However, there are some observers who expect COVID-response to translate into opportunities for innovation and entrepreneurial success. Media commonly presents a handful of mega-entrepreneurial firms that emerged after the 2001 crisis (such as Google, eBay, Groupon, and Pinterest) and after the 2008 financial crisis (such as Airbnb, Uber, Instagram, Dropbox, Square, and WhatsApp); these success stories relate to digital entrepreneurship. Although mainstream media promotes the implication that such successes are a standard outcome of entrepreneurial development, this is not correct. Nevertheless, there may be a number of entrepreneurial firms that are faster, agile, and more motivated to adjust their ventures post COVID-response, while a few successful start-ups or rapid expansions of existing firms may come about from this economic calamity.

Media furthermore encourages entrepreneurial development in the post COVID-response era through such slogans as: "tough times are the best times to start a firm" (i.e., a higher risk of failure), the "beauty of working from home" (i.e., more operational disruptions), "online is in the genes" (i.e., an interruption of critical in-person relationships), "do not waste a good crisis" (which encourages new venture creation in a suboptimal period and under difficult conditions), or "be agile and embrace change" (which, when done randomly and haphazardly, can be devastating to business). Entrepreneurs are also promoted in the media as indestructible, optimistic, and resilient business combatants; this appears to be somewhat propagandist as entrepreneurs are facing serious challenges post COVID-response. Thus, according to the media, entrepreneurs are expected to rise to the challenge of rescuing the entrepreneurial ecosystem, and the national economy, from the devastation caused by COVID-response. However, the start-and-stop approach of the state has proven to be exhausting not only for entrepreneurial structures, but also to the personal, physical, and mental health of entrepreneurs. It will likely be some time before entrepreneurs again become more vigorous, productive, innovative, and capable of sustaining prolonged mental stresses and strains.

Entrepreneurial struggles become real problems for the venture capital ecosystem at large for a number of reasons, not the least of which is because venture capitalists depend on entrepreneurs' ability to grow their firms, increase profits, improve cash flows, and invest in capital expenditures programs. When entrepreneurs struggle in all of these areas, there is limited potential for value creation or an increase in business valuation. Moreover, the depth and breadth of these challenges are likely to discourage both existing and new entrepreneurs alike. Additionally, the venture capital ecosystem relies on a flow of newly created firms with interesting ideas, concepts, and propositions to enter the entrepreneurial ecosystem, which are expected to later migrate into medium and larger firms. Venture capitalists also count on new and more mature firms to create an interesting deal flow of investable opportunities. In the age of COVID-response, venture capitalists are instead likely to encounter increasing instability and fragility within the entrepreneurial ecosystem. Finally, venture capitalists will also be forced to contend with more incomplete management teams, unstable markets, unpredictable competition, fluctuating profit margins, and choppy revenue growth in potential investee firms; these are hardly ideal investment conditions for venture capitalists.

Note

1. Analysis from Aswath Damodaran (see http://pages.stern.nyu.edu/~adamodar/).

Bibliography

Baker McKenzie. 2020. The COVID-19 pandemic: A corporate survival guide. www.psik.org.pl.

Bartik, Alexander W., Marianne Bertrand, Zoe Cullen, Edward L. Gleaser, Michael Luca, and Christopher Straton. 2020. The impact of COVID-19 on small business outcomes and expectations. *Proceedings of the National Academy of Science* 117: 17656–17666.

Calvino, Flavio, Chiara Criscuolo, and Rudy Verihac. 2020. Start-ups in the time of COVID-19: Facing the challenges, seizing the opportunities. June 23. www.voxeu.org.

Cubbon, Paul. 2020. Entrepreneurship and innovation post-COVID. June 22. www.thefutureeconomy.ca.

Derderian, Marie-France. 2020. What is the impact of COVID-19 on entrepreneurship? April 20. www.hospitalitynet.org.

Deutsch, Waverly. 2020. COVID-19 is changing key business relationships. August 27. www.review.chicagobooth.edu.

Dua, Andre, Deepa Mahajan, Lucienne Oyer, and Sree Ramaswamy. 2020. US Small-business recovery after the COVID-19 crisis. July 7. www.mckinsey.com.

Entrepreneurs Organization Toronto. 2020. Business post COVID-19: Is Canada headed for a stall in startups and support? May 6. www.eonetwork.org.

Haeffele, Stefanie, Anne Hobson, and Virgil H. Storr. 2020. Coming back from COVID-19: Lessons in entrepreneurship from disaster recovery research. April 28. www.mercatus.org.

Hawker, Emmy. 2020. Entrepreneurs vital for post-coronavirus economic recovery. May 14. www.businessbecause.com.

Klonowski, Darek. 2018. *The venture capital deformation: Value destruction throughout the investment process*. New York: Palgrave MacMillan.

Klonowski, Darek. 2014. *Strategic entrepreneurial finance: From value creation to realization*. London: Routledge.

Lafrance-Cook, Amelie, Ryan McDonald, and Michael Willox. 2020. Monthly business openings and closures: Experimental series for Canada, the provinces and territories, and census metropolitan areas. August 17. Statistics Canada. www.stacan.gc.ca.

Lino, Marc, Hubert Shen, Andrei Vorobyov, and Hao Zhou. 2020. Coping with coronavirus: How private equity firms can focus on what matters most. www.bain.com.

Looze, Jessica, and Sameeksha Desai. 2020. How does COVID-19 affect challenges facing entrepreneurs? Trends by business age. December 16. Ewing Marion Kauffman Foundation.

Meyer, Klaus, Carsten L. Pedersen, and Thomas Ritter. 2020. The coronavirus crisis: A catalyst for entrepreneurship. www.theconversation.com.

OECD. 2020. Coronavirus (COVID-19): SME policy responses. July 15. www.oecd.org.

Pressman, Jason. 2020. The fallacy of 'normal': How the coronavirus will reboot venture capital. April 30. www.venturebeat.com.

Rana, Tehseen. 2020. Implications of COVID-19 on entrepreneurship and innovation. October 19. www.blog.mdbinsight.com.

Sinha, Debasish. 2020. Post Covid-19 trends of entrepreneurship according to the changed market demand. July 20. www.entrepreneur.com.

Team Sequoia. 2020. Coronavirus: The black swan of 2020. March 5. www.medium.com.

Torkildson, Adam. 2020. How startup entrepreneurship will change post COVID-19. December 16. www.m.dailyhunt.in.

Tucker, Charlotte. 2020. How is coronavirus impacting the funding landscape for startups? April 30. www.eu-startups.com.

Zahra, Shaker A. 2020. International entrepreneurship in the post Covid world. *Journal of World Business* 56: 1–7.

CHAPTER 8

Amplified Challenges in Access to Entrepreneurial Finance in the Age of COVID-Response

Financial Management of Entrepreneurial Firms Post COVID-Response

Chapter seven provided an extended discussion of the challenges entrepreneurial firms have faced post COVID-response, which related to all factors that have proven impactful upon entrepreneurial success in the past, including the size and growth of the market, the management team, the business model or mode of operations, the nature of competition, money management, and profitability. This chapter will extend this discussion by focusing specifically on issues related to financial management and access to finance. Financial management issues will be examined separately in this chapter because of the significant financial vulnerability and fragility of many entrepreneurial firms post COVID-response, which is a trend that is expected to continue for the foreseeable future.

Financial management is a quantitative, analytical, descriptive, and dynamic discipline which effectively consolidates the fields of accounting, economics, law, and psychology, among other areas of study. In the context of entrepreneurship, financial management specifically relates to the financial practices that are employed by entrepreneurs to analyze, forecast, and allocate their various available financial and non-financial resources. To achieve their objectives and goals, entrepreneurs must utilize the appropriate financial management frameworks, models, ratios, structures, and mechanisms for successful financial decision-making.

D. Klonowski, *Venture Capital Redefined*,
https://doi.org/10.1007/978-3-030-83387-9_8

In broad terms, there are five core analytical components at the center of financial management: liquidity, capital budgeting, financial forecasting, capital structure decisions, and valuation. It is important to understand that financial management and its critical components are inherently connected to the five non-financial aspects of business operations discussed previously in Chapter seven. To fully understand the dynamics of entrepreneurism, these two areas (i.e., financial and non-financial) must be analyzed in tandem and with regard to the ways in which they jointly impact entrepreneurial firms, and the entrepreneurial ecosystem at large.

One of the most critical functions in financial management for any young or more mature entrepreneurial firm is the analysis of the firm's liquidity; basically, financial liquidity assures business survival. Of course, business survival becomes easier when the entrepreneurial firm generates sales, effectively controls costs, and competently manages working capital (i.e., inventory, accounts receivable, and accounts payable). Liquidity, which predominantly refers to the proper management of current assets and liabilities, is key to a firm's ability to stay alive. Liquidity also requires the right balance to be struck between consuming and generating cash in order to settle any current or outstanding liabilities the firm may have, including paying employees, loan payments, taxes, and additional payments or expenditures. Thus, an analysis of liquidity underscores the importance of cash as the lifeline of any business, since poor liquidity management will lead to imminent business failure.

Capital budgeting is a formal analytical process wherein the entrepreneurial firm decides which specific investment project is worthwhile; in other words, it is an investment appraisal mechanism. Decisions related to capital budgeting commonly refer to investments in fixed assets and may involve replacement, expansion, the introduction of new products, or mandatory investments. However, capital budgeting may also include investments in other types of projects such as marketing, promotion, human resource acquisition, research and development, innovation, or improvements to working capital.

Fundamentally, capital budgeting analysis includes the preparation of a capital budgeting schedule on the basis of the most appropriate analytical framework, such as a payback period, an internal rate of returns (IRR), or a net present value (NPV), when incremental revenue and costs are taken into consideration. Capital budgeting decisions impact the future success of every aspect of the entrepreneurial firm's operations; good projects may significantly increase the value of the firm, enhance its revenue growth, and improve profitability, while suboptimal projects can destroy the firm's value and result in negative financial and non-financial consequences. The importance of making the right capital budgeting decisions is especially critical for younger and smaller entrepreneurial firms because they are already hindered by limited financial resources, poor access to external finance, inadequate human capital, and less experience managing complex projects. Although mistakes can be considered less detrimental to the survival of more mature firms because they have other projects, excess financial and human resources, and more favorable access to additional finance, errors in capital budgeting can be fatal to young firms.

Financial forecasting is the process of determining the future financial success of an entrepreneurial firm. This mechanism serves as an important benchmark for comparing actual and budgeted financial performance, which, in turn, will lead to a revision of strategic considerations. Financial forecasting is not a one-time process, but rather an iterative exercise with the goal of developing realistic business and financial assumptions that allow for the crafting of achievable financial objectives. The repetitive nature of financial forecasting is grounded in the fact that a change in one assumption will automatically cause revisions in other parts of the financial forecast. While there are different methods of preparing financial forecasts, the process is normally done in stages and often begins with the preparation of a pro-forma income statement (this is the most critical building block of financial forecasts and involves precise estimations of revenue and cost), continues with the development of a cash flow statement, and concludes with the creation of the balance sheet. The process of financial forecasting ends with the calculation of financial ratios to verify how achievable the financial numbers reached in the assessment are likely to be in practice.

Furthermore, capital structure relates to the relative mixture of capital that the firm uses to finance the acquisition of resources necessary for its operation. In broad terms, the firm has two basic choices when financing its operations: debt or equity. Debt has a number of advantages, one of which is that interest payments on debt are tax deductible (thereby lowering the level of profit before tax); debt is thus a less expensive method of financing than equity. Additionally, if utilized for capital budgeting projects that are value-generative and transformative to the firm, debt can significantly enhance the firm's value. Of course, this discussion regarding debt and the optimal capital structure may be purely theoretical if the firm is unable to raise debt (or equity) due to problems with the supply of finance. Therefore, a critical challenge related to capital structure is the ease with which entrepreneurial firms can access different but complementary forms of finance.

Once the entrepreneurial firm chooses the most viable capital budgeting projects, develops appropriate financial forecasts, and decides how best to finance its operations, the natural next step may be to establish the firm's business valuation. The process of business valuation can be defined as the manner in which any asset (including the firm) is valued, although it is commonly established through the application of different valuation techniques that reflect the purpose and premise of the business valuation. Therefore, the most prevalent valuation methods include the discounted cash flow (DCF) method (which relies on adjusted values of projected cash flows) and the EV/EBITDA (enterprise value divided by earnings before interest, taxes, depreciation, and amortization) multiples method. The DCF method considers the most important interlocking components of financial management and value creation, namely cash flow size, cash flow timing, and cash flow risk. In the EV/EBITDA multiples method, enterprise value (EV) estimates the theoretical takeover price of the venture. Additional techniques may relate to liquidation and replacement valuation methods.

Business valuations can be constructed around any outcomes of financial forecasting, such as the income statement, the cash flow statement, or the balance sheet. Typically, a business valuation is performed for the purpose of a business transaction, personal circumstances, or legal disputes. However, business valuation is also critical if the entrepreneur wishes to know whether value was created or destroyed in the process of entrepreneurial development. Furthermore, the establishment of the firm's baseline value is critical in business development and serves as a useful benchmark for future decisions. And yet, despite the importance of business valuation, research and business practice suggests that less than one out of every three business owners actually understands the value of their firm; this is especially true for small firms.

Entrepreneurial Firms and Financial Management Post COVID-Response

This section of the chapter will specifically analyze the five core areas of financial management outlined above with regard to the key challenges entrepreneurs have experienced post COVID-response. Although some of these difficulties have already been discussed in Chapter seven, they will be further elaborated on in the context of financial management. A bullet-point summary of these critical financial management challenges is included in Table 8.1.

In terms of liquidity, cash is the primary vehicle of financial survival for entrepreneurial firms; this is especially true in the period of COVID-response. Cash preservation is essential for entrepreneurial firms because financial pressures are expected to worsen due to extended and fluctuating state restrictions and public orders. And yet, it appears that the "cash runway" for the vast majority of entrepreneurial firms during COVID-response is extremely short. Evidence from the Unites States (U.S.), for example, suggests that many firms only had cash resources available to cover between two and three months of expenses, while entrepreneurs were simultaneously limited in the ways with which to improve their cash cushion. While entrepreneurs could theoretically extend their cash runway by further reducing wages, laying off employees, decreasing investments, canceling promotional efforts, refusing to hire necessary personnel, and delaying purchases, these actions will reach a breaking point and ultimately prove to be detrimental to day-to-day operations and business survival. In other words, entrepreneurial firms may not be able to reduce cost in any meaningful manner without unduly hurting their operations. Moreover, and as previously stated, a combination of declining revenues (due to low market demand and disruptions of global supply chains), high fixed costs, problems with working capital management, stretched financial resources, and poor access to finance further reduce liquidity.

One of the components most critical to the maintenance of liquidity is revenue generation, which can be simply understood as the firm's ability to retain existing customers and procure new ones. Research supports the idea that revenue generation is difficult to achieve post COVID-response, as 70 to 80% of entrepreneurial firms have reported difficulty with this aspect of financial management. In order to increase the firm's liquidity, especially when the business underperforms and the current financial obligations exceed the firm's capabilities, there is a significant pressure on entrepreneurs to support their business with personal financial resources. An entrepreneur may therefore choose to use their personal property, movable assets (including their home or car), or lines of credit, as collateral for a business loan. Unfortunately, these personal or family assets may be liquidated to settle outstanding creditor claims in the case of business

Table 8.1 Five areas of financial management and their key challenges for entrepreneurial firms

Areas of financial management	*Key challenges for entrepreneurial firms*
Liquidity	• Declining revenue and fixed costs contribute to liquidity problems • Disruption of global supply chains leads to stock outs, thereby limiting sales • Limited financial resources of entrepreneurial firms • Reliance of entrepreneurs on non-traditional sources of finances, such as drawing on personal lines of credit, personal loans, and remortgaging personal assets • More difficulty in managing working capital as the entire entrepreneurial ecosystem is under financial stress • Persistent liquidity problems for entrepreneurial firms
Capital budgeting	• Inability to estimate incremental revenues and costs • Cash shortages, poor access to finance, and liquidity issues prevent entrepreneurs from pursuing capital expenditure programs • Disruption of innovation, invention, and discovery due to poor access to finance

Areas of financial management	*Key challenges for entrepreneurial firms*
Financial forecasting	• Difficulty in projecting key financial characteristics of entrepreneurial firms, namely revenue, costs, profit margins, and cash flows • Difficulty in establishing revenue growth • Inability to engage in long-term planning prevents entrepreneurs from proper estimation of actual financial needs • Downward pressure on margins • Poor reliability of financial forecasts
Capital structure	• More constraints in access to finance from equity and debt providers • Additional operational risks and uncertainties adversely impact access to finance • Inability to raise external capital in a timely manner • Challenges in optimization of capital structure • Increased reliance on different methods related to personal financing • Many entrepreneurial firms are likely to carry excessive levels of debt; this may cause an unprecedented wave of insolvencies, bankruptcies, and windups in the entrepreneurial ecosystem • Prevalence of excessive debt-to-equity and poor interest coverage ratios • Enhanced reliance on online finance providers • An increased role of fintech providers
Valuation	• Downward pressures on business valuation due to challenges in financial and non-financial aspects of entrepreneurial operations • Valuations unlikely to recover in the foreseeable future • Selected firms operating in specific segments of the economy may count on high valuations

failure or bankruptcy. Thus, if the business underperforms or outright fails, and personal assets and wealth are not separated from business property, the family essentially risks everything. In a less extreme scenario, the redirection of personal funds toward the business may result in fewer necessary funds available to meet important family needs, such as home renovations and improvements, family vacations, the requirements of children, or education. The financial security and wellbeing of the family is thereby put at risk on a daily basis for the sake of perpetuating the entrepreneurial venture from week-to-week. While these tradeoffs may occur for young entrepreneurial firms at any point in time, they are likely to be increasingly common post COVID-response. If business owners choose to financially support their venture with personal assets, the financial problems of the venture may translate into financial problems for the entrepreneur in the form of increased personal debt, personal bankruptcy, and the loss of everything which the entrepreneur and their family cherish.

With regard to considerations of capital budgeting, entrepreneurial firms face a number of challenges that have been exacerbated by COVID-response. Primarily, entrepreneurs intuitively realize that investment projects should not go forward without a detailed analysis. And yet, this is difficult to accomplish without the proper estimates of incremental revenue and costs that entrepreneurs are currently unable to develop due to market uncertainties, state restrictions, and other risks. The second obvious impediment to capital budgeting is a poor access to finance. In short, a lack of finance may completely stop contemplations of potential investment programs; this is, of course, subject to any investment made from internally generated cash flow.

The third obvious, but equally important, component that negatively affects capital budgeting relates to the availability of human resources that are critical to the successful implementation of capital budgeting programs. As concluded in Chapter seven, talented human resources will be increasingly difficult to hire, retain, and keep motivated due to workplace restrictions and volatile employment. Of course, the obvious danger of such personnel issues is that many entrepreneurial firms would not be able to continue their investment programs. On a macro-scale, this would prove devastating to national economies because the vast majority of inventions, innovations, and discoveries come from the small and medium-sized enterprise (SME) sector. Problems in this area not only leave firms unable to commence new investment projects, but they may also be unable to perpetuate existing ones. Since the continuation of both smaller and more substantial capital budgeting projects has been the cornerstone of entrepreneurship around the globe for the last 50 years, it is difficult to understand how such "creative disruptions" could be positive to either entrepreneurial firms or national economies.

The next critical problem for entrepreneurial firms is the preparation of financial forecasts. State-led COVID-response has effectively disabled entrepreneurs' ability to precisely estimate the revenue, cost, profitability, cash flow, and leverage of their entrepreneurial firms; these financial characteristics are at the heart of financial forecasts. An inability to prepare credible financial forecasts also prevents entrepreneurial firms from raising external finance since these forecasts are a critical tool of evaluation utilized by external financiers. Of course, without proper financial planning and documentation in the form of financial forecasts, entrepreneurial firms would not be able to provide evidence demonstrating their ability to cover interest payments, repay loans, or provide the returns expected by equity investors.

Problems related to capital structure, which are amplified by increased operational risks and financial uncertainties, are also complicated by difficulties with access to finance (this challenge will be discussed in more detail later in the chapter). Although entrepreneurial firms are normally able to adjust their capital structures for different phases of the economic cycle (more debt can be carried in a strong phase of economic development while less is appropriate in economic downturns), poor access to finance prevents firms from this continuous adjustment. In other words, entrepreneurial firms will likely struggle to balance the levels of debt and equity over their development, and thereby optimize their capital structures, which will create additional financial risks.

Therefore, entrepreneurial firms are now locked into the specific capital structure scheme that was initiated in 2019 or early 2020. Under these conditions, entrepreneurial firms may find themselves in two distinct financial predicaments. Firstly, they may have already relied on excessive amounts of external debt which, when combined with inadequate access to equity finance, would require the entrepreneurial firm to carry excessive debt loads into a period of economic downturn; excessive debt-to-equity ratios and poor interest coverage could be disastrous to firms in this circumstance. An over-weight debt structure can also instigate liquidity problems that will inevitably lead to an unprecedented wave of small business insolvencies, bankruptcies, and windups in the short-term. These adverse events, in turn, are likely to have a strong spillover effect on personal finance, leading to personal financial difficulties, including personal bankruptcies, in the long-term. In the second case, however, entrepreneurial firms that have not been able to raise sufficient debt in the past may actually be in a better financial position because of this previous inability. Since a rapid decline in revenue may not automatically translate into problems with financial institutions for these entrepreneurial firms, they may not experience the insolvencies and bankruptcies projected for those who already have large amounts of debt.

Lastly, there are financial management issues related to business valuation that were aggravated by COVID-response. Earlier chapters have already mentioned some critical issues associated with the business valuation of entrepreneurial firms in the context of the venture capital ecosystem; these issues, which included uncertain market demand, low consumption, multiple operational risks, and fragile financial wellbeing, are relevant here as well. In addition, the various political, economic, and social impacts discussed in Chapter two have indirectly (and negatively) influenced business valuation post COVID-response. It was also noted in Chapter five that the business valuations in 2020 fell between 20 and 40% compared to the 2019 levels; this decline may be expected to continue in 2021 as state-led COVID-response appears to be more restrictive and severe. Even in the case of more mature entrepreneurial firms that have already experienced success in growing revenue and profits, there may still be a decline in business valuation that is reflective of the uncertainty surrounding the sustainability of operations and finances in the short- and medium-term. Suppressed business valuations for younger firms also reflect uncertainties regarding their business survival, liquidity challenges, probability of financial insolvency, ability to raise the external finance necessary for further growth, financial performance, timing of reaching a break-even point, and steady cash flows. However, and as stated in Chapter five, selected entrepreneurial firms that have disproportionately benefited from COVID-response could experience higher valuations; this refers to a narrow universe of firms.

Problems with Access to Finance Post COVID-Response

Of the many challenges entrepreneurs face, one of their most critical hurdles is access to finance. In fact, securing capital may be the most demanding, exhausting, and time-consuming task for entrepreneurial firms, and as such, it is estimated that about 90% of entrepreneurial firms face significant problems in this area throughout the various periods of their entrepreneurial development and progression. These challenges have of course been intensified post COVID-response, so the objective of the following section of this chapter is to outline the difficulties entrepreneurial firms encounter under normal circumstances, as well as investigating how these issues regarding access to entrepreneurial finance have been amplified post COVID-response.

While it is generally well documented by academic literature that entrepreneurial firms struggle with access to finance, there is some debate whether this poor access, otherwise known as liquidity constraint, effectively binds entrepreneurs. Therefore, the key question is not if liquidity constraints exist, but instead if these financial obstacles effectively prevent entrepreneurs from starting and optimally growing their firms. Academics offer two viewpoints on this conundrum, the first of which is the argument that there are significant liquidity constraints to bind entrepreneurs and effectively prevent them from starting or continuing business development. These same observers further conclude that wealthier individuals are more likely to become entrepreneurs, while entrepreneurs who exhibit particular characteristics related to education, marital status, and business experience can alternately remove or worsen their liquidity constraints. The second group of academics, however, have determined that liquidity constraints are unlikely to prevent small business formation and development. Regardless of their ultimate impact on the venture, poor access to finance is especially detrimental to young entrepreneurial firms that have limited alternatives when procuring capital; these issues are more pronounced post COVID-response.

There are two critical moments in the expansion of an entrepreneurial firm when finance is essential to its continuation. The first of these critical moments occurs in the initial stages, during which there may simply be an idea, concept, invention, or vision that needs to be developed into a full business. The most fundamental issue at this stage of development is the ability to secure sufficient capital for the assurance of the business's survival and the day-to-day perpetuation of the venture. Young entrepreneurial firms may also require a vast range of assistance during these initial phases of the entrepreneurial process that go beyond the simple provision of capital, including careful strategic planning and cash management in order to effectively manage cash burn and their limited financial and human resources. The inability of the entrepreneurial firm to raise sufficient finance in this first critical phase will inevitably contribute to the firm's collapse. The second critical period in a firm's development is expansion, and should problems with access to finance occur in this subsequent stage, it can result in developmental inactivity, growth stagnation, and a greater sensitivity to external shocks. Thus, proper financial access is essential in expansion to allow entrepreneurial firms the opportunity to progress and migrate into another level of business development. However, insufficient access to finance at any stage of entrepreneurial progression can cause a negative ballooning reaction that can potentially impact the entire entrepreneurial ecosystem and economy on a national level.

Problems with access to finance may arise for a wide range of reasons, but they typically fall within two main categories: supply-side problems and demand-side concerns. In terms of the supply of capital, the provision of finance may be restricted due to general shortages of capital in the marketplace, which is the case if financial institutions, private individuals, investors, or public markets are unwilling to extend capital to firms. This unwillingness may be because the venture is perceived to be of high risk, the particular business sector in question is not a strategic area of focus, the firm or its products are unfamiliar, there is a lack of loan guarantees, or other reasons. Of course, it is always a possibility that an entrepreneurial firm may not warrant financing because it fails to meet the financing criteria set by financial institutions or other capital providers; these requirements could relate to profitability, liquidity, future growth potential, value of collateral, the specific sector of the economy in which their firm operates, or business valuation. Alternately, the venture could also lack key non-financial necessities established by providers of finance.

On the other hand, there are also issues stemming from demand-side concerns that impact a firm's ability to access capital. The most basic shortcoming in these cases is that the firm may not be ready to receive finance, the chief reasons for this being a lack of business plan or strategic vision, an incomplete management team or the existence of a solo entrepreneur, poor presentation skills, or other challenges. Entrepreneurs may also have complex business structures that obscure asset or business ownership; this must be disentangled before external finance can be provided. Furthermore, unaudited and problematic financial statements are another matter that must be resolved before capital will be extended to the entrepreneurial venture.

An additional hurdle to the entrepreneurial firm's access to finance that has been observed by academics is the variance with which capital providers will analyze funding proposals. For example, while capital providers seek distinctive information and assess business, financial, operational, and management risks in different ways, entrepreneurs often do not possess the insight to vary their finance presentations when attempting to raise external capital. Instead, entrepreneurs commonly present a general assessment of the firm's commercial achievements in addition to its financial performance and management. However, it is also important to note that entrepreneurs may not raise external finance on their own, especially in relation to equity finance; many entrepreneurs obtain assistance from external advisors who not only provide valuable advice, but also serve as important animators of the entrepreneurial ecosystem.

Problematic Access to Entrepreneurial Finance

Evidence from the initial research conducted post COVID-response confirms that access to finance is now more difficult for the vast majority of entrepreneurial firm. In the United States (U.S.), for example, about 70% of newly created firms (i.e., less than one year old), 60% of young firms (i.e., less than five years old), and 40% of more mature firms (i.e., more than ten years old) have experienced significant problems in this area. Undoubtedly, the most negatively affected are young firms in seed and early-stage development because financing is generally limited or even non-existent for new entrepreneurial firms. In comparison, there are typically multiple avenues of financing open for expanding firms, whose desire and ability to raise a specific form of finance depend on the firm's level of development, profitability, revenue, anticipated growth trajectory, market share, risk tolerance, and industry, among other factors. It is therefore pertinent to review the main modes of entrepreneurial finance to understand the difficulties, both new and continuing, that are relevant to each form.

Firstly, there are financial institutions (i.e., banks, co-operatives, and so on), which often represent an important source of entrepreneurial financing. In fact, commercial banks can satisfy a significant portion of the entrepreneurial firm's financial needs. Banks may even prove to be uncooperative with entrepreneurs who seek dedicated capital for activities which banks perceive as risky, such as research and development, the broadening of product offering, or expansion into markets outside of the entrepreneur's home region. Additionally, and when compared to venture capital, for example, banks are unlikely to provide any start-up or expansion assistance to entrepreneurial ventures. Of course, bank financing alone may not be sufficient to support the growth of entrepreneurial firms; they will require additional finance from other sources. However, in the era post COVID-response, evidence from different countries has revealed that entrepreneurial firms are experiencing even further problems accessing bank debt. For instance, indications from Australia suggest that banks have restricted loans to entrepreneurial firms that operate in the segments of the economy most affected by COVID-response (i.e., leisure, entertainment, restaurants, cafes, and so on).

Although it may appear counterintuitive, there is also decreased demand for loans post COVID-response, despite entrepreneurs' increased need for external capital and diminished ability to access entrepreneurial financing. One explanation for this major drop in market demand could be because entrepreneurial firms are engaging in cash saving tactics such as avoiding the replenishment of inventory, delaying anticipated investment projects, laying off staff, or postponing expansion plans. Thus, the external finance that is normally required to support these activities may simply not be necessary. A second reason for a reduction of loans relates to business owners' intuitive recognition that their firms may already be over-leveraged, so a further increase in borrowing may lead to imminent bankruptcy or issues with financial institutions. This is exemplified by evidence from the U.S. which suggests that, due to high investment and working capital needs, the level of debt in entrepreneurial firms may be so excessive that the cost of servicing debt could already be as high as 30% of revenue. Therefore, entrepreneurs may not be willing to borrow because they anticipate substantial operational risks and uncertainties. Business owners may also be reluctant to provide additional collateral, perhaps in part because a significant portion of their business loans already utilizes personal assets as collateral.

Additionally, entrepreneurs may be turning to less formal modes of entrepreneurial finance, such as friends-and-family, casual online lending channels (which may not be reflected in official lending statistics), and personal finance. However, in the most pessimistic scenario, entrepreneurs may be choosing not to pursue loans because they anticipate that their venture is not likely to survive in the short- or medium-term. Borrowing to pay rent, utilities, and other expenses in view of an impending failure is simply not prudent if there is no reasonable chance of perpetuating the venture in the future. If this indeed were the case, "not throwing good money after bad" would seem rational for entrepreneurs, who may instead direct available financial resources toward alternate ventures, business ideas, and investment opportunities.

If a firm has been operating for a while, is profitable, and generates cash, it may be able to support its operations and expansion through the use of its own financial resources. Even if the firm is not profitable, it may still manage its cash resources in such a way as to cover any cash needs. This form of entrepreneurial financing, commonly termed as "bootstrapping", is defined as the process of acquiring resources and developing the entrepreneurial venture with minimal capital. Bootstrapping represents the lowest cost method of entrepreneurial financing because it entails self-funding. It is an approach in managing a venture operation in a manner that conserves cash and limits spending. Bootstrapping is furthermore a process of acquiring, mobilizing, allocating, and coordinating financial resources through frugality and penny pinching. The most common bootstrapping techniques include relying on trade credit, customers (i.e., pre-payments and advances), equipment suppliers, bartering, personal resources (i.e., credit cards, lines of credit, personal real estate, and savings), peer-to-peer lending, factoring, resource sharing (i.e., equipment, employees, raw materials, and financial resources), group purchasing, and leasing.

However, bootstrapping may not be a viable solution for all entrepreneurial firms; some firms are limited in their ease of utilizing bootstrapping activities by the nature of their operations. Thus, entrepreneurial firms that can benefit from this approach are those that require low capital outplay, can rely on word-of-mouth (i.e., low cost) promotion, have "captive audience" (i.e., repeatable) customers, and can depend upon cash payments from customers while delaying supplier payments. The key advantages of bootstrapping include a lack of financial obligations (i.e., loan payments), the ability to test-drive a venture without overcommitting resources, and no dilution of ownership. Under the conditions of COVID-response, entrepreneurial bootstrapping has become more difficult to implement because the entire entrepreneurial ecosystem is under financial strain. Primarily, supplier credit may be less available; customers require more optimal terms to generate a sale and are generally unwilling to prepay (they have limited financial resources and tend to hoard cash in times of crisis); creative inventory access may be suppressed (suppliers may not be willing to provide inventory on consignment); favorable trade terms are typically unavailable (suppliers may be unwilling to extend trade credit); the entrepreneurs' personal savings may be exhausted; personal lines of credits and credit card usage could be limited; and family-and-friends may be less compassionate or willing to provide "love money". Therefore, entrepreneurial firms are provided limited opportunities to rely on bootstrapping post COVID-response. On the other hand, firms are more likely to obtain state assistance due to the implementation of new programs, and their increased eligibility to access existing programs, designed to aid entrepreneurs impacted by widespread state restrictions.

A third financing option for entrepreneurial firms is business angels, who provide both capital and advice to entrepreneurial ventures. This type of external finance is one of the most significant sources of capital for start-ups and early-stage firms; some evidence estimates that business angel financing exceeds the value of institutional funds by a factor of at least five times. These private, non-institutional investors, who are often former entrepreneurs themselves, are typically passive investors that will take an ownership interest in a venture created by another entrepreneur. However, business angels do occasionally assume an active role in the management of the funded venture. The goal of business angel financing is to aid the venture in terms of revenue growth, profitability, and competitive position while simultaneously reducing some operational risks and uncertainties. Although business angels aim to maximize the value of their investment, which differs from the goal of institutional capital, they may remain involved in the investee venture for a long period of time. Evidence also suggests that business angels are able to realize returns in excess of 20% while managing to generate few write-offs, which exemplifies a better record of financial performance compared to traditional institutional investors (i.e., venture capitalists). Entrepreneurial ventures financed by business angels are frequently characterized by enhanced performance, higher business survival rates, greater employment, and better exit opportunities.

Despite the positive benefits of their involvement within an entrepreneurial firm, access to business angels is generally difficult to attain. Some methods that are utilized to attract business angels can include relying on business referrals, accessing organized business angel networks, and participating in online digital platforms. However, research evidence collected post COVID-response suggests that the deal volume for business angel investments declined by 58% between quarters two of 2019 and 2020, while deal value fell by 38% during this same period. Evidence also indicates that while some business angels are still willing to finance seed and start-up opportunities post COVID-response, which is similar to institutional investors, business angels are also focused on problems with their portfolio firms. Furthermore, business angels are adhering to a strategy of conserving cash that would normally be directed toward new investment opportunities in anticipation of potential follow-up financing to portfolio firms whose financial position has become more challenging due to COVID-response.

Although there are many benefits to the involvement of business angels, portfolio firms financed through such capital can also be characterized by low revenue, a high cash burn rate, poor liquidity, inadequate access to finance, and problems breaking-even. Post COVID-response, business angels will likely take some time to re-assess their own financial situations, determine the cash needs of their portfolio firms, and strategize for future investments. As proven by the 2008 financial crisis, it will take a few years before business angels, and other financiers, are able to return to their normal practices and levels of investment activity. For example, larger firms required four years to reach their pre-crisis level of contribution to gross domestic products (GDP) post 2008; smaller firms needed about six years. However, business angels may be more amenable to pursue opportunistic investments because of fewer institutional restrictions, which would initiate a steady increase in deal volume and signal a return to normal levels of investment activity for all types of entrepreneurial finance. And yet, it appears that business angel financing currently remains more difficult to access for entrepreneurial firms as a facet of COVID-response.

One of the final forms, and fastest growing modes, of entrepreneurial finance is crowdfunding. Undertaken by individuals as opposed to institutions, crowdfunding represents a collective, commission-driven, and Internet-based effort to pool financial resources with the aim of financing entrepreneurial ventures and other types of projects. Put simply, crowdfunding is a social networking event aimed at generating a desired amount of capital for an entrepreneurial venture that may be unable to access entrepreneurial finance through other channels. Crowdfunding activities generally fall into one of four categories of financial activity: lending, provision of equity, donations, and reward-based approaches. Since crowdfunding normally occurs through the use of online digital platforms, capital providers are often diverse and may include experienced financiers, novice investors, product or service enthusiasts, philanthropists, and others; these assorted financiers may exhibit various return expectations, some of which may be non-financial in nature. This type of finance is beneficial to entrepreneurs because it fills an existing gap in the marketplace for financing projects within a specific range of capital needs, democratizes access to finance for a wide range of individuals and firms (extending finance to those who would normally have problems securing capital from other sources), provides sufficient capital to young entrepreneurial firms to test-drive their business ideas, and allows the underlying business concept to be promoted to a wider audience.

The value of the crowdfunding market was estimated to equal about $100 billion in 2019, with lending- and equity-based platforms generating the largest amounts of capital, although the industry is expected to exceed $200 billion by 2024. However, the crowdfunding market is also anticipated to be significantly impacted post COVID-response, which is supported by evidence to suggest that there has been a 20% decline in seed and early-stage investment financing. For example, Kickstarter, one of the leading crowdfunding platforms, experienced a 35% decline in the number of projects in April of 2020 alone, leading to an inevitable layoff of staff. There is also proof that fewer pledges have been committed to crowdfunding platforms. And yet, despite its current challenges, there are multiple indicators to suggest that crowdfunding will become an important contributor to entrepreneurial finance in the future. In the first case, such signs include the professionalization of operations, testing of alternate online finance delivery methods, and the significant popularity entrepreneurs and other social circles have gained in the last decade across many crowdfunding platforms. These platforms are also uniquely positioned to provide finance through digital channels, particularly in comparison with other types of finance providers (i.e., traditional financial institutions) that are currently in the process of partially shifting their business models to accommodate online delivery. Thus, crowdfunding platforms currently offer the most advanced form of digital entrepreneurial finance. Should these finance providers be in a position to expand their operational models to include the provision of other resources, such as access to the know-how, mentoring, consultancy, and advisory services entrepreneurial firms often desperately require, crowdfunding may come to rival the capacity of the traditional modes of entrepreneurial finance. Nonetheless, the main challenge for crowdfunding platforms post COVID-response relates to the stabilization of contribution levels from individual funders.

Figure 8.1 provides a pictorial representation of various forms of entrepreneurial finance in both pre and post COVID-response situations, and was developed on the basis of available academic studies prior to COVID-response. Different forms of finance are presented along two dimensions: the level of know-how assistance and the probability of obtaining finance. The level of hands-on assistance is of specific importance to younger entrepreneurial firms (although more mature ventures of course benefit from such support) because they are often characterized by poor strategic management, incomplete management team, market and competitive uncertainties, and significant operational risks. The dotted and shaded ovals of various sizes represent the size of the market for each capital source and its availability to entrepreneurial firms pre COVID-response, while solid ovals denote these same features for each form of finance post COVID-response; to distinguish them from other sources of finance, state assistance programs are illustrated in a rectangular shape.

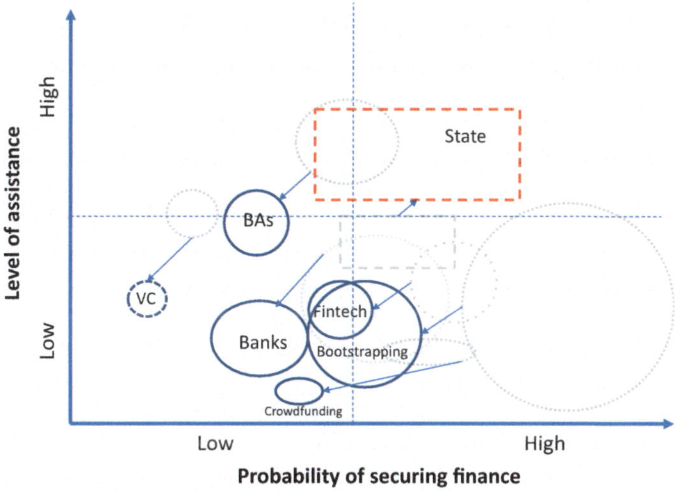

Fig. 8.1 Evolution of entrepreneurial finance in pre and post COVID-response conditions (*Source* Adjusted from Klonowski [2018])

The arrows between the solid and broken line ovals signify the migration of the market size and availability of entrepreneurial finance methods from pre to post COVID-response levels.

Of the numerous conclusions that may be reached with regard to trends evidenced in Fig. 8.1, the most obvious is that many, if not all, forms of entrepreneurial finance have migrated to occupy different areas on the graph than they previously held pre COVID-response. However, these new positions have generally worsened entrepreneurial firms' access to finance and ability to obtain hands-on assistance. Furthermore, the deterioration in accessing entrepreneurial finance is represented by a difference in size between the dotted ovals and their smaller, solid counterparts, while the heightened difficulty in access is shown by a leftward movement of the ovals on the graph. The visibly smaller solid ovals are further evidence of the decreased level of deal or transaction volume, which is estimated to have declined somewhere between 10 and 30% from 2019 levels; these statistics are confirmed, and debated, by various sources. However, the most meaningful decline in oval size occurs in the area of bootstrapping due to the entrepreneurial ecosystem's inherent financial difficulties. This negative shift in the viability of bootstrapping is undoubtedly worrisome for entrepreneurs because it often functions as a fallback method of entrepreneurial finance when the firm has exhausted all other finance options.

Additionally, the level of hands-on assistance that some providers of finance are now able to offer when compared to their previous abilities has also deteriorated post COVID-response. Venture capitalists and business angels are more prominently impacted in this area, although business angels are generally capable of providing more comprehensive and valuable know-how assistance. A final observation that can be made with reference to Fig. 8.1 is the state's emergence as one of the largest providers of entrepreneurial finance, due to the size of its assistance programs post COVID-response. And yet, given the state's track record of assistance to entrepreneurial firms, this may prove troublesome to both firms and the entrepreneurial ecosystem as a whole.

The Growth of Fintech as an Important Contributor of Entrepreneurial Finance

Beyond the modes of entrepreneurial finance mentioned previously, the provision of entrepreneurial finance is also supported, enabled, and enhanced through the implementation of technology-driven innovations and inventions that are comprised of software, business processes, and other modern technologies known collectively under the term "fintech". Primarily, financial technology purports to improve the efficiency with which various financial services are delivered. The fintech model of delivery is based on the use of the Internet, smartphones, and other online technologies, which is then applied to a wide range of finance options, including investments, securities trading, banking, risk management, the monitoring of financial performance, and financial activity reporting. Fintech also appears to fill a gap in the finance-oriented marketplace that has not been satisfied by the traditional channels of entrepreneurial and consumer finance. Evidence from the U.S., for example, suggests that fintech lending accounted for about 40% of the unsecured lending market in 2018; this value increased rapidly from about five percent in 2013. Research has also confirmed that global fintech lending grew by 115% in 2016 and 49% in 2017, reaching $400 billion in loan value and representing about 0.5% of global GDP. The two main categories of fintech relate to business loans, which account for about 70% of fintech financing, while the remaining 30% comprises consumer lending. Of course, fintech offers a number of functional advantages to financial institutions, such as a reduction of operational costs, necessary personnel, and other expenses (i.e., rent, utilities, etc.).

However, the most important component of fintech with relation to entrepreneurs is its ability to secure their access to alternate channels of entrepreneurial finance. One such channel is online lending, and in this case, fintech providers may rely on artificial intelligence, algorithms, big data analytics (i.e., methods of extracting and analyzing data from various sources), blockchain technologies (i.e., a list of various data structures that are linked together), biometric identification, and other technologies to assess the borrower's risks and make lending decisions. These non-traditional and fintech-based sources of entrepreneurial finance may include balance sheet lending, which involves the online platform lending directly to the borrower from its own financial resources, or peer-to-peer lending, which connects the two distinct pools of borrowers and lenders through the use of a technological platform. Online lenders can also offer other non-traditional finance products within the fintech framework, which can include revenue-based lending or royalty-based financing (a lender receives a percentage of revenue until the loan and interest are repaid), invoice factoring (using acquired contracts or issued invoices as the basis of obtaining a loan), or invoice discounting (providing funds equal to the value of the invoice, which is discounted by some percentage amount and commission). Online fintech providers may also emerge as an important source of independent entrepreneurial finance in the future.

The online processes offered by fintech may be relatively straightforward and timely in comparison with traditional channels of lending (i.e., banks, financial institutions, co-operatives, and so on). Online loans are provided on the basis of the applicant's input of basic information and data into a digital platform, which can include the number of years the business has operated, their level of sales, and the type of business. Once the loan has been approved, the borrower's financial data and banking information may be automatically linked to the fintech provider for the purpose of making payments, monitoring the financial standing of the borrowers, or perhaps some other purposes. The fintech lender is also permitted to charge an origination fee, interest rates (which may be more competitive when compared to traditional lenders), and other fees. Furthermore, borrower-lender arrangements under fintech may be more permitting in their allowance of delayed loan payments than traditional forms of entrepreneurial finance, although this flexibility is usually accompanied by additional fees.

Despite their ease of use, it is important to note that services offered by fintech firms are still not easily understood. While entrepreneurs are increasingly open to using various fintech solutions, surveys confirm that many potential users are unsure as to how fintech tools work or how they can enhance entrepreneurs' financial decision-making, reporting, management, and control; some may even struggle to see any benefit to fintech solutions at all. Nevertheless, there is evidence to suggest that fintech firms are able to make faster loan decisions, reach a wider range of consumers and entrepreneurial firms, and offer competitive interest rates, all without requiring collateral. On the other hand, fintech providers are known to aggressively pursue clients with late payments or delinquent loans.

Early analysis of the impact of COVID-response on fintech demonstrates a number of negative consequences, such as a tightening of lending practices and loan requirements by fintech providers; this is in line with practices introduced by traditional lending channels post COVID-response. Secondly, the provision of fintech finance has proven to have declined in the early period of COVID-response. This has necessitated a significant reduction in fintech lenders, while other financial operators have experienced outright failure. As a result, this industry problem has led to a wave of consolidations and buyouts of smaller fintech providers. Furthermore, fintech has suffered a decline in investments from venture capital firms, thus limiting their ability to innovate or provide additional capital to foster invention within entrepreneurial firms. However, the perpetuation of fintech's development may be one of the first major steps toward the full digitization of the relationship between suppliers and demanders of capital, which would disintermediate venture capital fund managers (a conclusion noted in Chapter three). The rise of fintech may also diminish the traditional channels of informal lending or the provision of finance, such as "love money", informal money lenders, microfinance institutions, and so on; this would be an unfortunate outcome of an otherwise positive industry development.

Government Assistance Programs Post COVID-Response

As argued throughout this book, the strict measures, restrictions, and constraints imposed post COVID-response by political leaders, unelected public officials, and local authorities has contributed to entrepreneurial crisis in a meaningful manner. However, the effectiveness of state assistance programs dedicated to the support of entrepreneurial firms has been alternately lauded and criticized by academics. These programs generally fall into six main categories and include financial aid, training and retooling assistance, advisory and consultancy services, marketing support, the provision of infrastructure, and research and development funding. An additional area of support can occasionally manifest in the form of business incubation, which is defined as targeted programs aimed at accelerating the development of entrepreneurial firms through a range of various support services.

While there are some potential benefits of these state programs to entrepreneurial firms, many academics find little empirical evidence to confirm that these programs actually translate into growth and prosperity for the entrepreneurial ecosystem. Furthermore, outright problems with these state programs may relate to the duplication of resources (many different agencies are usually involved in the delivery of these programs), the broad-based nature of the programs (which may cause problems when attempting to quantify their actual results and benefits), widespread bureaucratic restrictions and requirements, and misjudging actual entrepreneurial needs. There are also concerns about the quality and focus of state assistance programs, which often fail to recognize the complexity of the challenges facing entrepreneurial firms. In many cases, small firms would benefit more from a lack of restrictions, a return to business as usual, and most importantly, sales, than they would from state assistance.

States around the world have resorted to unprecedented stimulus packages post COVID-response (thereby increasing public debt to previously unseen levels), many of which were directed at the SME sector. This state assistance broadly fell into four categories: labor-related (i.e., wage subsidies, payroll protections, payment for hours not worked, and quarantine wage protection), assorted deferrals (i.e., social security and pension payments, tax deferrals, property tax postponements, a moratorium on debt payment, and bans on commercial evictions), financial assistance (i.e. grants, subsidies, loan guarantees, direct lending, and bridge loans), and structural adjustments and incentives (i.e., innovation, digitization, and safety or hygiene protocols). However, qualification for these programs was often predicated on the business meeting specific criteria, requirements, and minimums, which excluded many entrepreneurial firms. In some cases, access to these support programs rested on the firm's ability to secure a "matching" amount of financing from another type of financier, which, of course, likely proved difficult due to limitations in the provision of entrepreneurial finance post COVID-response. Other state programs have chosen to emphasize and foster innovation.

Furthermore, some states have co-operated with financial institutions and requested that banks grant a moratorium on all interest payments or loan repayments for a specific period of time. An additional unique program offered by the state is the loan guarantee, which aims to incentivize financial institutions to extend loans to the SME sector. In these cases, state programs guarantee up to 80% of the loan amount, the value of which can be quite substantial. For example, a program in Austria guarantees the repayment of 80% of a loan's value equal to €10 million. Some of the largest loan guarantee programs were offered by the U.K. (£330 billion) and France (€300 billion), while other countries have significantly increased the capacity and scope of their preexisting programs.

Conclusions: Access to Finance and the Financial Management of Entrepreneurial Firms in the Age of COVID-Response

The numerous benefits of engaging with successful financial management for young and more mature entrepreneurial firms alike include better planning, a clear focus, more optimal choices, and a greater appreciation of underlying risks. In addition, financial management can become an important platform to test-drive various strategic and financial scenarios before they are implemented in practice. Financial planning, along with strategic management and specific financial practices (i.e., capital budgeting, valuation, liquidity management, and so on), can identify a firm's key areas of value creation while also illuminating decisions that can convert into value destruction.

However, the period following COVID-response is likely to redefine financial management as it was formerly understood by entrepreneurs. Many of the previous financial practices of traditional financial management that relied on stable access to information and the analysis on historical trends are now less valuable to entrepreneurs. For example, the historical records of many entrepreneurial that were previously depended upon as a guide to develop future strategies and financial forecasts are now essentially less usefull. This uncertainty forces the vast majority of entrepreneurs to operate in a state of operational and financial "blindness" post COVID-response.

The inability to engage in meaningful financial planning has many operational impacts, including a failure to hire employees, safely commit financial resources, enhance products and services, and pursue innovation. Furthermore, a negative consequence of entrepreneurs' incapability to create financial forecasts is a further challenge in their access to finance. Obtaining financial forecasts is a cornerstone of a financier's ability to evaluate the entrepreneurial firm's likelihood of generating adequate levels of financial returns (for equity providers) or to make loan payments and repay the principle (for debt providers). Issues relating to the development of financial forecasts is likely to further exacerbate a decline in the amount of capital various types of financiers are able to extend to entrepreneurial firms post COVID-response.

Bibliography

Arundale, Keith and Colin Mason. 2020. Private equity & venture capital: Riding the COVID-19 crisis. *Innovation in Business, Economics & Finance 1*, eds. Monica Billio and Simone Varotto, 193–220. Ca' Foscari University Press: Venice.

Bartik, Alexander W., Marianne Bertrand, Zoe Cullen, Edward L. Gleaser, Michael Luca, and Christopher Straton. 2020. The impact of COVID-19 on small business outcomes and expectations. *Proceedings of the National Academy of Science*, 117: 17656–17666.

Brown, Ross and Augusto Rocha. 2020. Entrepreneurial uncertainty during the COVID-19 crisis: Mapping the temporal dynamics of entrepreneurial finance. *Journal of Business Venturing Insights*, 14: 1–10.

Brown, Ross, Augusto Rocha, and Marc Cowling. 2020. Financing entrepreneurship in times of crisis: Exploring the impact of COVID-19 on the market for entrepreneurial finance in the United Kingdom. *International Small Business Journal*, 38: 380–390.

Calvino, Flavio, Chiara Criscuolo, and Rudy Verihac. 2020. Start-ups in the time of COVID-19: Facing the challenges, seizing the opportunities. June 23. www.voxeu.org.

Caplain, Judd. 2020. Banks balance surge in SME business loans. April 16. www.kpmg.com.

Carman, Ashley. 2020. Kickstarter plans layoffs after new projects on the site drop off by 35%. April 20. www.theverge.com.

Collier, Paul and Colin Meyer. 2020. Reforming the UK financial system to promote regional development in post-COVID Britain. *Oxford Review of Economic Policy*, 36: 270–280.

Cook, John. 2020. Caution ahead: Startup report predicts venture capital drought, layoffs as COVID-19 crisis mounts. April 27. www.geekwire.com.

Corredera-Catalan, Felix, Fillipo di Pietro, and Antonio Trujillo-Ponce. 2021. Post-COVID-19 SME financing constraints and the credit guarantee scheme solution in Spain. *Journal of Banking Regulation*, March, 1–11.

Deloitte. 2020. Private equity opportunities post-COVID-19. August 7. www.deloitte.com.

Deutsch, Waverly. 2020. COVID-19 is changing key business relationships. August 27. www.review.chicagobooth.edu.

Dua, Andre, Deepa Mahajan, Lucienne Oyer, and Sree Ramaswamy. 2020. US Small-business recovery after the COVID-19 crisis. July 7. www.mckinsey.com.

Farhoud, Mohamed, Sheeza Shah, Pekka Stenholm, Ewald Kibler, Maija Renko, and Siri Terjesen. 2021. Social enterprise crowdfunding in an acute crisis. *Journal of Business Venturing Insights*, 15: 1–6.

Grabow, Jeffrey. 2020. Venture capital before and after the pandemic. April 21. www.ey.com.

InnoCell. 2020. Venture capital post-COVID-19: Trends in the entrepreneurial and investment environment. July 22. www.medium.com.

Klonowski, Darek. 2014. *Strategic Entrepreneurial Finance: From Value Creation to Realization*. London: Routledge.

Klonowski, Darek. 2018. *The Venture Capital Deformation: Value Destruction throughout the Investment Process*. New York: Palgrave MacMillan.

Lewis, Michelle and Qiang Liu. 2020. The COVID-19 outbreak and access to small business finance. September. Reserve Bank of Australia.

Looze, Jessica and Sameeksha Desai. 2020. How does COVID-19 affect challenges facing entrepreneurs? Trends by business age. December 16. Ewing Marion Kauffman Foundation.

Nadkarni, Anuja. 2020. Crowdfunding campaigns struggling after COVID-19. June 18. www.stuff.co.nz.

OECD. 2020. Coronavirus (COVID-19): SME policy responses. July 15. www.oecd.org.

Rice, Zabediah. 2020. A venture capitalist's 3 lessons from the last two tech crushes. March 16. www.startupdaily.net.

Robinson, Mark, Jamie McLaren, and Matthew Wentz. 2020. Pressure points: Venture capital in Southeast Asia post-COVID-19. June 24. www.herbertsmithfreehills.com.

Shepherd, Dean A. COVID 19 and entrepreneurship: Time to pivot? *Journal of Management Studies*, 57: 1750–1753.

Simmons, Lee. 2020. VCs and COVID-19: We're doing fine, thanks. September 22. www.gsb.stanford.edu.

Team Sequoia. 2020. Coronavirus: The Black Swan of 2020. March 5. www.medium.com.

Technavio. 2020. Crowdfunding market analysis highlights the impact of COVID-19 (2020–2024): Increasing use of social media to boost market growth. August 4. www.businesswire.com.

Thorne, James and Priyamvada Mathur. 2020. Venture capitalists to adopt new script on fundraising. June 2. www.pitchbook.com.

Tucker, Charlotte. 2020. How is coronavirus impacting the funding landscape for startups? April 30. www.eu-startups.com.

Wintermeyer, Lawrence. 2020. COVID-19 has put many British businesses on life support systems–Can Fintech help save U.K. SMEs? December 17. www.forbes.com.

PART VI

Conclusions: Venture Capital in the Age of Covid

CHAPTER 9

Descent or Revival of Venture Capital in the Age of COVID

The last eight chapters provided a detailed analysis of the various internal and external components within the venture capital ecosystem that have been affected by COVID-response. This analysis has proven to be more pessimistic than optimistic and paints a grim picture of venture capital's immediate future while also suggesting a prolonged, long-term negative impact on the entire industry. The presented material reflects this initial evidence from the venture capital ecosystem, which has been documented in multiple industry studies (consulting firms have been quick, responsive, and reflective), newspapers, magazines, business and financial dailies, state reports, Internet-based articles and blogs, research institutes, and think-tanks. However, there has unfortunately very limited academic inquiry into venture capital post COVID-response at the time of this writing. A number of academic articles related to the state of entrepreneurship post COVID-response have also been relied upon; these studies have been descriptive and observational (based on secondary data, various information sources, and deductive reasoning), and empirical.

This chapter's content will continue to reveal the broken nature of the venture capital industry and the vulnerability of the small business sector. The current economic, political, social, and structural adjustments that are occurring globally are likely to place additional pressures on the venture capital ecosystem and will be discussed further in the following sections.

D. Klonowski, *Venture Capital Redefined*,
https://doi.org/10.1007/978-3-030-83387-9_9

Four Pillars of the Global Venture Capital Ecosystem

An estimation of the venture capital industry's future success is inherently difficult to predict because the emerging picture still has many moving fragments, conflating information, and opposing trends, as well as several unknowns. The objective of this section of the chapter is to elaborate on the key components that are likely to influence the future shape of the industry. Of course, there may be additional meaningful undercurrents not discussed here, which in due course may sway the industry in a specific direction; this is difficult to anticipate at the moment. One such trend may be the sudden disappearance of the novel coronavirus and a complete stoppage of state-led COVID-response. Alternatively, there could be more insistent restrictions, lockdowns, and restraints that surpass those implemented thus far to further hinder the industry.

Figure 9.1 presents the four pillars of the global venture capital ecosystem that are estimated to be most critical to its future development: the entrepreneurial sector (or the entrepreneurial ecosystem),

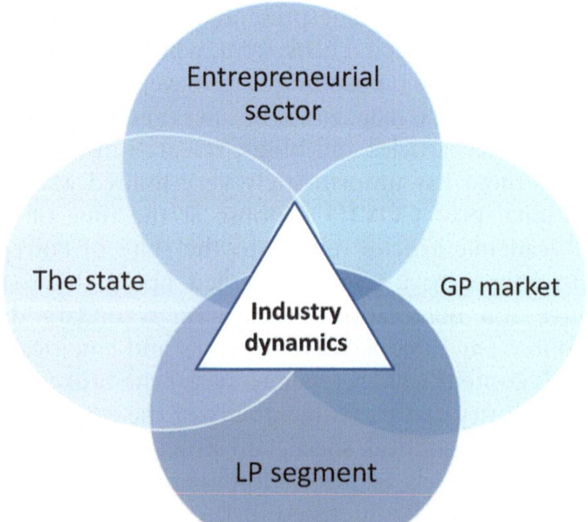

Fig. 9.1 Key components of the venture capital ecosystem

operational and market dynamics related to general partners (GPs), networks associated with limited partners (LPs), and actions of the state. These components are discussed separately, although they are interconnected; they cross-influence each other in a synergetic, cooperative, and enhancing manner to jointly affect the venture capital ecosystem. As an example, the existence of a flourishing entrepreneurial sector translates into a thriving economy (i.e., economic growth, low unemployment, strong consumption, and so on). The entrepreneurial ecosystem is especially fertile when firms are able to effectively transition from a small company to become medium-sized, large, and eventually even a mega corporation. For venture capitalists, a strong entrepreneurial ecosystem and the steady migration of firms from one development stage to another allows for a steady inflow of deals; this, in turn, is beneficial to the LP market segment, which indirectly supports these firms with financial means of development that are delivered through intermediaries (i.e., GPs). In return for this indirect provision of finance, LPs may receive above-average returns.

Of course, entrepreneurial firms grow best in an environment with friendly institutional infrastructure, limited business interference, manageable business establishment and registration requirements, low regulations, reduced taxes, fewer bureaucratic restrictions, and an effective court and legal system. Accessible and business-oriented institutional infrastructure (i.e., laws, accounting regulations, corporate governance standards, etc.), in turn, provides further incentives for entrepreneurial development and perpetuation. Steady infrastructure is also critical for a strong capital inflow into the market from domestic and foreign LPs, as well as the expansion of local financial intermediaries (GPs). Furthermore, the existence of a reasonable number of GPs assures that entrepreneurial firms can pair with the most suitable and optimal financiers who understand their specific sector of the economy, are able to properly assess business and financial risks, and have the internal capability to provide optimal hands-on assistance. A selection of GPs that is commensurate with the opportunities available in the marketplace also allows LPs to focus on the unique segments of the economy which they view as most attractive; LPs can thus allocate their capital both efficiently and optimally. Additionally, the state can be an important conduit for the development of the venture capital ecosystem by establishing minimal regulations, offering low taxation (including capital gains tax) and state fees, limiting business interference, and allowing the industry to develop its own system of checks and balances (i.e., self-regulation).

As noted in previous chapters, the small and medium-sized enterprise (SME) sector plays a key role in shaping national economies. In fact, SMEs represent over 95% of all firms, account for between one half to two-thirds of national employment, and make up about 50% of the GDP within many different countries. For example, SMEs account for 99.9% of all businesses and employ about 47.1% of the workforce in the United States (U.S.). These firms create about 1.5 million jobs per annum, which account for about two-thirds of all newly created jobs. SMEs also generate innovations, while the sector as a whole is characterized by resiliency, flexibility, and agility. However, the entrepreneurial ecosystem is not only critical for national economies, but it also fuels the venture capital industry. Thus, the fact that the SME sector has been one of the hardest-hit segments of the economy post COVID-response, which was discussed in Chapters 7 and 8, has many additional consequences for firms, the venture capital industry, and the economy at large. In different countries, between 30 and 50% of firms from the SME sector suspended their operations, while up to 80% of firms reported both demand-side and supply-side issues due to the severity of external shocks that arose post COVID-response. It is also important to clarify that many SMEs have not yet fully recovered from the 2008 financial crisis and, consequently, were already operating under significant financial and operational constraints and pressures prior to COVID-response.

The operational aspect of the venture capital fund partnership is vested with GPs, who manage about seven thousand active funds within the entirety of the global GP market segment. Since entry barriers into the industry are relatively low, there is a regular influx of new players into the venture capital ecosystem; there are over two hundred new funds created every year in different geographic markets. GPs compete with each other on two main counts: investing in attractive entrepreneurial firms and securing capital from LPs to successfully manage these firms. Competition for deals is intense and often spurs aggressive retaliation among GPs. When promoting themselves to potential investee firms, GPs rely on their market reputation and past track record of success to distinguish their services in terms of the level of hands-on assistance offered, the industry focus, the size of capital they may provide, their speed when closing deals, the geographic market of coverage, and so on.

Another critical area of competition is capital, which is typically more intense among GPs after an economic downturn; LPs tend to hoard capital and seek more stable and liquid modes of investing during these economic periods. In this case, GPs compete to pitch their allegedly unique market approaches to LPs, which are grounded in GPs' focus on the nature of entrepreneurial firms (i.e., start-ups, early stage, expansion), the types of deals (i.e., traditional, buyouts, buy-ins, restructuring, turnaround, etc.), the industry, and the amount of capital required per deal. Although GPs attempt to occupy a distinctive and favorable segment of the market with respect to some of these parameters, the most significant differentiators between GPs are returns. Ultimately, the size and consistency of returns are the only true measures of GPs' abilities to find deals, screen and analyze opportunities, and work with investee firms effectively; returns directly reflect GPs' talents and capabilities.

In addition to the entrepreneurial sector, the LP market segment and its provision of actual capital is another critical building block of the venture capital ecosystem. Capital contributions may come from various types of LPs, including pension funds, endowments, corporations, insurance companies, financial institutions, banks, multinational corporations, or wealthy individuals. LPs are passive investors who only contribute capital to the partnership because, as stated previously, GPs are responsible for day-to-day operations of the fund; they effectively buy investment management services from GPs. LPs' capital contributions normally occur in phases or stages following GPs' capital calls for drawdowns, which reflects the timing of investing into portfolio firms. However, LPs have become increasingly mindful of GPs' patterns of poor financial record, excessive fee structures, extraordinary amounts of carried interest earned, and limited information disclosure. In spite of these challenges, most LPs have maintained fixed allocations to venture capital, which rarely exceeds 15% of capital under management. LPs may be motivated to invest in venture capital because of their desire to achieve suitable portfolio diversification, gain access to premium investment opportunities they would otherwise be unable to access, or to generate above-average returns. And yet, LPs simultaneously recognize that venture capital funds are more risky and highly illiquid when compared to other types of investing. While many LPs continue to embrace the industry and nourish underperforming GPs when they do not have access to the top quartile GPs, other LPs have learned to ignore the asset class in favor of other forms of investing, such as public equities markets and other aspects of private capital (i.e., debt, infrastructure, real estate, resources, and so on). Regardless of the critical role LPs play in the venture capital ecosystem, they have traditionally held a relatively weak bargaining position vis-à-vis GPs, which may reflect LPs' erroneous belief in GPs' ability to access the most attractive investment opportunities and generate premium returns.

The state is a significant and active component to most economies around the globe, and as such, it necessarily plays an important role in the development of a strong economy. However, the state can also hurt the economy through over-active involvement, suppression of rights and freedoms, destruction of private initiative, over-regulation, excessive taxation, and various other means. And yet, it is the "systemic competitiveness" promoted by the state that is relevant to this discussion, which broadly encompasses the state's provision of appropriate institutional infrastructure and administrative support to the private sector. The key components of this system may relate to legal infrastructure (i.e., property rights, ownership laws, corporate laws, judicial and court systems), accounting regulations (i.e., accounting standards, tax reporting, assuring compliance with accounting legislation), and taxation (i.e., fiscal policies, tax collection policies, and tax rates). In terms of the venture capital industry, the state can positively influence its growth by establishing a favorable tax treatment of capital gains, further limiting regulation, and refraining from any direct interference. And yet, since the 2008 financial crisis, the positive predisposition of the state toward venture capital has been altered in many countries as more academic studies have raised questions about the industry's actual contributions to economic growth, job creation, and innovation. In short, the 2008 financial crisis spurred more intensive scrutiny, and potentially greater interference, of the venture capital industry by the state.

Lastly, it is important to note that various schools of economics, such as Marxism and Keynesianism, praise the positive role and involvement of the state. There are examples of many countries, including South Korea, Taiwan, Japan, Singapore, Indonesia, and Hong Kong, where industrial policies were successfully drafted and implemented by the state. Other countries with an active state and an expanded welfare system (such as Sweden, Norway, and Finland) have also seen some of the fastest economic growth in the world. The key features of an economy in which the state is heavily involved can be identified by the substantial size of the state and the subsequently elevated level of control it wields, high public spending (including social programs), increased regulation, and deficit spending. On the other hand, other economic schools of thought, including the classical and Austrian schools, blame the state and its ensuing regulations, taxes, and ownership for all human and economic ills. Many schools of modern liberal economics similarly declare that the state's involvement in the market is overwhelmingly negative, suboptimal, and obstructing; modern economics argues that the state is incapable of looking after national wealth and the common interest because state officials are corruptible and may behave solely in their own interest. The key features of an economy where the state is minimized include a limited size of the state, decreased state spending, active participation of the private sector, deregulation, and balanced budgets.

The Revival of Venture Capitalism

Given the previous discourse in the last eight chapters, it is difficult to prophesize a positive outcome for the venture capital industry in the short- and medium-term; negative effects are easily visible, while positive evidence is challenging to locate. Nevertheless, the main objective of the discussion in this section is to outline the conditions that will need to be fulfilled to realize the venture capital industry's revival and revitalization. In other words, the revival of the venture capital industry would be predicated on a number of positive changes in the four pillars outlined above. The following section will define these required conditions, as well as offer comments regarding the likelihood of these positive developments occurring in the future (see the left-hand side of Table 9.1 for a brief summary of this discussion).

Stimulation of the Entrepreneurial Ecosystem

The venture capital ecosystem could be revived if the entrepreneurial sector embraced new developments, innovations, and general industrial restructuring while at the same time avoiding the destruction caused by COVID-response within key segments of the economy where entrepreneurial firms have traditionally flourished. Of course, a vital assumption behind the revitalization of the entrepreneurial ecosystem is that the impact of COVID-response can somehow be converted into entrepreneurial opportunities on a massive scale. Chapter 4 identified some segments of the economy which are likely to experience strong growth in the future; these segments may include fintech, cyber

Table 9.1 Four pillars of the venture capital ecosystem

Key pillar	*Revival of venture capital*	*Descent of venture capital*
Entrepreneurial sector	• Possible emergence of new, high-growth segments of the economy • Emergence of new disruptive technologies and innovations may revitalize the SME sector • Firms may become more efficient and productive • Productivity growth may translate into economy-wide growth	• Continued restrictions, limitations, and restraints devastate the SME sector • Recovery of the entrepreneurial ecosystem likely to take time • Firms in most affected segments of the economy likely to struggle • Strong disincentives for business formation • Difficult access to finance likely to thwart business growth • Market consolidation and monopolization likely to negatively affect the SME sector
GP market dynamics	• GPs to become more selective in investment decisions; this may enhance returns • More focus on portfolio firms, which would enhance GPs' skillsets • GPs may provide financing to a wide range of firms	• Limited number of attractive investable projects • Significant issues in GPs' portfolio firms; GPs unprepared to handle such problems • Increased numbers of write-downs and write-offs in GP portfolios • Sustained low returns in the foreseeable future • Continued decline in GP performance • Widening disparity between top quartile and remaining GPs
LP infrastructure	• LPs likely to be more selective, which may improve performance • LPs continue to exhibit long-term view of the venture capital asset class • Unclear whether re-adjustment to LP-GP arrangements may be possible	• Poor financial performance of GPs may discourage LPs • LPs may continue normal asset allocation strategies • Continued lack of recognition of divergent interests between GPs and LPs

Key pillar	*Revival of venture capital*	*Descent of venture capital*
State	• State to provide assistance to the SME sector • Improved institutional infrastructure • State may provide various incentives to the venture capital industry	• State likely to play a negative role for the SME sector and GPs • Continued restrictions, lockdowns, limits, new regulations, and "preventive" measures • State to continue its actions in spite of data and evidence suggesting this is counterproductive

Abbreviations: *GPs* general partners, *LPs* limited partners, *SME* small and medium-sized enterprise security, online shopping, social media platforms, digital entertainment, telemedicine, online health screening, digital education, biotechnology, and medical technology. In order to view these developments positively, it would also need to be presumed that these sectors would lead to significant new venture creation and the progression of existing firms toward higher levels of entrepreneurial development. This notion is also predicated on the belief that opportunities in these sectors would be open to new or existing entrepreneurial ventures, which is not a guarantee. Additionally, many of these new and high-growth sectors are likely to require access to significant amounts of capital.

Therefore, it is important to ask: How likely is it that these assumptions and conditions can be met? Initial evidence suggests that the SME sector is struggling with a wide range of issues, including financial management (i.e., loss of revenue, liquidity and cash flow problems, etc.), adjusting existing business models, human resource modifications (i.e., staff reductions, decrease in wages, low morale, etc.), product alterations, and new product development. These struggles are multiple, severe, and simultaneous, which prevents entrepreneurial firms from devising timely and effective solutions. Although there may be opportunities to develop successful ventures, these prospects may be limited to relatively selective and narrow segments of the economy. There is also evidence that the on-and-off fluctuation of state restrictions acts as an effective deterrent for new business formation and business continuation. Many entrepreneurs who put their life savings into their venture, mortgaged their houses to survive, borrowed from friends and family, dedicated all available "sweat equity", and eventually bankrupted their business ventures, are unlikely to come back as business owners or *serial entrepreneurs* even if attractive opportunities emerge; their proverbial "entrepreneurial spines" have been broken.

Another critical assumption about the entrepreneurial sector that one would need to make is regarding the availability of capital to fund these emerging sectors of the economy. Here again, background investigation confirms that access to entrepreneurial finance in the form of banks, venture capital, business angels, crowdfunding, and fintech is more difficult post COVID-response. Although state programs are more readily available, their access is based on the fulfillment of a wide range of pre-conditions and requirements, which may preclude many firms. Furthermore, the ability of friends-and-family financing to fill the wide gaps resulting from declines in the accessibility of other forms of finance post COVID-response is difficult to predict.

While there have been many evidence-supported arguments provided to outline the struggles of the SME sector post COVID-response, it is important to acknowledge the positive developments, which, in due course, may provide some impetus for growth to the sector. Firstly, the current crisis can provide multiple opportunities to re-adjust, re-align, and re-organize the entrepreneurial ecosystem; for example, the crisis may force firms to relocate available resources, thus leading to more innovation, efficiency, and productivity. Of course, productivity gains can be achieved by shedding a significant part of the labor pool, although if this were to occur on a massive scale, the minor economic activity achieved would be at the expense of significant increases in unemployment. Evidence suggests that about 80% of entrepreneurial firms have already had to deal with major adjustments to their operations, which included addressing a reduction in customers, dealing with products and services that no longer fit their customers' needs, accommodating customers' increased sensitivity to prices, changing modes of delivery (i.e., curbside pickup), and so on. If these adjustments are successfully done, emerging and fast-growing entrepreneurial firms could potentially absorb employment losses arising from business reductions and closures.

Secondly, entrepreneurial firms that survive the current economic devastation would be in a favorable marketplace position to potentially become high-growth ventures. These firms would grow at the expense of firms unable to survive the period of COVID-response, so the net effect on employment would be limited.

Thirdly, evidence indicates that these high-growth entrepreneurial firms could tap into a talent pool of university-trained engineers, scientists, and MBAs whose employability is lower during recessions; these university graduates may be employed by developing entrepreneurial firms at an affordable cost due to their limited employment opportunities.

Possible Enhancements in the GP Market

There is no evidence to support the idea that the vast majority of GPs are seeking to proactively change their business models in a way that would revitalize the venture capital industry, improve entrepreneurial firms' access to finance, or provide much-needed hands-on assistance. There have been limited changes in the venture capital industry in the last 50 years, which has resulted in a poor and still declining financial performance. Because participation in the venture capital industry has remained financially rewarding for GPs, there has been no real incentive for them to change their behaviors. So, under what conditions would GPs contribute to a profound revival of the industry? Primarily, GPs would need to begin recruiting a completely new stream of talent with significant practical industry experience; in other words, fund managers would need to begin increasingly employing "superior venture capitalists" who exhibit the characteristics outlined in Chapter 6. Although hiring from a new talent pool is feasible for the industry, such action would need to be grounded in the industry's deep self-reflection and self-diagnosis, which may simply not be possible when the industry is filled with MBA-type actors that gravitate toward hiring the same types of professionals. Sadly, there has been a mass departure of professionals with the right industrial backgrounds and the aspiration of being in the "business of building businesses" (i.e., "superior venture capitalists") in the last twenty years due to retirement, thereby leaving a disproportionate number of inferior venture capitalists in the industry.

Another requirement of GPs to revitalize the venture capital industry would be their voluntary agreement to right-size their operations to match the volume of attractive investment opportunities available in the marketplace. In terms of operational changes, this would mean limiting the scope of fundraising drives, reducing the size of current operations, lowering fees, restricting the number of professionals in the industry, and decreasing salaries. However, current evidence suggests that follow-on funds are generally bigger than they were in the past, and GPs are not willing to contemplate such systemic adjustments. As noted throughout this book, the motivation to secure additional fixed fees is difficult to resist by GPs because these fees provide a financial cushion against prolonged economic cycles. This addiction to fixed fees, high salaries, and employment stability may be one of most critical impediments to change within the venture capital industry. Furthermore, there has been very limited alteration to the venture capital investment process over the last 50 years; it has broadly consisted of the same five stages. Venture capitalists have, however, experimented with varying their approaches toward conducting due diligence, negotiating deals, and working with investee firms in a more proactive way over a longer period of time. And yet, because the venture capital process is designed to achieve the highest financial returns in the shortest possible increment of time, GPs swiftly move from one investment project to another in search of premium returns.

Another result of venture capitalists' haste for optimal financial returns over short intervals, and which is also an impediment to the industry's revival, is the suboptimal assistance GPs provide to entrepreneurial firms. Only a small subset of venture capitalists are able to provide robust hands-on assistance, and this is not likely to change without an influx of new professionals into the industry. Additionally, while GPs often seek investee firms with superior technological innovations, they have resisted upgrading their own internal operations. Other operators in the broadly defined finance industry have fully embraced artificial intelligence, algorithms, big data analytics (i.e., methods of extracting and analyzing data from various sources), blockchain technologies, (i.e., a list of various data structures, which are linked together), and other technological tools; with the exception of a small group of GPs, such technologies have not been widely adopted in the industry.

LPs as the Engine of Change in the Venture Capital Ecosystem

If there is one area where a much-needed spark for the venture capital industry's revitalization could originate, it is with LPs. These important stakeholders of the venture capital ecosystem could easily contribute to the industry's swift revival if LPs were to submit GPs to gentle moral suasion or exert even small amounts of pressure. Such efforts could include cutting the "fuel supply" to underperforming GPs, changing GPs' compensation structures by establishing new methods of aligning interest in the LP-GP relationship, negotiating more strict legal terms, right-sizing the industry by curtailing fundraising activities to the actual volume of deal flow, and changing automatic "bucket-filling" allocation. By implementing these measures, LPs could restore the venture capital system's natural equilibrium by allowing it to predominantly rest on LPs and entrepreneurial firms, rather than on GPs. However, the chance of such an adjustment is unfortunately low given LPs' track record of documented LP-GP arrangements over the last 50 years. There is also no evidence that any fundamental changes to LP-GP engagements are underway in the current economic climate, the reasons for which have been provided in detail in previous chapters.

Assistance from the State for the Venture Capital Ecosystem

The fourth pillar that may be able to reinvigorate the venture capital industry is the state, which can also simultaneously impact the entrepreneurial ecosystem, the LP and GP markets, and its own institutional infrastructure in a positive way. Additionally, the state could conceivably play an important role in aiding the SME sector; by carefully evaluating their currently available assistance programs, the state could potentially expand to provide facilities and resources for business incubation, acceleration, and development. As some academics suggest, preexisting programs could be even more effective if the state selectively chose to assist the most promising ventures rather than spreading its limited resources to firms that are unlikely to generate strong growth, increase employment, and enhance productivity. Furthermore, the state could become an important hub for providing financial support to start-ups, innovative firms, and capable exporters. There are also numerous opportunities for the state to create public–private equity fund-of-fund programs (i.e., Israel and South Korea) or state venture capital (i.e., the U.S. and Canada). Obvious impediments to the implementation of these programs would be the state's ability to obtain the resources to finance such initiatives, and potential long-term implications for the venture capital industry, the state, and the economy.

By choosing to focus on various proactive structural programs promoting innovation, internalization, and specialization, the state could foster entrepreneurial resilience post COVID-response. Contemporary surveys of entrepreneurial firms suggest that they would appreciate some assistance in the areas of salary subsidies, access to loans and credit guarantees, rent deferrals, utility subsidies, loan repayment deferrals, and tax postponements. Entrepreneurs also indicate that they would specifically benefit from zero-interest loans, which could be extended for longer periods of time until their operations were restored to the previously anticipated levels of their development trajectory. Moreover, and in terms of institutional infrastructure, the state could ease the accessibility and cost of business registration, simplify tax structures, provide tax incentives to the SME sector, limit various rules and regulations, and generally be more business-friendly. The most critical need of the SME sector, however, is for the state to remove the COVID-response restrictions so the sector can begin its rebuilding efforts. And yet, and as noted in previous chapters, the state does not have a positive historical record regarding their assistance programs, so it is prudent to be skeptical of their ability to develop effective programs on a massive scale post COVID-response.

Evidence for the Descent of Venture Capital

The case for the descent of the venture capital industry post COVID-response is strong, particularly in light of numerous drifts and inclinations that may act as destructive undercurrents within the industry now and continuing into the future (these trends are summarized on the right-hand side of Table 9.1). Negative trends that are evidenced now may represent a cascading effect through the entire venture capital ecosystem; COVID-response has destabilized the SME sector, thereby causing problems with GPs' portfolio firms, which will ultimately lead to the weak financial performance of GPs and poor net returns for LPs.

Prolonged State of Entrepreneurial Crisis

Previous chapters have highlighted a wide range of problems that the entrepreneurial sector has suffered post COVID-response. The most affected segments of the economy, many of which are part of the SME sector, include hotels, restaurants, cafes, construction firms, logistics service suppliers, and a wide range of personal services (i.e., barber shops, fitness operators, retail boutiques, entertainment and leisure centers, and so on). If the state and public officials continue along the current path of restraints, restrictions, and limitations, the inevitable outcome will be irreparable devastation to small businesses and their owners. As previously noted, the most significant problems to arise in the SME sector post COVID-response are related to revenue generation (this is the most prominent issue), profitability, cash flow management, liquidity, and the unavailability of financial resources. Since there is evidence to suggest that business owners are unsure if they will be able to secure adequate financing to maintain their firm's survival, they may resort to state assistance, personal savings, friends-and-family, community donations, and other means, to cover any unanticipated cash emergencies.

As stated in Chapter 8, entrepreneurs, perhaps recognizing the fragility of their business operations, poor financial standing, and already high levels of debt, are careful to only raise debt incrementally; they understand that this could exacerbate their already dire business and personal situations. Under conditions of higher debt levels, entrepreneurs are at the risk of losing their business, their homes, and personal assets, while simultaneously threating their family with bankruptcy. Research indicates that between 50 and 70% of entrepreneurial firms among different countries struggle in the area of financial management, with concerns predominantly related to covering wages, operating expenses (including accounts payable), lease or rent payments (which may consume up to 50% of revenue), and loan payments. A lack of demand for products and services is an economy-wide problem, which is driven by mass unemployment, poor job prospects, a downward pressure on wages, and limited savings. These conditions precipitating weak economic consumption are unlikely to change until employment stability (i.e., normal fulltime hours, restoration of wage growth trajectories, etc.) and confidence in the economy re-emerges; this is likely to take years.

Furthermore, entrepreneurial firms have struggled to revamp their existing business models, adjust daily operations, modify levels of staffing, refashion products and services, and make other alterations post COVID-response. Although these are major adjustments that were required to be made in a short period of time, they were sometimes not sufficient to ensure a business's survival. For example, while some firms adjusted somewhat to online sales, online customer interactions, and digital payments, such actions do not appear to adequately restore revenue. Many of these adjustments also do not directly address demand-side and supply-side challenges, as the entrepreneurial ecosystem has not seen or dealt with these types of issues previously. In addition to the speed with which government restrictions were implemented and changes were thus required to be made, a further barrier for entrepreneurial firms was the high cost of many of these adjustments.

Along with operational and financial issues, many entrepreneurial firms have also been forced to make human resource adjustments in the form of lay-offs, which is supported by evidence from various countries. Data from Canada, for example, suggests that about half of all firms in the SME sector laid off up to 80% of their workforce. Not only do mass lay-offs represent a disruption of production workflow, teamwork, and the flow of information, but it also fuels undue staff turnover and negatively impacts the morale, commitment, and loyalty of personnel who remain employed. Moreover, a sustained disruption of the workforce can detrimentally affect creativity and innovation while also being costly, due to training expenditures, lower efficiency of newly hired personnel, work disruption and stoppages, high levels of scrap, and so on. The rate of rehiring currently remains low, as research from the U.S., for example, suggests that only 45% of firms claim to rehire personnel to the same level held prior to COVID-response.

It is also prudent to mention the mental health of business owners, which has been detrimentally affected post COVID-response but is a problem often omitted in public discussions. In addition to significant worries and stress about their ventures, entrepreneurs are also increasingly concerned about their families from both a financial and health standpoint. Research indicates that nearly half of all business owners experience higher levels of burnout, stress, and anxiety, which are mental strains that may also disproportionately affect female entrepreneurs.

The multiple problems that impact the entrepreneurial ecosystem post COVID-response can lead to a continual downward spiral of revenue, profitability, and cash resources, which, if sustained over the medium- or long-term, could result in declining levels of operational efficiency and productivity. The most significant adversaries to entrepreneurial continuation are the on/off switches in business operations brought about by COVID-response and fluctuating government restrictions. Evidence from past recessions suggests that it will take a number of years for the SME sector to recover from the current crisis. As already noted, this is likely to discourage new business formation and prevent existing businesses from transitioning to new levels of development. Of course, there have been some clear beneficiaries of COVID-response, including "big-box" retail outlets (i.e., Walmart), "big pharma" (i.e., Pfizer, Johnson & Johnson, Moderna), "big tech" (i.e., Amazon, Alibaba, Shopify, Alphabet), and social media platforms (i.e., Facebook, Twitter).

A Spillover Effect of Entrepreneurial Challenges to GPs

Problems in the entrepreneurial sector can only exacerbate problems for GPs. As demonstrated in Chapter 5, numerous and severe challenges are anticipated at every phase of the venture capital investment process. Firstly, one of the most adversely affected areas of venture capital is deal flow, although the venture capital community already struggled in this area prior to COVID-response. Secondly, many portfolio firms have been affected; their fortunes are also compounded by comprehensive challenges from other market segments as well. However, portfolio problems have likely not yet been fully manifested for the majority of GPs, as they are anticipated to crystalize in the next 12–18 months. Thirdly, most GPs are unprepared to handle extensive damage to their portfolio firms due to a lack of practical experience, strategic vision, and industry knowledge, among other factors. GPs are generally untested and unprepared for situations in which the majority of their time is dedicated to portfolio firms rather than deal-making activities; this represents a complete re-adjustment to the daily patterns of venture capital operations. Additionally, COVID-response is likely to continue revealing the many weaknesses and disadvantages inherent to the venture capital ecosystem, which are primarily grounded in the inability of most GPs to provide value-added assistance to firms. Fourthly, financial challenges within the SME sector would continue to put significant downward pressures on the business valuations of portfolio firms, which, in turn, is expected to initiate a massive wave of write-downs and even write-offs. Thus, GPs should anticipate a tsunami of portfolio firm fatalities and major problems in the future. Of course, the net effect of these negative trends is a continuation of the already declining returns that were seen by the industry prior to COVID-response.

LPs' Continued Dislocation

Historical evidence from the venture capital industry illustrates that LPs have failed to recognize the continued divergence of interest between GPs and themselves. Academics have persistently, albeit wrongly, argued that the 80/20 compensation scheme and carried interest arrangements are sufficient for aligning LP and GP interests. While these structures are likely to prevail for some time in the future, they are bound to be reversed, although this erroneous belief in the proper alignment of interest between GPs and LPs is bound to accelerate the decline of the industry in the meantime. Careful observers have deduced a clear misalignment of interest between LPs and GPs, which is primarily associated with fixed fees and a strong upside potential for GPs. The 1% that GPs may contribute to partnerships with LPs is not sufficient to provide strong financial congruity of interest; this 1% contribution may indirectly come from LPs anyway. Moreover, this divergence in the LP-GP relationship is not only visible in financial objectives, but also in strategic considerations: LPs seek financial returns while GPs' main objective is to perpetuate their operations from fund-to-fund.

The consequence of poor deal flow, the struggling entrepreneurial ecosystem, and a continued misalignment of interest between GPs and LPs can only lead to poor financial performance for LPs. When returns eventually fall significantly below those achieved in public equities markets, and maintain this suboptimal position for a period of time, LPs may actually react and seek to reevaluate the dynamics of their relationships with GPs.

Continued Negative Interference from the State

As observed in Chapter 2, the vast majority of states around the globe simultaneously decided to implement a vast range of restrictive public measures when the novel coronavirus initially appeared. These mandates included the closure of public spaces, stay-at-home orders, travel restrictions, border closures, forced home quarantine of healthy people (which has not been enacted in the history of modern medicine), curfews, restrictions on social gatherings (including visitations of family members and friends), the enactment of social distancing measures, and widespread mask wearing requirements. The state also distinguished between essential and non-essential services, and subsequently forced all businesses and services they deemed non-essential to close. Restrictions were implemented by the state to avoid overwhelming the healthcare system and thus "flatten the curve".

With public declarations of subsequent waves and new coronavirus variants, various states continued to implement continual lockdowns and restrictions worldwide throughout 2020 and 2021. More than a year after the initial restrictions came into effect, these states still do not have a clearly defined and actionable plan to ease restrictions, reduce lockdowns, lift curfews, or restore normal everyday life. This lack of planning and strategy is becoming increasingly visible in lawsuit proceedings undertaken against local and federal governments. Meanwhile, the entrepreneurial ecosystem continues to be negatively impacted by persistent state restrictions. Entrepreneurial firms have not recovered from financial and operational challenges that they experienced in early 2020, while the fluctuating on-and-off restrictions further prevent firms from beginning their rebuilding process. Some estimates suggest that 20–30% of entrepreneurial firms will not survive another wave of lockdowns and restrictions, primarily because their financial resources are already thinly stretched.

Beyond the state's external impact, their own institutions have experienced significant operational problems post COVID-response; court systems have been paralyzed, social programs have provided suboptimal assistance, educational systems have delivered compromised levels of education, and public telemedicine (i.e., providing health advice without seeing patients) has largely neglected patients.

Revival or Descent of the Industry in the Age of COVID

This part of the chapter will discuss whether the venture capital industry is likely to undergo revival or descent post COVID-response. Although there are some hints at its revival, there are stronger arguments in support of the descent of the venture capital industry, especially in the short- to medium-term. It is also anticipated that the venture capital industry will emerge in a more adjusted (although it is currently unclear whether in a revitalized or reinvigorated) mode, but with a completely different shape. By revisiting previous chapters, the following discussion will illustrate how this conclusion has been reached.

Chapter 3 describes the possible evolution of the venture capital industry through a three-stage process, which may include the global consolidation of GPs (i.e., growing emergence of mega-funds), global pooling of LPs (i.e., emergence of mega global LPs), and the development of more futuristic structures based on the digitization of the investment process and a wide-ranging disintermediation of GPs. Table 9.2 presents the evolution of the venture capital industry in each of these three stages and outlines the key characteristics of each stage, its likely length, an evaluation of possible financial performance, and the anticipated dollar amounts for fundraising and investing activities.

The first stage of the venture capital industry's evolution is anticipated to relate to the consolidation of GPs. This phase is highly necessary in the evolution of the industry because there are an excessive number of underperforming and borderline GPs currently in the ecosystem. Due to the normal longevity of a typical venture capital fund (i.e., funds are normally set up for a period of ten years), it is difficult to make timely adjustments to the industry; in other words, underperforming GPs are abridged

Table 9.2 Evolution of the venture capital industry in the future

	Stages in the evolution of the industry		
	Consolidation of GPs	*Pooling of LPs*	*Digitization of the industry*
Key characteristics	• Rise of global leaders and mega-fund GPs • GP market consolidation driven by performance, hands-on assistance, and innovation • Inability to raise subsequent funds by underperforming or borderline GPs • Emergence of new technologies and innovation among leading GPs • GPs rely on close connection with the state, industrial partners, and banks • Consulting firms to become an increasingly important part of the venture capital ecosystem	• Development of mega-financial structures on the LP side • LP consolidation reflects mega-structures already present in other segments of the finance industry • Reduced negotiating power of GPs • Pooling financial resources allows for a reduction of LP cost • Increased reliance on external advisors • Independent GPs command smaller share of the market • Slow decline in "dry powder" • Better coordination of financial resources	• Full digitization of relations in the venture capital ecosystem • Disintermediation of GPs • Significant reduction of venture capital's complexity and cost • Other capital suppliers and major stakeholders become an integral part of the system • Independent GPs command even smaller share of the industry
Financial performance	• Declining performance of the industry • Increased divergence in GP performance • Industry size begins to decline, which can improve returns	• Decreased industry size begins to improve returns • Lower cost of the venture capital industry further enhances performance	• Returns will become more stable and repeatable (unlikely to reach previous levels)

(continued)

Table 9.2 (continued)

	Stages in the evolution of the industry		
	Consolidation of GPs	*Pooling of LPs*	*Digitization of the industry*
Time period	5–10 years (2020 to 2025–2030)	7–15 years (2027–2035)	10–20 years (2030–2040)
Fundraising ($ billion)[a]	$196.0 ($175.1)	174.6 ($139.4)	$148.6 ($115.7)
Investing ($ billion)[a]	$232.6 ($189.0)	$247.9 ($192.4)	$228.8 ($177.7)

Note [a]These numbers represent averages for the period per annum. The second number in brackets refers to a pessimistic scenario from the industry by attrition only when they are unable to raise subsequent follow-on funds. The elimination of these suboptimal GPs during this first phase of the industry's evolution is also likely to coincide with the rise of mega-funds and a general increase in marketplace consolidation, which may even lead to industry monopolization. GP leaders, who would clearly be distinguished from others by their improved financial performance, superior hands-on assistance capabilities, and more innovative approaches to the investment process, would drive this consolidation and subsequent monopolization. Achieving such a consolidation would lead to higher rates of digitization of certain processes and a reduction of unnecessary costs, which would ultimately result in lowering the cost of venture capital services. An elimination of inferior players and simultaneous domination of superior venture capitalists may also coincide with GPs' increased co-operation with the state, different industrial partners, financial institutions, and other stakeholders. Furthermore, consulting and advisory firms are anticipated to emerge as a more important part of the venture capital ecosystem.

While it may be difficult to precisely estimate the timing of the consolidation process, this phase is expected to continue for a period of five to ten years, or until approximately 2030; this is one of the most inefficient stages of the industry's adjustment. Significant activity is also expected to take place in venture capital's secondary market, including the trade of ownership stakes in GPs, as this has already been underway for a number of years. However, COVID-response can also be expected to perpetuate the significant problems already impacting portfolio firms and the financial performance of GPs, although this period of consolidation will only aggravate the growing divergence of performance between superior and inferior GPs, thereby further perpetuating a trend that has already been visible in the industry for several years. The normal consequence of such disorderly structural adjustments will be declining returns for the entire industry. Alongside the market consolidation process, the size of the industry is likely to get smaller, which, at its most basic adjustment, can lead to a restoration of returns. The average annual fundraising and investing levels during this period are estimated to equal $196.0 billion and $232.6 billion, respectively (note that these numbers reflect the consideration of an optimistic scenario).

The next phase of the adjustment to the venture capital industry relates to the pooling of financial resources. This stage of evolution can be characterized by consolidation on the opposite side of the venture capital ecosystem, namely the true suppliers of capital, or LPs. The prediction of LP consolidation is based on the existence of mega-financial structures in other segments of the finance industry (i.e., financial management). Pooling LP resources has many benefits, including promoting the better coordination of financial resources (which can go a long way toward right-sizing the industry and reducing over-commitment of capital to under-performing GPs), restricting the negotiating power of GPs, decreasing LPs' costs related to GP selection and capital allocation, and lowering the overall cost of GP services. In preparation of a more intense digitization phase of the venture capital ecosystem, LPs (and perhaps even some GPs) may become increasingly reliant on external advisors and consultants. While the consolidation of GPs and the creation of mega-funds is predicted to continue during this second phase of the industry's evolution, smaller and non-consolidated GPs are likely to take an even smaller share of the venture capital industry once LP consolidation begins. The amount of dry power is also expected to slowly decline, given the inevitable decrease in fundraising activities and increase in investing that will occur at this phase.

The second phase of the venture capital industry's evolution is expected to take place in the next seven to 15 years, with its peak in the mid-2030s. The most significant benefit of this phase is the reversal of negative GP performance; returns are expected to improve due to the better allocation of available capital to promising investment opportunities and a reduction in operational costs throughout the entire venture capital ecosystem. The level of annual fundraising will continue to decline, when compared to estimates from the previous phase, and will equal about \$174.6 billion (in an optimistic scenario). Flat fundraising activity reflects significant amounts of available dry powder, but also LPs' skepticism with regard to the volume of attractive investment opportunities. Better coordinated LPs are also more likely to require real evidence of GPs' performance, rather than relying on the clever investment themes being pitched to them by GPs as proof of financial prowess. The average annual level of investing is predicted to increase to about \$247.9 billion over this period, which is significantly lower than the annual average value of \$322.4 billion in investment activity between 2000 and 2020.

The prediction regarding the last phase of the venture capital industry's evolution, namely the full digitization of the venture capital investment process, is based on the increased usage of online tools and platforms, the introduction of the Internet-of-things, and greater implementation of artificial intelligence (AI). It would also reflect the continued emergence of blockchain technologies, big data analytics, robotic processes, algorithms, and so on. These technologies have not been previously used in the venture capital industry on a massive scale, although they have been applied on an exceptional basis by a small universe of GPs. Beyond the bold, albeit uncertain, prediction that the industry will become entirely digitized, this hypothesis is similarly audacious because it assumes the almost complete disintermediation of GPs from the venture capital ecosystem. Major advantages of this third phase of venture capital's evolution include the reduced complexity of the ecosystem, its lower cost, and the elimination of costly intermediaries. Consequently, returns are expected to increase in size, stabilize, and become repeatable. One of the most significant drawbacks of a digitalized structure is the de-personalization of relationships within the venture capital ecosystem (which has vastly negative consequences on the ecosystem as a whole), and it is still unclear how this issue could be resolved in a satisfactory manner.

The timing of this structure's introduction and implementation is uncertain, although it may occur in the next 20 years or so. The level of annual fundraising during this final phase is expected to decrease even further and reach $148.6 billion per annum, while the level of investment would climb to an annual average of $228.8 billion.

The Possibility of Accelerated Evolution Within the Venture Capital Industry

It is also worthwhile to consider whether the venture capital industry could resuscitate itself faster than what has been previously anticipated. The answer is in the affirmative, primarily because the industry has never shown any interest in changing. Many GPs, LPs, and other stakeholders (such as lawyers, consultants, accountants, and various other advisors) appear satisfied with the industry's current structure, which can be characterized by an over-bloated size, fragmented and confusing architecture, job security, high salaries, prestige, and positive media coverage; GPs are especially protective of their fixed fees. On the other hand, LPs do not wish to admit that they allocated capital to suboptimal GPs or that their net returns from the asset class are equal to or even below those achieved in the public equities markets.

The spark to change the venture capital industry in a more expedited manner could come from many sources within the ecosystem. The first and most obvious agents of change in the industry are LPs, who are growing increasingly skeptical of the venture capital industry, and particularly with its financial performance. This issue is compounded by GPs who are often unable to produce empirical evidence in support of their alleged superior performance. Secondly, entrepreneurs who are new to the venture capital industry are quickly disillusioned with venture capital, and especially with its inability to provide much needed hands-on assistance (note that *serial entrepreneurs*, whose objective is often to move from one financially rewarding project to another, may be more aligned partners to venture capitalism). Thus, due to suboptimal hands-on assistance and similar to other forms of entrepreneurial finance, venture capital increasingly presents itself as a commodity service. Thirdly, GPs who sense an opportunity to assume a leadership position in the industry and become the drivers of industry consolidation may be more willing to amend their financial, compensation, technological, and operational modes of behavior. Like LPs, these GPs may intuitively realize that the current structure of the industry is not sustainable for the foreseeable future and therefore wish to set future precedents for the entire industry.

It is evident that the venture capital industry will be smaller, more consolidated, and different post COVID-response when compared to its previous iterations. Of course, the best-case scenario would be the venture capital industry's return to its true roots of being in the "business of building businesses" that arose in the late 1960s and the early 1970s. Unfortunately, this idealization does not seem possible today, as it is unclear how digitization would fit into this historical system and philosophy. There is, however, one possible area of interest for both LPs and GPs that may inspire growth and opportunity within the venture capital industry over the next decade: emerging markets. Venture capital in emerging market was highlighted in Chapter 1 as one of the most attractive market segments in the global venture capital landscape. The primary attraction of emerging markets reflects the fact that many countries in these markets have been able to achieve strong economic growth, a vigorous expansion of the middle class, substantial local investments, extraordinary rural-to-urban migration, a reduced dependence on exports, and responsible public finance. Of course, venture capital opportunities in emerging markets are not spread homogenously, as the most common investments are within the BRIC countries (i.e., Brazil,

Russia, India, and China). Potential investment opportunities for GPs in emerging markets may also be available in countries such as Indonesia, Malaysia, or Taiwan.

However, one of the best examples of a unique emerging market was Poland, although the market unfortunately does not seem to offer such attractive opportunities today. Between 2000 and 2010, Poland was not only one of the best performing emerging market countries, but also the most consistent provider of returns worldwide; venture capital returns averaged about 15.6% per annum for a period of ten years (note that returns from public equities markets were equal to about 16.9% between 1991 and 2011 and 14.8% in a comparable ten-year period). The case of Poland confirms that the best investment opportunities may emerge in a local venture capital industry's second decade of development. Of course, in order to fully participate in these opportunities and realize a consistently strong return performance, GPs must be sufficiently established in emerging markets. In other words, GPs must accurately predict and subsequently financially commit to a specific geographic market ahead of the curve to even be able to participate in the opportunities emerging market countries may hold. Early entry into some of these unique markets could be used to build strong and proprietary deal flow, develop and train a solid local deal team, and cultivate a respected market reputation among local entrepreneurs.

Venture Capital and Key Numbers

Having discussed the evolution of the venture capital industry, it is important to chart its development in terms of key fundraising and investing statistics. The amount of "dry powder", which is the final by-product of these two key numbers, will also be considered.

Of course, these projections have been prepared under the assumption that past trends are useful to the process of developing financial forecasts for the industry, the simplest of which presume that the future mirrors the past. However, the following proposed projections are founded on the likelihood that future trends, which were noted in detail in Chapter 4, will change the nature of the industry, its competitive dynamics, preferences for investee firms, return expectations, and so on. The contemplation in this chapter is also based on subjective assessments of the four critical areas within the global venture capital ecosystem.

The forecasts of fundraising, investing, and dry powder levels are reflective of an analysis of historical trends over the last twenty years, with particular interest paid to the impact of the 2008 financial crisis. When predicting these key numbers, it was necessary to rely upon averages of fundraising and investing dollar amounts, percentage changes in these figures from year-to-year, the cyclicality of the industry, and the assessment of the destructive impact of COVID-response on the SME sector, among other factors. The key financial projections are presented in Fig. 9.2 and represent an optimistic scenario (the pessimistic scenario assumes a protracted period of recovery and it is not shown in Fig. 9.2). The optimistic scenario includes higher percentage growth rates in fundraising and investing, more robust recovery after COVID-response, and a slower resolution of the accumulated dry powder.

The impact of COVID-response on the venture capital industry is projected to be much more severe than that of the 2008 financial crisis for a range of reasons that were outlined throughout this book. For example, the forecasts demonstrated in Fig. 9.2 predict that the average level of global fundraising would decline to \$171.2 billion per annum from the level of \$414.8 billion seen in the last 20 years (i.e., 2000–2020); this level of fundraising may still be excessive given the estimate

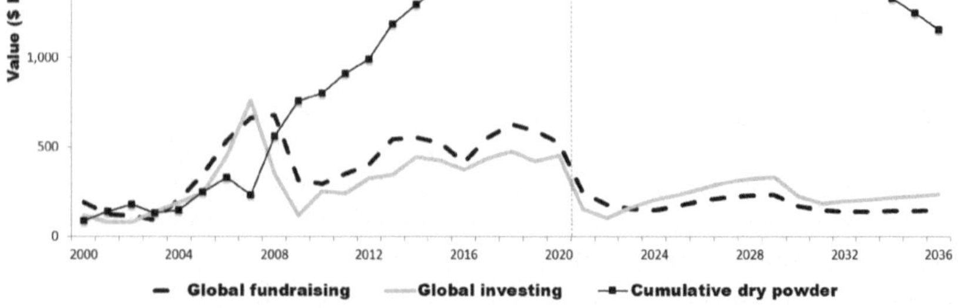

Fig. 9.2 Fundraising and investing activity in the venture capital industry up to 2036

provided at the end of Chapter 1 that the optimal annual fundraising would be around $100 billion if the value of annual realizations (i.e., exits) was taken into account. The basic premise behind decreasing global fundraising is that it would simply not be needed to fund new investment opportunities in light of excessive amounts of dry powder. The level of investing is also anticipated to decline by about $91.6 billion from an average of $322.4 billion to $230.8 billion, which reflects the destruction of the entrepreneurial system and a slow emergence of new investment opportunities on a larger scale.

Lastly, it is important to note that accumulated dry powder will continue to accumulate until it reaches $2.1 trillion in 2023. At this point, it will begin to steadily decline, reaching $1.1 trillion in 2036 and $0.8 trillion in 2040; however, these are still substantive amounts. It is conceivable that LPs may need to direct this capital to different forms of private capital investing, including private debt, to support the entrepreneurial ecosystem.

Bibliography

Albaz, Abdulaziz, Marco Dondi, Tarek Rida, and Jorg Schubert. 2020. Unlocking growth in small and medium-sized enterprises. July 2. www.mckinsey.com.

CTV News. 2021. 22 percent of Alberta businesses in danger of closing: report. January 21. www.ctvnews.ca.

Eggers, Fabian. 2020. Masters of disasters? Challenges and opportunities for SMEs in times of crisis. *Journal of Business Research*, 116: 199–208.

Etemad, Hamid. 2020. Managing uncertain consequences of a global crisis: SMEs encountering adversities, losses, and new opportunities. *Journal of International Entrepreneurship*, 18: 125–144.

Facebook. 2020. State of small business report. Facebook and Small Business Roundtable, volume I. May. www.about.fb.com.

Haines, Lucy. 2020. Bucking the trend of business closures. November 19. www.albertaprimetimes.com.

Hudes, Sammy. 2020. COVID-19 pandemic caused 'significant' spike in Alberta business closures: Statistics Canada. August 6. www.calgaryherald.com.

Jackson, Jon. 2020. COVID-19: Venture capital perspectives and reactions. May 8. www.cvca.ca.

Juergensen, Jill, Jose Guimon, and Rajneesh Narula. 2020. European SMEs amidst the COVID-19 crisis: Assessing impact and policy responses. *Journal of Industrial and Business Economics*, 47: 499–510.

Klonowski, Darek. 2013. *The venture capital investment process: Principles and practice*. New York: Palgrave Macmillan.
Klonowski, Darek. 2014. *Strategic entrepreneurial finance: From value creation to realization*. London: Routledge.
Klonowski, Darek. 2018. *The venture capital deformation: Value destruction throughout the investment process*. New York: Palgrave Macmillan.
Lim, Dominic S.K., Eric A. Morse, and Naryoung Yu. 2020. The impact of the global crisis on the growth of SMEs: A resource perspective. *International Small Business Journal*, 38: 492–503.
Michelin, Lana. 2021. Nearly 5% of Alberta businesses closed during 2020 pandemic: Will more closures happen before it's over? April 20. www.reddeeradvocate.com.
Sequoia. 2020. Coronavirus: The black swan of 2020. March 5. www.medium.com.
Verster, Liam. 2021. New report paints bleak picture of Alberta's small business. January 21. www.everythinggp.com.

Index

D. Klonowski, *Venture Capital Redefined*,
https://doi.org/10.1007/978-3-030-83387-9

The manufacturer's authorised representative in the EU is Springer
Nature Customer Service Centre GmbH, Europaplatz 3, 69115 Heidelberg,
Germany. If you have any concerns regarding our products, please
contact ProductSafety@springernature.com

Printed and bound by CPI Group (UK) Ltd, Croydon, CR0 4YY
30/09/2026
02225703-0001